AMERICA FOR AMERICANS

RECENT TITLES IN
CONTRIBUTIONS IN AMERICAN HISTORY

AMERICA
FOR
AMERICANS

*ECONOMIC NATIONALISM AND ANGLOPHOBIA
IN THE LATE NINETEENTH CENTURY*

Edward P. Crapol

**Contributions in American History
Number 28**

GREENWOOD PRESS, Inc.
Westport, Connecticut • London, England

Library of Congress Cataloging in Publication Data

Crapol, Edward P
   America for Americans.

   (Contributions in American history, no. 28)
   Bibliography: p.
   1. United States—Foreign economic relations—
Great Britain. 2. Great Britain—Foreign economic
relations—United States. 3. Nationalism—United
States. I. Title.
HF1456.5.G7C7   382'.0973'042   71-176287
ISBN 0-8371-6273-4

Library of Congress Catalog Card number: 71−176287
ISBN: 0−8371−6273−4

First published in 1973

Greenwood Press, Inc., Publishing Division
51 Riverside Avenue, Westport, Connecticut 06880

Manufactured in the United States of America

CONTENTS

PREFACE

The purpose of this book is to provide a thorough and integrated analysis of Anglophobia in the United States during the late nineteenth century. It goes beyond the traditional explanation that the anti-British nationalism of the period can be understood essentially as the result of the historical enmity for the former mother country and the consequence of Irish-American agitation in the political arena. While a number of extant scholarly works deal adequately with the diplomatic, political, and strategic aspects of the "Great Rapprochement" between the United States and Great Britain at the turn of the century, none, rather ironically, describes the full contours of the widespread antipathy for England that prevailed in the United States during the previous decades. Hopefully, this book will satisfactorily explain the phenomenon of Anglophobia and in the process pave the way for a more complete understanding of the rapprochement phase of Anglo-American relations.

I wish to thank the William F. Vilas Trust and the Graduate School of the University of Wisconsin for fellowships and research grants while this study was at the dissertation stage. My gratitude is also extended to the Society of the Alumni of the College of William and Mary for a faculty research grant that allowed for a summer of research in England.

My greatest debt, intellectually as well as personally, is to William Appleman Williams. He freely shared the results of his own research and encouraged me with his insights and criticism. I should like to express my appreciation to Howard Schonberger, Tom Terrill, and Brady Hughes for their helpful suggestions and perceptive comments. A word of thanks for help along the way to Stanley Kutler, Anthony Esler, Thad Tate, and Joy Barnes. Finally, thanks to Jeannette Lindsay and Betty Pessagno of Greenwood Press for their patient assistance in preparing the manuscript for publication.

AMERICA FOR AMERICANS

1

Introduction

Republics, above all other nations, ought most studiously to guard against foreign influence.

Henry Clay, 1811

The people of England will never respect us as we merit until we give them a right down good flogging. War is always a sad alternative, but let it come when it will, we must never leave it until we drive our old enemy from the continent, not even leaving them a spot of ground upon which they leave a footprint.

Senator Lewis Linn, 1839

It is easy enough for Europeans to sneer at the Monroe Doctrine and Manifest Destiny, but if they were better acquainted with the Americans they would know that these ideas are in their very blood and in the air they breathe. There are twenty millions of Americans, every one of them a free man and filled with the idea that America is for Americans.

Admiral Alexander Popov, 1860

The tide should be turned if the United States is to keep in her onward course toward supremacy. It was the English workshop which gave to Britain her strength, her real strength. That nation

3

which assists in erecting the workshops of the world within her bor-
ders is destined to become the industrial and commercial ruler of
the world. The United States should be that nation, it can become
that nation.

Terence V. Powderly, 1893

Why should England be the only power upon whose dominion the
sun never sets? Why should England have the world for her field?
Let us be fellow-Americans in the conquest of the world.

Albert Beveridge, 1894

America for Americans, and to hell with Britain and her Tories.

Ben Tillman, 1896

Americans traditionally have distrusted, feared, and disliked England. And while this anti-British side of the national character has virtually disappeared since 1945, it was a distinct and predominant feature of the national consciousness from the birth of the republic to the early years of the twentieth century. A clearly discernible pattern of Anglophobia—one that admittedly shifted and varied in emotional and geographic intensity—extends from the Revolutionary patriot cursing English tyranny with its suppression of personal and economic liberties, to the aroused farmer of the 1890s berating British plutocrats and denouncing the shackles imposed by British financial power. Anti-British nationalism, running like a red skein through American history, apparently served a negative but nonetheless essential role in the development of an American patriotism and loyalty. In addition to shaping an emerging sense of identity among Americans, this anti-British outlook clarified and focused what became a commonly shared vision of the future. For if the United States was to fulfill its mission and become a nation of great wealth and power, as well as the beacon and haven of liberty, it initially had to wrench free of England's economic orbit and ultimately overtake and surpass Great Britain in the markets of the world. Not surprisingly, in the years between the American Revolution and the Spanish-American War the popular perception of England was as an amalgam of oppressor, rival, and nemesis. British actions throughout the period did little to allay

or temper this view, and frequently confirmed the existing prejudices and preconceived notions of many Americans.

Almost immediately after the successful fight for independence
the main components of the phenomenon of Anglophobia became
apparent. As might be expected, Americans deeply resented such
English practices as the hiring of mercenaries and Indians to sup-
press their bid for freedom. British abuses in the 1790s did nothing
to erase the memory of past grievances. Engaged in a life-and-death
contest with France, Britain harassed American commerce, cap-
tured American merchantmen, and rather wantonly disregarded the
nation's neutral rights. Equally irritating to a generation that
vividly recalled the revolutionary struggle, American trade within
the British Empire was restricted, redcoats still occupied the western forts a decade after the peace treaty calling for their removal
had been ratified, and English instigation of the Indians to border
warfare seemed a threatening likelihood. To those Americans who
eventually rallied around the banner of Jefferson and the Republicans, the British transgressions were salt in old wounds and appeared ominously as the first stage in recolonization. Although the
Jay Treaty was to have rectified many of these grievances, in their
eyes the Washington administration had sold out to the British and
they denounced the agreement as the "badge of American dishonor
and disgrace."[1]

At first glance it would appear that Americans unhesitatingly
would support France, their ally and recent benefactor, in its bitter
international battle with England. Such was not the case. French
depredations of the United States' neutral shipping were as flagrant
as those of the British, and the political indiscretions of the French
emissaries Edmond C. Genet and Pierre A. Adet were a highly
visible reminder of the danger of foreign influence. Perhaps more
disturbing, France was undergoing a sweeping and bloody social
revolution that not only appalled some Americans but led them
to shrink from their ally in horror and disbelief. Unlike many later
manifestations of Anglophobia, particularly in the years before the
Civil War when all elements of the political spectrum verbally
flayed Great Britain and "twisted the lion's tail," the anti-British
outbursts of the Federalist era were decidedly partisan and reflected
a pronounced and obvious dichotomy that shaped, and to a considerable extent created, party alignments and loyalties. In that sense

the 1790s were rather unique, as Francophobia competed with Anglophobia and one's position for or against France and Great Britain fairly accurately reflected party allegiance. Hence, in this political equation, Federalists were essentially anti-French and nominally pro-British; the Jeffersonian Republicans were basically anti-British and pro-French.

However, the situation changed rapidly as anti-French feelings virtually disappeared with the settlement of the quasi war and the termination of the alliance of 1778. And when Napoleon offered Louisiana to the young republic the purchase not only fulfilled American expansionist ambitions, it also effectively removed France as a threat and rival to the United States in the Western Hemisphere. As a result Great Britain became the undisputed and unchallenged national rival. Not even French violations of American neutrality in the continuing conflict with England in the early 1800s rekindled anti-French passions. France simply did not influence American economic and political life to the same degree that Britain did at the opening of, and for that matter throughout, the nineteenth century. Great Britain had the upper hand in the existing client-patron trade pattern in which the United States supplied England with raw materials and foodstuffs and served as a major outlet for the products of Britain's looms and factories. England was also seen as imposing a financial stranglehold on the United States in the first decades of the century through its role as the largest foreign holder of American bonds and national bank stock.[2] As Senator William B. Giles of Virginia complained in 1811, "the enormous British influence, which notoriously pervades this country . . . affects the proceedings of Government so seriously, that it can hardly be said to be independent."[3] Those years witnessed as well an increasing Anglo-American rivalry for markets in Latin America that further reinforced the national attitude that the British lion blocked America at every turn.

If any doubt remained, the experience of the War of 1812 made the identification of England as the national nemesis and rival complete. Britain's blatant disregard for American neutral rights and its arrogance in impressing seamen, based on the philosophy of "once an Englishman, always an Englishman," wounded the national pride and intensified an already budding anti-British nationalism. In their second struggle with the world's greatest industrial power, Americans fought to protect their rights at sea and to defend their national honor. But they also were intent on preserving their admittedly precarious and decidedly limited economic independence. If Britain recolonized American trade and inundated the home market with its manufactured goods, warned President James Madison, that "would drain from us the precious metals, endanger our Monied Institutions, arrest our internal improvements, and would strangle in the cradle, the manufactures which promise so vigorous a growth."[4] However, fear and distrust of Great Britain was not limited solely to the concern for freedom of the seas and economic integrity. As war-hawk Henry Clay believed, "the real cause of British aggression was not to distress an enemy but to destroy a rival." England, Clay informed his countrymen, "sickens at your prosperity and beholds in your growth—your sails spread on every ocean, and your numerous seamen—the foundations of a Power which, at no very distant day, is to make her tremble for naval superiority."[5] And in their land-hunger for Canada, the war-hawks were partially motivated by the prospect that they could end British meddling on the frontier and rid the continent of this despised competitor.

Unfortunately for American nationalists, none of these objectives was wholly or satisfactorily reached in the stalemate that ended with the Treaty of Ghent. The United States had suffered extensive damage (including the destruction of its capitol), had been frustrated in its desire to conquer Canada, and had failed to secure recognition of neutral rights from Great Britain—all of which further accentuated the popular enmity for John Bull. Yet, despite these setbacks, the United States had once again fended off Great Britain and in the process gained confidence, cohesion, and increased industrial strength. Important Anglo-American diplomatic settlements such as the Rush-Bagot Treaty and the Convention of 1818 followed in the immediate postwar years, but these successes by no means allayed or diminished the bitter memory of the war. Throughout the remainder of the century, Anglophobes such as James G. Blaine repeatedly cited in their litany of British crimes the War of 1812, and in particular characterized the burning of Washington by British troops as an atrocity that symbolized the barbarity and rapacity of England. This type of distortion, which among other things ignored the American burning of York in Canada, was typical of the impassioned oratory that would become institutionalized in the Fourth of July speech. Such was the pattern during the century, as the general perception of England and its policies became increasingly oversimplified and inaccurate. However, the images drawn from the emotions and passions of national rivalries rarely display an affinity for objective analysis or subtle truth.

The 1812 conflict may have been dubbed the second war for independence, but the goal of economic independence remained elusive even though domestic manufacturing had mushroomed during the war. As they had after the settlement of the Revolutionary struggle, British merchants flooded the American market with their cheap goods, thus accelerating the dislocation and distress of the postwar economy. To further arouse American suspicions and fan the fires of anti-British nationalism, Henry Brougham openly recommended in a speech before Parliament in 1816 that British traders take a loss in their exports to America so that the glut might "stifle in the cradle those rising manufactures in the United States which the war had forced into existence contrary to the natural course of things."[6] The speech was highly publicized in the United States, first as concrete proof of malevolent British intentions to subvert American industry, and second, to inspire American consumers to purchase and take pride in articles of domestic manufacture. Even Thomas Jefferson admitted that "experience has taught me that manufactures are as necessary to our independence as to our comfort" and he appealed to the patriotism of his countrymen in urging them to buy domestic so that home supply might equal demand and they might "wrest that weapon of distress from the hand which has wielded it."[7]

The desire to retain and expand upon the impressive gains in manufacturing gave renewed vigor to the economic nationalism which had been spawned in the 1790s during the debates surrounding Secretary of the Treasury Alexander Hamilton's national program for economic development. Using Hamilton's basically unimplemented *Report on the Subject of Manufactures* as a springboard, such economic nationalists as Mathew Carey, an Irishman who had emigrated to the United States in 1784, desired to break the shackles of economic insufficiency in order to make American political freedom a reality and not just a high-sounding phrase.

Carey, followed by his son Henry C. Carey, and their supporters campaigned throughout the century for government support and aid to promote economic development and increased industrial self-sufficiency. The consistent and unaltering aim of all economic nationalists in propagandizing and lobbying for legislation, whether in behalf of a protective tariff, transportation subsidies, or currency and banking measures, was to serve "the nation by making it not richer, but freer, by promoting not its material welfare but its independence of foreign influence."[8] Within this framework, the goals were a greater degree of diversification of production and a better balanced national economy. Hopefully, wealth, material well-being, and world power would ultimately accrue to the nation as well. For Mathew Carey, Great Britain may have been the avowed enemy, but at the same time his conception of a viable economic system for the United States was substantially influenced by his admiration and respect for British industry and enterprise. This ambivalent outlook—distrust and hatred of England joined with the desire to duplicate the successful British model—evolved in America until it became a dominant feature in the thinking of most late nineteenth century Anglophobes.

In the ante-bellum period the patterns of response to Great Britain that had existed since the formation of the republic remained intact. The passage of time did little to dim or soften the American memory. Instead, over the years American grievances, real and imagined, accumulated. The French commentator on life in the United States, Alexis de Tocqueville, found it difficult to imagine a more intense hatred than that of Americans for England. Among other things, Americans constantly grumbled about the condition of semivassalage that the trade relationship with Britain inflicted. Andrew Jackson, for one, complained that Americans "have been too long subject to the policy of British merchants," and he felt that "it is time we should become a little more Americanized, and instead of feeding the paupers and laborers of Europe, feed our own." Another vestige of England's control over the American economy that rankled President Jackson was the considerable amount of national bank stock held by Britons. In his 1832 message vetoing the recharter bill for the Second Bank of the United States, Jackson not only cited the foreign ownership of bank stock as objectionable, he also asserted that if such an institution with private stockholders was an absolute necessity, at the very least "every impulse of American feeling admonishes that it should be purely American."[9] Such appeals to national pride and a sense of Americanism became a standard response among opponents of British financial control and critics of British investment in the United States.

The atmosphere between the United States and Great Britain was poisoned further by the hassle over the repudiation of state debts, the absence of an American copyright law, and the venomous accounts of American life projected by a number of English travelers and literary periodicals. The individual states had borrowed approximately $150 million from British capitalists to finance internal improvements. With the financial collapse at the end of the 1830s and the ensuing depression, several states defaulted on their payments and ultimately a number repudiated their debts. In the early 1840s recriminations bounded back and forth across the Atlantic. The English denounced American dishonesty and fraud. Americans, for their part, lambasted "the bloated British bondholder," as the debtor's disdain for the creditor became an integral part of their anti-British mentality.[10] Another sore spot for the English was the lack of international copyright provisions in the United States. At one point in the 1830s a number of embittered British authors vainly petitioned Congress for protective legislation to halt the unauthorized publication of their literary works. And when a series of Englishmen (including Charles Dickens) who had visited the young republic published highly critical travel books that condescendingly appraised all phases of the American experiment, a battle of words ensued between English and American literary journals. Clearly, no love was lost on either side of the Atlantic in those years.[11]

The fear that Britain would prevent the fulfillment of America's manifest destiny to secure a continental empire that stretched from ocean to ocean prompted repeated outbursts of Anglophobia in the 1840s. In their desire for Texas, Oregon, and California, American expansionists quite literally were afflicted with a phobia about the machinations of the British. In this instance, however, it was not completely irrational. In reality England in the mid-nineteenth century was the one power that could, and occasionally did attempt to, place obstacles in the path of American territorial ambitions.

A case in point was Britain's courtship of the Lone Star Republic to guarantee the independence of Texas which, among other things, would erect a permanent barrier to United States expansion and give English abolitionists a possible base from which to undermine southern slavery. That prospect infuriated southerners, especially John C. Calhoun, who bitterly lashed out at the meddling policies of John Bull. In the Oregon dispute and with England's alleged interference in California, the apostles of manifest destiny found further justification for their charge that Britain conspired to contain and restrict the development of the United States. To overcome the British threat and alleviate their insecurity, Americans rationalized that England must be eliminated from the whole of the continent if the United States was to be safe. Total expulsion of British influence was an often expressed, if never attained, goal of expansionists who fully expected American dominance and control to follow British evacuation.[12]

In the twenty years preceding the Civil War there existed great concern that Britain's activities in Central America and the Caribbean also endangered American security. Considerable anti-British agitation arose over British encroachments in the isthmian region, which threatened to foreclose any future American control of an interoceanic canal. The controversial Clayton-Bulwer Treaty of 1850 guaranteed joint construction of an isthmian canal and ostensibly halted any further British expansion in Central America. However, the ambiguous language of the agreement and the absence of a retroactive feature dealing with past British territorial infringements led many Americans to agree with the appraisal of Stephen A. Douglas that the treaty was simply "truckling to Great Britain." The specter of the British bogey was raised as well by the fear that England was maneuvering to gain control of Cuba. Cuba in the hands of "Great Britain or any strong naval power," argued Secretary of State James Buchanan in 1848, would "prove ruinous both to our domestic and foreign commerce, and even endanger the Union of the States."[13] To forestall this challenge to American security, Buchanan and a host of other Americans invoked the Monroe Doctrine. They recommended not only that Britain be prevented from acquiring Cuba, but ultimately justified virtually any tactic "to detach" the island from Spain. But Spain's refusal to part with the Pearl of the Antilles and the sectional tensions engendered by the slavery issue defeated the various American efforts to acquire Cuba in the 1850s. Ironically, amidst all the anti-British rhetoric over English aggression in the Caribbean and the frequent appeals to the sanctity of the Monroe Doctrine, the United States was more than willing to penetrate China on the crest of the British imperial wave to secure treaty privileges that Britain had forcibly wrung from the Chinese.

Despite the oft-voiced apprehensions about England and its efforts to stymie the national destiny, Americans at mid-century pointed with unabashed pride to their own recent territorial gains as a wave of nationalistic fervor momentarily swept the nation. The continental limits of the country had been completely carved out with the annexation of Texas, the settlement of the Oregon dispute at the forty-ninth parallel, and the war booty taken from conquered Mexico. The projected and desired hegemony in the Caribbean seemed within grasp, as did ultimate dominance in the entire hemisphere. And during the 1850s American clipper ships boldly challenged Britain for supremacy of the commerce lanes of the world. "Brother Jonathan," Philip Hone observed, "is growing to be a 'big boy' and must be treated with a little more respect."[14] The United States had become an incipient imperialist nation eager to flex its muscles in the international arena, and had not the slavery issue intruded, America undoubtedly would have launched its career of overseas territorial expansion in those years.

The outbreak of the Civil War dashed those imperial ambitions; the bitter conflict threatened the existence of the Union and its future position as a world power. Both the North and the South deemed Britain's stance on the war as crucial to the outcome. The South openly courted English recognition of the Confederacy in the hope that British financial assistance and possible military intervention might guarantee the success of their struggle. Among northern leaders the feeling was fairly widespread that England intended to take advantage of the conflict to strengthen its commercial supremacy by destroying an economic and commercial rival. Not only was such a policy wholly consistent with the American perception of England's historic record, but British actions during the war did little to dispel that view. To begin with, the Union resented Britain's recognition of southern belligerency and the early sympathy expressed by a number of English leaders, including William E.

Gladstone, for the Confederacy. More infuriating were the efforts of a group of Tories in organizing the private Southern Independence Association, with its campaign to raise funds for the Confederate cause. Mr. J. A. Roebuck, a leader of the organization, made it abundantly clear why he hoped the South would never rejoin the Union: "America while she was united ran a race of prosperity unparalleled in the world. Eighty years made the Republic such a power, that if she had continued as she was a few years longer she would have been the great bully of the world."[15] The North's ire was also aroused by such transgressions of neutrality as the laxity of the British government in suppressing the construction of the two armored ships known as the Laird rams, the role of Canada as a base for Confederate attacks, the support given blockade runners in the West Indies, and the aid provided the *Alabama* and other raiders in the African and Asian colonies of Britain. To be sure, England never granted diplomatic recognition to the Confederacy, but that only served to anger and embitter southerners. All in all, Britain's actions during the Civil War left a legacy of ill-will in both the North and the South.

Although the dominant themes of Anglophobia were already fairly well developed in the years before 1865, the main purpose of this study is to demonstrate that anti-British nationalism reached its peak during the late nineteenth century as a manifestation of the United States' strident economic nationalism and its increasingly aggressive quest for commercial supremacy in the Western Hemisphere. Anglophobia went hand in hand with the nation's expanding power and its awakening national consciousness. However, in the post–Civil War period fear was no longer the principal emotional ingredient of anti-British sentiment, as it had been in the 1840s and 1850s when the nation nervously anticipated that Great Britain would thwart American territorial expansion. After the purchase of Alaska in 1867, continental expansion was essentially complete, although many Americans still coveted Canada. Instead of instilling fear, England's actions during the Civil War embittered both the North and South and intensified anti-British feelings throughout the nation. This led to an unusually explosive display of Anglophobia in the immediate postwar years, marked by demands for retaliation and vengeance and motivated by a sense of righteousness directed to rectifying the alleged injustices perpetrated by England during the conflict. Then, in the last decades of the century, as the United States directly confronted Britain for economic and political hegemony, this Anglophobic response was characterized by an emotional and psychological combination of jealousy and resentment, frustration and hostility.

As such, these expressions and overt displays of anti-British feeling reflected two distinct features of the national consciousness. At the domestic level this phenomenon appeared as the result of an increasing popular awareness of the dominant role played by Great Britain in American economic and political life. This was particularly true among agrarians of the trans-Mississippi West and the South, regions where the impact of British capital was highly visible and where a sense of dependence upon England as a market for agricultural exports prevailed. The farmers of the West and the South not only understood that the existing trade pattern dictated that the price for their wheat and cotton be set in the Liverpool and London commodity markets, they also clearly perceived their position within that system as colonial and compared their plight with that of the wretched of other colonial societies, especially British-controlled India and Ireland. In addition, farmers suffered from the deep-seated abuses that were implicit in the American economy of the 1880s and 1890s; Anglophobia and the agrarian upheaval were symptomatic of these inequities.

At the second level, involving foreign policy, a new aggressiveness marked American diplomacy as the nation directly challenged Britain's commercial and economic supremacy in the Western Hemisphere and the Pacific. The ensuing confrontation with England's power and influence evoked a mixed emotional response among Americans; intense distrust and hostility for the national rival were accompanied by a considerable degree of jealousy of Britain's position in the world. Ironically, while England was resented and envied by its former colony, many Americans desired to imitate the success of the British Empire. This ambivalent attitude toward Great Britain was displayed frequently in the thinking of Anglophobes in the late nineteenth century. Thus, at the conscious level, the tendency for Americans was to denounce England and all that it stood for, while at the subconscious level, Britain epitomized America's image of the successful world power.

These two levels of national thought—one demanding America's

economic, financial, and political independence and the other calling for the United States' commercial supremacy in the Western
Hemisphere—were fused under the banner and rallying cry of
"America for Americans." This contemporary slogan demanded
the elimination of British influence from the economy and was the
watchword for the nation's economic expansionists in their crusade
to displace the English, and Europeans generally, in the markets
of Latin America. To be sure, Anglophobes and critics of England
were not alone in raising this nationalistic cry. It also was employed
by nativist groups agitating for immigration restrictions and by the
anti-Chinese forces of the West Coast. Occasionally these various
strands of national feeling would be united, as in the case of the
ephemeral American party, which organized in Philadelphia in September of 1887 to coincide with the centennial commemoration of
the Constitutional Convention. This neonativist group was
dedicated to maintaining "the power and supremacy of American
born citizens," to guaranteeing "that American lands should be reserved for American citizens" and to pursuing "a firm and consistent foreign policy and vigorous assertion of our national dignity
and respect to our flag on land and sea."[16] Nevertheless, it remains
accurate to identify the slogan with the widespread Anglophobia
and general hostility for Great Britain that existed during the period, as exemplified by "Pitchfork" Ben Tillman when he bellowed
"America for Americans and to hell with Britain and her Tories."[17]

While it is convenient for the purpose of historical analysis to
delineate the domestic and foreign policy aspects of Anglophobia,
it must be remembered that these levels were not independent nor
mutually exclusive. Actually, they were closely interrelated and in
numerous instances reinforced each other. Also, conspiratorial in-
terpretations of the past that defined Great Britain as blocking
American economic progress were transferred, and modified
somewhat in the process, from eastern industrial groups to the later
agrarian protest movements of the West and South. This was the
case with the explanation of Britain's role offered by Henry C.
Carey and his cadre of economic nationalists. They campaigned
throughout the period against English influence and hailed the protective tariff as the "way to outdo England without fighting her."[18]
These representatives of eastern manufacturing interests formulated
and propagated a thesis that defined any agitation for tariff reform

as part of a British plot to subvert the nation's industrial development, and hence, delay its financial and economic independence.
Admittedly these charges of conspiracy were grossly exaggerated
and basically false. But many Americans were receptive to this explanation because England's power as the most mature industrial
society, further strengthened by its surplus capital, placed the
United States, still a developing country, in an economically dependent position. And it was this analysis, no longer exclusively
tied to the tariff debate, with its conspiratorial portrayal of Great
Britain, that was adopted and expounded by the Populists in the
1880s and 1890s.

In the last decades of the nineteenth century British power and
influence were everywhere apparent, and this country felt hemmed
in and frustrated in its ambitions by Britain. Previous
confrontations with England, especially during the Civil War, had
sensitized the American populace so that in later encounters they
responded and reacted within a psychological context of rage. That
emotional set existed at two levels. One concerned the United
States and England as nations. Britain was identified and understood as thwarting American aspirations for commercial and economic preeminence in the Western Hemisphere in particular, and
the world in general. Americans in all walks of life and in all sections of the country felt that England—through its economic and
financial power—was simply using the United States to further its
own ends. The predominant issues of the period—the
remonetization of silver, the tariff and reciprocity treaties, the call
for a revived merchant marine, an American-controlled isthmian
canal, the battle for expanded foreign markets, the campaign for
alien land legislation—can be more clearly analyzed and understood in this light. Americans concluded that England presented
the principal obstacle to the achievement of their destiny, and British actions in the years between the Civil War and the Spanish-
American War supported and reinforced this analysis.

This psychological sense of rage at the national level was paralleled by an identical phenomenon at the individual level of
perception, especially among the agrarians of the South and West.
People in those areas, defining themselves in a colonial status, concluded that they were being employed, on the one hand by England
and on the other by the financial and commercial interests of the

Northeast, not as human beings, but as instruments to serve purposes other than their own. Their response to these real and apparent grievances was to organize politically and offer concrete and relevant solutions to improve their condition. Among other things, the farmers and their allies demanded the elimination of British influence from the American economy, an end to the client-patron trade relationship that kept them in a state of subservience to England, and they actively supported programs that would foster overseas economic expansion and find alternate markets for their agricultural exports. However, in the campaign to overcome the agricultural majority's deteriorating economic position, one issue above all others integrated the various emotional and psychological responses to Britain, whether at the national or individual level: the drive for free silver.

Anglophobia became more active and widespread in the late nineteenth century than it had been in the ante-bellum era primarily because the United States was in the process of becoming one of the world's major economic powers. Americans recognized that the country was on the threshold of world power and true economic independence. Yet, despite its staggering agricultural production and industrial capacity, its increased control of the home market and its burgeoning export trade, the nation appeared incapable of breaking free of the British economic orbit and asserting its supremacy in the markets of the world. In response a dynamic economic nationalism erupted, dedicated to ending the humiliation of the United States being "tail to the British Kite," and to making "America for Americans." That in turn stirred and sustained the vehement anti-British nationalism that marked the last decades of the century.

NOTES

1. Kenneth W. Rowe, *Mathew Carey, A Study in American Economic Development* (Baltimore: Johns Hopkins Press, 1933), p. 41.

2. Bradford Perkins, *The First Rapprochement, England and the United States 1795 – 1805* (Philadelphia: University of Pennsylvania Press, 1955), pp.11–13.

3. Remarks of February 11, 1811, *Annals of the Congress of the United States,* 11th Cong., 3rd Sess., 1810–1811, p. 206.

4. William A. Williams, *The Contours of American History* (Chicago: Quadrangle Books, Inc., 1966), p. 193.

5. Remarks of December 31, 1811, *Annals of the Congress of the United States,* 12th Cong., 1st Sess., Part 1, p. 601.

6. Hansard, *Parliamentary Debates,* 1st Series, XXXIII (1816), p. 1099.

7. Paul L. Ford, ed., *The Writings of Thomas Jefferson,* Vol. X (New York: G. P. Putnam's Sons, 1899), p. 10.

8. Michael A. Heilperin, *Studies in Economic Nationalism* (Paris: Librarie Minard, 1962), p. 18.

9. James D. Richardson, *Messages and Papers of the Presidents 1789 — 1897,* Vol. II (Washington: Government Printing Office, 1898), p. 58.

10. Reginald C. McGrane, *Foreign Bondholders and American State Debts* (New York: The MacMillan Company, 1935).

11. Glyndon G. Van Deusen, *The Jacksonian Era 1828 — 1848* (New York: Harper & Row, Publishers, 1959), p. 172.

12. Richard W. Van Alstyne, "The Oregon Question," in W. A. Williams, *The Shaping of American Diplomacy,* Vol. I (Chicago: Rand, McNally & Co., 1970), pp. 149—53.

13. Buchanan to Mr. Saunders, June 17, 1848, in John Bassett Moore, ed., *The Works of James Buchanan,* Vol. VIII (Philadelphia: J. B. Lippincott Co., 1909), pp. 90—102.

14. Entry of February 5, 1848, in Allan Nevins, ed., *The Diary of Philip Hone* (New York: Dodd, Mead & Co., 1936), pp. 869—70.

15. James G. Blaine, *Twenty Years of Congress: From Lincoln to Garfield,* Vol. II (Norwich, Conn.: Henry Bell Publishing Company, 1884), pp. 478—85.

16. *Appleton's Annual Cyclopoedia 1887,* New Series, Vol. XII (New York: D. Appleton & Co., 1891), pp. 659—60.

17. Remarks of May 1, 1896, *Congressional Record,* Vol. 28, Part V, p. 4662.

18. Henry C. Carey, *The Way to Outdo England Without Fighting Her* (Philadelphia: Henry Carey Baird, Industrial Publisher, 1865).

2

Economic Nationalism and History as Conspiracy

England is ready to give up empire in government for dominion in the trade of America. The only supremacy she cares for now is that of her labor. Her only fleets and forces for invasion and conquest are her mercantile vessels and her manufactures, and our defences are not in our monitors and forts, but in our customhouses.

William Elder, 1865

The trained legions of England are fighting us from her mines and workshops, under guidance more subtle and more ruthless than that of military rule, and from those secure fortifications they launch the missiles which are to subjugate and impoverish us. Her mines and factories are pitted against our mines and factories in a struggle wherein our independence is at stake, and every industrial establishment upon our side which is forced to succumb in the struggle is one of our batteries silenced, with its soldiers cast into the hospital.

This struggle is one which we cannot avoid, and in which defeat must be fatal. The continent is ours to subdue and to possess, ready to yield all its treasures to us and to our posterity, but only upon the condition of our being able to develop all its capacities and to maintain ourselves against all comers. Any dreams of a merely agricultural wealth and civilization are utterly illusory, for no merely agricultural people have ever long maintained their independence ex-

19

*cept when both they and their country were too poor to excite
cupidity.*

> *House Committee on Manufactures
> Majority report, "Examination of
> statements in the Report of
> Special Commissioner of the
> Revenue."   1870*

*Let free trade remain on the banners of England, but let our
policy be in all the years to come what it has been in the past. Let
us seek to make a market here for all our products...let us stand
by the idea that America is a Government for Americans and American ideas and principles.*

> *Newton W. Nutting, 1884*

In the immediate aftermath of the Civil War, American political,
industrial, and agricultural leaders proudly and repeatedly declared
that the United States now would become the most important and
powerful nation in the world. Many of them believed the United
States had been on the threshold of global preeminence in the 1850s
and had only been denied its destiny by the bitterness and rancor
of a civil war. They viewed the war as having temporarily delayed
overseas territorial and commercial expansion and the fulfillment
of America's destiny. If, as some historians and economists now
contend, the Civil War actually served to retard America's industrial development, it can also be interpreted as having retarded American imperialism in the Western Hemisphere and the Pacific. This
delay caused dismay and disappointment, but most American
leaders, among them many radical Republicans, confidently predicted that reunion and recovery would enable the United States
to arise from the ashes and become the marvel of the world.

Henry C. Carey led the prophets of the new age. He was aided
by such disciples as William Elder, Joseph Wharton, William D.
Kelley, Henry Carey Baird, Robert Ellis Thompson, and James
Moore Swank, all of whom represented and spoke for the coal and
iron interests of Pennsylvania. They propagated a doctrine of economic nationalism that promised to convert the United States, then
faced with the established supremacy of Great Britain, into the
world's foremost industrial and commercial power. This pioneer social scientist, following in the footsteps of his father, Mathew

Carey, created an American school of political economy that denied the dismal forecasts of such Englishmen as Malthus and Ricardo, and instead propounded an optimistic program for the realization of American industrial, commercial, and financial independence. The younger Carey stressed the harmony of all producing economic interests in America; he believed there existed a basic community of interest among the agricultural, wage earning, and industrial classes.[1] This harmony of interests among all producing classes dictated that industrialization benefited the entire nation, not simply the manufacturers and industrialists. But more important, industrialization was crucial for the United States to overcome the lead possessed by the early starters in the industrial revolution.

Carey frequently lamented that America's independence was "a mere form of words," and until his death in 1879 this inveterate economic nationalist continually exhorted his countrymen and fellow Republicans to strive for the United States' complete and unhampered economic and financial independence. As did his father before him, Carey stressed—indeed, made it one of his principal tenets—the essential need of the nation to be freed from the yoke of foreign domination.[2] The protective tariff was deemed crucial to the realization of his nationalistic vision, and with the defeat of the Confederacy assured, Carey, one of the authors of the 1860 Republican tariff plan, moved to consolidate and extend the economic legislation of the war years. In 1865 he argued, through a series of public letters to Schuyler Colfax, Speaker of the House of Representatives, that the protective tariff would be "the way to outdo England without fighting her."[3] The policy of protection provided "a peaceful, pleasant road towards that thorough independence which will enable us to respect ourselves while commanding the respect of other nations of the world."[4]

The Philadelphia economist had not always embraced protection, but became an advocate in the 1840s when prosperity returned after the adoption of the 1842 tariff.[5] Carey's conversion also resulted from his historical analysis of the world economy and the position of the United States within that international system. A deep-seated antipathy and distrust for England accompanied his shift to protectionism, and he believed that "the tendency of the whole British system of political economy is to the production of discord

among men and nations."[6] And quite naturally, British free trade
policy was defined as the single most important obstacle to
America's economic development; it represented, Carey asserted,
the fulfillment of Lord Brougham's strategy for preserving English
commercial and industrial preeminence by destroying foreign manufacturers in the cradle.[7] England exploited the world by increasing
and enhancing the role of the trader, as opposed to the producer,
and kept many parts of the world underdeveloped and without industry. "The object of protection," Carey proclaimed, "is that of
aiding the farmers in the effort to bring consumers to their
sides . . . while aiding in the annihilation of a system that has
ruined Ireland, India, Portugal, Turkey and all other countries subject to it."[8] This historical interpretation was accepted by a host
of Carey adherents, most notably James G. Blaine, and it undoubtedly influenced the thinking of the many prominent leaders and
politicians who attended the weekly "Carey Vespers."[9]

In the post—Civil War period and throughout the remainder of
the nineteenth century, the Carey school identified tariff revision
with allegiance to Great Britain and one phase of the overall British
plot to squelch American industry. Consequently, any American
citizen or political party that advocated tariff reform ipso facto
served British interests and was a de facto ally of the British. This
conspiracy thesis, hammered into shape in the tariff debates of the
late 1860s and early 1870s, pervaded the protectionist literature of
the era, and appealed to a public convinced of Britain's hostility
and evil intentions and concerned for the economic health and
growth of their nation.

But Carey's denunciation of Great Britain did not end there, for
in addition to destroying foreign industry, England aimed to "gain
and keep possession of foreign markets,"[10] while at the same time
confining Americans to the role of producers of raw materials and
agricultural products. England desired "that the distant farmer
shall have no market near him, that he shall be compelled to limit
himself to the production of the commodities of which the earth
yields little, and that can, therefore, go to that distant market in
which Russian, Polish, German, Egyptian and American food
producers are to contend with each other as to which shall sell most
cheaply."[11] The American farmer would remain subservient, for the
"market whose prices for food regulate those of all the world is

that of Great Britain."[12] The entire British system was repugnant to Carey, for in addition to denying the principles of his idol, Adam Smith, he believed it created unnatural monopolies that enriched the English commercial classes at the expense of the producing classes of the world. Ironically, Carey failed to foresee that in the long run his policy created the same disparity between developed and underdeveloped nations, the only difference being that the United States displaced Great Britain as the exploiter of the world's producers.

Protection was thus essential for the whole nation. It was the basis of a true harmony of interest. For if British designs for free trade were successful, then British manufacturers would be allowed to flood the American market with their cheap industrial goods. That would upset American industrial growth and cause widespread unemployment and depression with resultant misery and deprivation for American labor. And that, in turn, would cripple or eliminate the home market for farmers, leaving them defenseless in an uncertain international market dominated and controlled by Great Britain.

William Elder, an official in the Treasury Department and perhaps Carey's closest associate, spelled out this thesis in several pamphlets published immediately after the Civil War. Elder stressed to the farmer that he must have the home market, for the European market remained uncertain and "contemptible at best."[13] Protection provided the best policy, present and future, for the American farmer (of the western states in particular), because it would guarantee the home market and ultimately permit those states to diversify their industries. Industrial independence would allow the western states to lift themselves out of the category of America's "Anglo-Saxon colonies," and ultimately they might become the seat of empire in the Union.[14]

Elder stressed that before industrialization and the creation of a stable and expanding home market, it was most important to secure foreign markets for agricultural surpluses. America's security and prosperity demanded an "extension of the Monroe Doctrine to the commerce of the continent."[15] The farmers of the western states "must find a shorter route from the mouth of the Mississippi to South America than by the way of Liverpool."[16] The Treasury Department official recognized that Great Britain had abandoned formal colonialism in the Western Hemisphere and was "ready to give up empire in government for dominion in the trade of America."[17] To meet this challenge, Elder urged, the United States must seek new markets for agricultural surpluses in South America and in Asia. This would free the American farmer of the tyranny of a European market dominated by England.[18]

President Ulysses S. Grant, who occasionally had attended sessions of the "Vespers," supported this analysis in his December 1869 message to the Congress. He pointed out that:

> The extension of railroads in Europe and the East is bringing into competition with our agricultural products like products of other countries. Self-interest, if not self-preservation, therefore dictates caution against disturbing any industrial interest of the country. It teaches us also the necessity of looking to other markets for the sale of our surplus. Our neighbors south of us, and China and Japan, should receive our special attention. It will be the endeavor of the Administration to cultivate such relations with all these nations as to entitle us to their confidence and make it their interest, as well as ours, to establish better commercial relations.[19]

David A. Wells, the special commissioner of the revenue and a Carey student, also argued in his 1869 *Report* that the home market would never absorb the agricultural surplus, and consequently the farmer needed to export. However, his answer to the problem of securing expanded foreign markets was to lower the tariff. Throughout the late nineteenth century Wells remained a tariff reformer, but in the late 1870's he shifted the emphasis of his economic expansionism to the need for expanded markets for manufactured goods as a means of alleviating the social consequences of industrial depressions.[20]

Another obstacle to full economic independence in the immediate postwar period was the scarcity of capital to finance the development and expansion of American industry. In the years before 1875 industrialists and manufacturers, under the influence of Carey, favored "soft money" and easy credit to overcome the retarding effects of scarce capital and high interest rates.[21] The inavailability of capital and the resulting enormously high interest rates particularly aroused the Carey coterie, who were the major defenders of American industry, especially of Pennsylvania manufacturers. They directed their attack against "money lenders" as the primary enemy of productive capital, and, as with the protective tariff, the ultimate enemy and all too familiar nemesis was the world's great money power—England.

In creating the scarcity-of-capital thesis, the Carey school appealed to the anti-British nationalism rampant throughout the country while simultaneously promoting and intensifying American antipathy for England. Later, in the free silver campaign of the 1890s, this interpretation appeared as an integral segment of the charge that a conspiracy existed among English and Jewish bankers to keep the United States shackled in financial bondage. To be sure, the farmers and their silverite allies did modify the original version offered by the anticontraction forces when they emphasized the idea that the moneylender, American and British, was the enemy of the "producing classes" and not of productive capital. Nonetheless, the point that has eluded many historians is that the agrarians and Populists did not originate this view of history as conspiracy; the initial formulation of the money conspiracy emanated from eastern, urban, industrial groups when they utilized the thesis in their "soft money" campaigns of the 1860s and 1870s.

Carey was the chief intellectual spokesman for American industry in the years following the Civil War; although his influence among the academic community and more orthodox economic analysts waned somewhat in the postwar period, his political influence remained intact, and indeed was enhanced by the emergence of the GOP as the dominant party. He continually fired the imagination of American political leaders, many of whom undoubtedly shared his vision of the United States' future as an industrial giant and commercial colossus. Carey's influence did not end there, however, for he and his followers were also activists who campaigned vigorously for the fulfillment of their program. They were skillful pamphleteers who propagandized for their goals throughout the 1870s, and after the master's death in 1879, they continued their agitation in the tariff debates of the next decade.

Protectionists of the Carey stripe employed the alien-agent argument with great effectiveness during the controversy arising over the reports of Special Commissioner of the Revenue David A. Wells. Tariff revisionists had discovered a valuable ally in Wells, a situation particularly galling to high-tariff men, for Carey had tutored Wells in political economy. The Philadelphia nationalist's influence was paramount in Wells' thinking and the New Englander gratefully acknowledged his debt; nevertheless, Wells initially doubted the value of protection. He wrote fellow New Englander Edward Atkinson on July 17, 1866:

> I have changed my ideas respecting tarriffs [*sic*] and protection very much since I came to Washington and am coming over the ground which you occupy. I am utterly disgusted with the rapacity and selfishness which I have seen displayed by Pennsylvania people and some from other sections on the subject.[22]

However, Wells did not reveal publicly what he admitted privately until publication of his 1869 *Report*. The Carey group then heaped all their wrath upon him and ultimately drove him from public office by branding him an apostate who had been corrupted by British gold.

Ripples of discontent had appeared earlier within the protectionist camp, but Wells in his previous reports had not revealed the full extent of his transformation. Thomas H. Dudley, United States consul at Liverpool, wrote Wells expressing his concern over what appeared to be his friend's conversion to free trade. Wells replied and assured Dudley of his orthodoxy, claiming only to seek moderation to head off a public reaction that would disrupt the Republican party.[23] Wells was not being entirely candid, but as yet he did not wish to alienate his old comrades and ruin his position within the Republican party.

Wells journeyed to England in 1867 to investigate the British system and study for himself the protectionist argument that downward revision of the tariff necessitated a corresponding reduction of wages. That summer he published articles in the *Times* of London and the *New York Times* contrasting the British and American views on the tariff.[24] Although he did not reveal it in those articles, Wells' investigation of costs, wages, prices, and the conditions of manufacture supported the ideas he had already accepted before he left the United States. Instead of confirming the protectionist claim that high duties guaranteed high wages, the reverse held true. Countries such as Italy and Russia, with the highest protective duties, had the lowest wages and longest hours.

Wells did not reveal his altered views upon his return nor did he tip his hand in his *Report* of 1867. He avoided a discussion of the tariff on the ground that he lacked space.[25] Some industrialists might suspect Wells and his allegiance to protection, but he still maintained, even to Carey, that tariff reform would serve the long-run interests of the GOP and protection. He denied the charge that he had converted to free trade; he knew that a complete disavowal of protection would destroy his influence within the Republican party and close the way to further opportunity and advancement.

Some congressional criticism of Wells emerged in the spring and summer of 1868. But those who questioned his loyalty to protection were quickly quieted by his vigorous campaigning in the fall for the Grant ticket. In his *Report* for 1868, which appeared after the election, the tariff was given priority and Wells urged revision, asserting that the tariff "is in many respects injurious and destructive, and does not afford to American industry that stimulus and protection which is claimed as its chief merit."[26] Wells did not recommend specific reform legislation, and that approach caused confusion. But it did not prevent immediate opposition from the protectionist press.[27] The reform press gleefully praised Wells' report and took heart from what they termed a courageous stand.

The implications of the special commissioner's *Report* alarmed William D. "Pig-Iron" Kelley, a staunch protectionist and member of the Carey cadre. The Pennsylvania representative moved to prevent Congress from printing 20,000 copies of the *Report*. Kelley had been particularly angered by Wells' assertions about the decline in the position of American labor, especially his claim that the worker was less well off in 1868 than he had been in 1860. In a long and rather ill-prepared retort, the Pennsylvanian attempted to discredit the *Report* by showing that Wells had manipulated and juggled the figures. It failed to block congressional publication of the *Report*.

But more important (and perhaps in tacit recognition of the weakness of his logic), Kelley firmly set the pattern for all future protectionist attacks by arguing that Wells' advocacy of tariff revision was in the interest of Great Britain. To complete the false syllogism, Kelley waved the "bloody shirt" (a political smear tactic that rekindled the passions and emotions of the recently concluded Civil War), by identifying Wells with the traitorous policy of the Confederacy; "the southern leaders, holding to the revenue-tariff doctrines of the Special Commissioner of the Revenue, preferred having their ships and their workshops on the other side of the Atlantic."[28]

For Kelley the issue was clear: if the United States followed

Wells' suggestions it would remain England's "chief commercial dependency."[29] Kelley did not explicitly charge that Wells was in the pay of England. But through innuendo the relationship was implied, and when needed and under circumstances that allowed him more time to prepare, Kelley would not hesitate to make the connection clear. And while Kelley temporarily refrained from labelling the special commissioner an employee of the British, other members of the Carey group exhibited no such discretion.

The tariff reformers used Wells' 1868 *Report* more frequently throughout the spring of 1869 to support their demands for tariff revision, and as their movement gained momentum the protectionists angrily responded by denouncing Wells and his work. The gloves were removed and Carey led the attack. In a series of open letters to the *Tribune,* Carey rhetorically asked his former pupil: "Why is it that your report is so precisely in accordance with the views and wishes of these great British 'capitalists' who were accustomed in their efforts to gain and keep foreign markets to distribute money very freely among those of our own people who are supposed to be possessed of power and to influence public opinion?"[30] This approach proved quite effective and it remained an integral segment of the protectionist argument in the years between the Civil War and the turn of the century.

Horace Greeley, the editor of the *Tribune,* formally accused Wells in June 1869 of having been bribed by British gold. Greeley abandoned innuendo and insinuation:

> Mr. David A. Wells, revenue commissioner, was earning, at least receiving a great deal more than is paid him from the Treasury. We say this not because he favors what is called Free Trade—men as honest as live do that—but because he makes an exceedingly crooked trail from his premises to his conclusions. His late report is surcharged from the outset with just such venom as the foreign interest would have injected into it had they known how; yet he winds up by professing to be a protectionist! Honest men doing honest work do not make that sort of special track. Such is our reason for believing that Wells is bought and paid for by foreign interests.[31]

Not surprisingly, Wells, by being less than candid about his changed views in deference to his political career, contributed to the effectiveness of this charge.

Shortly before making the formal charge against Wells, Greeley had gained access to the records of the Free Trade League. What he uncovered undoubtedly contributed to his decision about Wells, and in his mind confirmed the whole argument that there existed a British conspiracy to undermine the protective tariff policy. Three-fourths of the entire amount subscribed to the league up to that time "came either directly from foreign houses, from their recognized agencies in New York City, or from those affiliated with foreign houses."[32] He also joyously noted that one-fourth of the entire amount came from family relations of the Barings. It all proved grist for the mill, further evidence of the British plot to subvert the American economy.

The special commissioner's *Report* for 1869 was a comprehensive attack on the tariff structure, and its appearance signaled another series of protectionist attacks through the press and in Congress. In this report (Wells anticipated it might be his last because his appointment would soon expire), he called for specific reforms of the national currency and the taxation process, especially the tariff system. It was the culmination of Wells' five-year study of the national economy and it was to serve as the platform of tariff reform for years to come. Wells acknowledged America's economic progress, but manifested a deep concern about factors that were contributing to the unequal distribution of wealth, and he reiterated his conclusion of the previous year that "the rich become richer and the poor poorer."[33] The inflated irredeemable currency and the excessive and unequal taxation also tended to disrupt and inhibit commercial relations with foreign nations, and in the long run would retard American industrial development. Then, in an essay of approximately 150 pages, Wells outlined the specific reforms he thought essential, hitting particularly hard at the tariff.

This time the protectionists lashed back in all their fury and on all fronts. "Pig-Iron" Kelley directed the attack in the House of Representatives and on January 11, 1870, he personally opened fire on Wells. Kelley charged that "the prominent characteristics of Mr. Wells' report are audacity and advocacy of the interests of England and her American colonies."[34] He implied that Wells was bribed by British gold by making allusions to his "Sheffield employers."[35] Kelley also noted that Wells' transition from protection to free trade was curiously synonymous with his official visit to England in 1867. But the crux of Kelley's remarks concerned the United States' continuing economic rivalry with Great Britain, especially the British awareness that they were losing their supremacy in the American market. America's industries were supplying its domestic needs and the British were being edged out in their most important and most lucrative market. In response they were freely employing the tactic that the protectionists had frequently warned against: through a liberal use of gold they were bribing certain influential American leaders to labor for free trade and thus curtail American industrial development and prosperity.

Representative Kelley's diagnosis of Britain's decline in the American market was somewhat premature and exposed only a portion of the economic reality. While it was true that English imports comprised less of the total of American imports, that relative decline was insignificant until the mid-1870s. More important, from the British viewpoint, was the fact that the dollar value of their shipments to the United States steadily increased up to 1875. For example, British imports rose from $519,962,621 in the years 1861–1865 to $1,042,179,670 for the period 1871–1875, while Britain's overall position in the American market during those same years declined from 40.71 percent of all imports to 36.07 percent of the total. Then, probably as a consequence of the depression of the 1870s, came a drastic fall; English imports plummeted to $663,550,722, or 26.94 percent of the total, in the years 1876–1880. This trend continued so that by 1891–1895, when American imports from all countries totaled $3,125,344,017, the British share amounted to $800,340,150, or 20.39 percent of the market.[36]

To prove that Wells provided an example of his analysis, Kelley presented a schedule of tariff rates suggested by Sheffield iron manufacturers and compared it to Wells' suggested schedule. Although not absolutely identical they were very similar, enough so to weaken the plea of coincidence. For "Pig-Iron" Kelley, the close similarity was convincing proof of Wells' chicanery, and he concluded with the remark that "I think I have sufficiently disclosed the devotion of our Special Commissioner of the Revenue to the interests of England."[37]

Greeley again denounced Wells as being in the pay of the British, and Carey quickly joined the attack with a pamphlet exposing

Wells' errors.[38] The protectionists were by that time consistently charging that Wells was in the hire of the British. In Congress they repeated their earlier tactic of blocking official printing of the report. Henry L. Cake, a coal operator from Pennsylvania, led the assault in the House of Representatives. The charges undoubtedly were familiar to the members of the House, but Cake repeated them again, emphasizing the trip to England as the "mistake" that corrupted Wells. The direct tie between Wells, the Free Trade League, and the British iron masters and manufacturers, was explicitly revealed and stressed. The campaign was important for it further advanced the pattern and strategy of the protectionist argument in the continuing struggle against tariff reform throughout the next two decades.

In the debate over the publication of Wells' report, the protectionist Republicans justified their position by pointing out that the Free Trade League planned to publish an edition. They cited this as evidence of the bias of the report and denied the necessity of another edition, especially one authorized and paid for by the Congress. The protectionists lost their battle to prevent Congressional publication, but were able to have the House direct the Committee on Manufactures to investigate the veracity of the report. The results of this inquiry were basically partisan; the seven-member majority concluded that "the report seems to have been written in the interest of foreign producers and manufacturers, and its suggestions and recommendations, if followed by consequent legislation, would be hostile to the best interests of the people of the country, and tend to make us dependents on foreign nations, when we have the means and ability to be independent of the world."[39] The minority report of Democratic Congressmen Orestes Cleveland and John M. Rice essentially agreed with Wells' conclusions.

Throughout the controversy the protectionists perfected the argument that became the basis of Republican opposition to tariff reformers and advocates of free trade. In all future debates they cleverly associated the idea of tariff reform with British free trade. The Wells affair, as interpreted by the protectionists, served to expose the danger that they continually warned against—Great Britain would use all means, fair or foul, to weaken and destroy American industry. That was the standard analysis of the Carey school, and the activities of the English during the Civil War were interpreted as verifying the argument. As Thomas H. Dudley, American consul at Liverpool, had warned in 1866, "they are making great efforts on this side to repeal our tariff and admit British goods free of duty. If effort and money can accomplish it, you may rest assured it will be done. The work is to be done through the agents of foreign houses in Boston and New York. Their plan is to agitate in the western States and to form free-trade associations all over the country . . . . No stone will be left unturned to break down our manufactures."[40] This theme remained dominant; the protectionist Republicans used it throughout the late nineteenth century as a replacement for the fading effectiveness of the "bloody shirt" as an issue to politically club the Democrats.

Although the allegations that Wells was in the pay of the British were never verified or substantiated, the attacks against him proved effective. The protectionists gained their general tariff law and virtually drove Wells from office. He early recognized the smear tactics and campaign innuendo as an old and favorite device, as he revealed to his friend James A. Garfield in 1868: "It is the same old game which slavery played. When argument and investigation were becoming too powerful, abolitionist was the potent word invoked to stifle free thought and end discussion as free trade is now."[41] And during the House debate over whether to print Wells' 1869 *Report*, James Brooks, Democrat of New York, angrily replied to the charges that advocates of tariff reduction were bought by "British gold," by reminding the Republicans that the special commissioner was their appointee, in a job they had created. Brooks defended Wells' right to change his view and then turned his attack on the protectionists, especially the Pennsylvania representatives, by denouncing the hypocrisy of those who had "fed and fattened" on federal bounties and now maligned anyone who opposed protection. Representative Garfield also rose in defense of his friend by praising him as an "able and industrious officer." It was, Garfield concluded, "a lamentable exhibition of weakness" to judge Wells unworthy and corrupt simply because he no longer agreed with the theories and opinions of the protectionists.[42]

The rebuttals had little impact. The charges that his report benefited only the British proved telling, and during the remainder of his career, which included his role as presidential advisor during both administrations of Grover Cleveland, Wells continually had to confront the accusation that he was a tool of England. The 1867 trip to Great Britain and then his election to the Cobden Club in May 1870 made him especially vulnerable. Wells himself contributed to the conspiracy aspect by being disingenuous about the change in his views; his subsequent championing of free trade only seemed to confirm the charges.

This success in the immediate years after the Civil War led the protectionist Republicans to employ the argument throughout the election years of the 1870s and 1880s. The country was flooded with protection pamphlets in each campaign. The Republicans directed their appeal to the Midwest farmers, but the argument was not lost on the region's growing industrial class. The approach was effective in overcoming the agrarian skepticism about the tariff; for, as much as they desired tariff reduction, the idea of free trade as a British policy upset the farmers. One Iowa farmer, expressing a fear common to his fellows, remarked that free trade "put gold in English coffers."[43] That prospect troubled agrarians, and the tariff in the 1880s "remained a quasi-patriotic economic question to many farmers in the Midwest and Far West."[44]

Several eastern manufacturers' associations, such as the American Iron and Steel Association and the Industrial League, provided the financial support for printing and distributing the pamphlets throughout the country during the election campaigns. James M. Swank, a Philadelphia industrialist, was a driving force in both groups, especially the American Iron and Steel Association, which he headed for 40 years. Swank's major effort came in 1887—1888, when he directed the protectionist campaign against President Cleveland, the Democracy, and tariff reform. The industrial associations' pamphlets were a major weapon in the protectionist arsenal, which in each campaign year repeated the analysis originally formulated by the Carey group. As late as 1892, for that matter, Swank himself authored a typical protection tract entitled "British Efforts To Prevent The Development of American Industries."[45] Swank repeated the historical analysis formulated by Carey years earlier, that Great Britain's policy had been to thwart American industrial growth, and he emphasized that it was still a reality in the 1890s.

The Republican strategy in these campaigns was to promote the idea of protection in the northwest states on the basis of a sectional home market argument. They maintained that the tariff protected the region's infant industries and guaranteed the national home market from the rapacious British. While this approach had psychological appeal to midwestern and western agrarians who resented their dependence upon the British market, and who distrusted the machinations of John Bull, it began to wear thin as the farmers' overall economic position remained grim and the benefits of protection appeared illusory. When the home market failed to materialize and the agricultural surpluses mounted, the farmers became impatient and their opposition to the tariff became stiffer with each passing year. As early as the 1870s some agrarians were attracted to tariff reform because it promised to open additional foreign markets, cut the costs of constructing railroads which would presumably result in lower rates to market, and reduce the cost of implements and consumer items.

The Republicans, conscious that the western agrarian was crucial to the continued success of the party, responded in several ways. First, GOP leaders stressed the necessity for expanded foreign markets, a course earlier charted by President Grant and William Elder, and proposed reciprocity treaties with the countries of Latin America as one way to secure additional outlets for farm products. Second, they were unwilling to abandon their emotional appeal to the farmers' anti-British nationalism, and increasingly relied on the theme that tariff reform meant free trade and domination by Great Britain. Despite these efforts many agrarians despaired of relief through the tariff and by the late 1880s and early 1890s turned to free silver as a more viable alternative.

The protectionist press and pamphlet corps also stressed the point that British agriculture had been destroyed by free trade. Increased importation of American cereals and meats during the years 1870 through 1896 proved disastrous to the British farmer.[46] This tremendous influx of agricultural products "made farming in Britain unprofitable as early as 1879."[47] Agricultural depression in Great Britain prompted a steady criticism of free trade, climaxing in 1893 at the National Agricultural Conference. At this meeting English farmers called for an abolition of free trade and asked for protective duties on imports.[48] In addition, English farmers envied the position of the American farmer and the tremendous development of American agriculture. To the protectionists, and they hoped to the farmer, the point was clear: "England had free trade, America did not."[49]

Democrats and other tariff reformers continually stressed the failures of protection in their appeal to farmers. As Representative William R. Morrison, Democrat of Illinois, pointed out in 1876: "After protection unequalled for half a generation the home market has not come to us, but is as far as ever removed from the fields of agriculture. Our surplus of grain has outgrown the wondrous growth of our population; it has not abated and will not abate."[50] Beneath all the propaganda of each group, however, it was clear that both protectionist Republicans and reform tariff Democrats understood that the agricultural surpluses demanded foreign markets. The protectionists did not abandon either their dream of, or their preference for, the home market; but they did recognize, as President Grant, William Elder, and others had previously, that expanded foreign markets were essential in the interim.

In the race for foreign markets American free traders acknowledged that Great Britain was the nation's chief rival. This realization, however, did not evoke any hostility or anti-British sentiment. They viewed the struggle as strictly commercial competition in which the United States eventually would be victorious. Protectionists, on the other hand, especially the actual manufacturers and producers, were less sanguine, and more insecure. The protective tariff represented the guarantee of America's success in the economic battle. Each group manifested the economic nationalism of the period, but the protectionists displayed a narrower, capitalistic outlook and they preferred to alleviate competition as much as possible to assure American success.

The tariff debate really concerned the question of means, not ends. Both groups desired commercial expansion and a strong, independent United States that would be commercially, financially, economically—and therefore politically—free of Great Britain and Europe.[51] The Republican tactic became reciprocity; the Democrat strategy favored tariff reduction to stimulate commerce with an emphasis on free raw materials to allow continued American industrial growth.

Not all members of either camp, of course, made their case in terms of such a general, integrated view of the national interest.

Tariff reformers, partially to deflect the charge that they were pro-British, alleged that protection promoted special interest, that the advocates of heavy industry represented by the Swank group saw American industrial growth through a distorted lens, and in reality sacrificed national interest for personal gain. The protectionist claim that tariff reform served Great Britain was not without foundation either, especially as revealed in the activities of such advocates as Thomas Worrall. Worrall, an English immigrant with commercial interests in the Mississippi Valley, saw direct trade with Great Britain as the way for the people of the upper Midwest to free themselves of commercial dependency vis á vis the Northeast metropolis.[52]

In the midst of the depression of the 1870s he dismissed as an illusion the hope that American manufactures could compete in world markets. Free-trader Worrall denied the home market argument; he believed that direct trade provided the West the means to overcome its commercial dependence on the Northeast. Goods were rusting in Great Britain for want of a market; crops were rotting in the Mississippi Valley for the same reason. Worrall's solution was to bring them together for the mutual benefit of both areas.

This was exactly what the protectionists warned against, for through this course the western states would remain a subservient region: "if restricted to agriculture, debarred from manufactures themselves, and undefeated by conterminous manufacturing, communities belonging to the same great nation would merely fall a prey to the trade plunder and rapine of Europe, and would vainly exhaust the riches of their soil for the benefit of the cotton lords of Manchester."[53] Protectionists viewed Worrall's cure for the Mississippi Valley's colonial status as worse than the disease, since it would have relegated that area to the position of a permanent British commercial dependency.[54]

But in the view of tariff reformers, protection was retrogressive legislation. It had destroyed the American merchant marine and limited the nation's foreign commerce. They argued the need for commercial expansion on the grounds of a constant redundant surplus. Thus they called for expanded markets and foreign commerce—that was "the life of the nation."[55] This group, instead of despising and fearing Great Britain, saw the system of "commercial freedom" as the secret of its success. David A. Wells had seen the need for foreign markets for agricultural surpluses and had recommended lowering the tariff to help open markets. To others, such as John Allen, England was at once America's rival and its model. He bore no malice and denied a conspiracy. Instead, he stressed that Great Britain was vulnerable because it had few resources. The United States, on the other hand, had magnificent potential. Yet Great Britain was on top, and its free trade policy was the reason. In addition, the tariff policies of other nations aided Great Britain. American tariff policy allowed England, for example, to obtain "all she wants of it at her own price" primarily, Allen believed, because protection "has operated in loosening our grip in foreign markets by depriving us of the power to make prices for those things we have to sell."[56] Allen believed the way to succeed was to emulate Great Britain; the United States must adopt free trade and displace England as *the* commercial nation of the world.

In response to Allen's and similar arguments, the protectionists reminded the electorate that the United States was Great Britain's greatest market. They contended that free traders and tariff reformers ignored protection's importance in preventing the English from crippling and destroying American industrial development. On that point the Republicans were correct. The British recognized the importance of the American market, and used their influence, discreetly to be sure, for tariff revision. In a long dispatch to Lord Salisbury dated August 4, 1879, Sir Edward Thornton discussed the prevailing duties and British hopes for tariff reform. He candidly acknowledged that any reform would be difficult since any benefit for British interests "is immediately attributed to the use of British gold."[57] Nevertheless, Thornton suggested that British importing merchants use their "influence" with members of Congress for tariff reform. He also informed his superior that he would be glad to do all in his power to influence those American officials whom he knew.[58]

Thornton's proposals for British participation in the tariff debate lent support to the Careyite explanation of agitation for tariff reform as conspiracy. Other British activities, such as the actions of the Cobden Club and its influence with the Free Trade League, further supported this view. Thomas Bayley Potter, head of the

Cobden Club, denied in 1891 that his organization was engaged in bribery in the United States. He admitted that "a large number of leaflets" had been distributed prior to 1879, but pointed out that the Club had stopped that activity because it became convinced that "the circulation of these leaflets was causing a feeling of great irritation and jealousy."[59] Admittedly, the protectionist charges of conspiracy were exaggerated and generally inaccurate, but the allegations were not entirely fabrication and a measure of truth existed in the explanation. And, as the Republicans shrewdly understood, many Americans were receptive to this interpretation because England's power as the most mature industrial society, further strengthened by its surplus capital, placed the United States, still a developing country, in an economically dependent position.

Americans were in a truculent mood toward Great Britain following the Civil War, and that accounts to some degree for the success of the Carey school in agitating this view of the tariff battle. Northerners remembered England's behavior during the war: the role of Canada as the base for Confederate attacks, the profits of the West Indian colonists collected by sustaining the blockade runners, and the indispensable aid given the *Alabama* and other cruisers in the African and Asiatic colonies of England. Even Australia had enabled the *Shenandoah* through "illegitimate privileges allowed to it at Melbourne to destroy the American whaling fleet in the Arctic seas."[60] Nor were the feelings of hatred and bitterness any less conspicuous in the South, where the refusal of England to grant recognition "left a feeling that Great Britain was wholly responsible for the ensuing catastrophe."[61] Americans not only felt some compensation was due, they easily accepted and responded to the protectionist explanation (and defamation) of Great Britain as the power blocking America in its efforts to fulfill its destiny.

This public perception of Great Britain as the power denying American aspirations was reinforced in the depression of the 1870s, when other issues directly linked to the overseas expansion option offered by Grant, Elder, and Wells dominated the thinking of American leaders. President Rutherford B. Hayes and his secretary of state, William M. Evarts, acted upon the foreign market solution to alleviate the domestic stress and strife caused by the depression, and in the process confronted Britain's commercial and financial supremacy in the Western Hemisphere and the Pacific. This shift of emphasis and concern, from the narrow tariff solution to a wider variety of expressions of economic nationalism—such as the construction of a first class navy, federal support for steamship service to South America and the restoration of the merchant marine, the question of which nation was to build and control an isthmian canal, and the struggle over the use of silver—sustained and in some instances intensified the anti-British nationalism of the immediate postwar years.

NOTES

1. Henry C. Carey, *The Harmony of Interests* (Philadelphia: Henry Carey Baird, Publisher, 1865).

2. Henry C. Carey, *The Way to Outdo England Without Fighting Her* (Philadelphia: Henry Carey Baird, Industrial Publisher, 1865), p. 95. For a discussion of the elder Carey's views see Kenneth W. Rowe, *Mathew Carey, A Study in American Economic Development* (Baltimore: The Johns Hopkins Press, 1933).

3. Ibid., Carey, p. 40.

4. Ibid.

5. A. D. H. Kaplan, *Henry Charles Carey, A Study in American Economic Thought* (Baltimore: The Johns Hopkins Press, 1931), p. 46. Arnold W. Green, *Henry Charles Carey Nineteenth-Century Sociologist* (Philadelphia: University of Pennsylvania Press, 1951), pp. 20—21.

6. Carey, *Harmony of Interests*, Preface.

7. Carey, *The Way to Outdo England*, p. 40.

8. Henry C. Carey, *Principles of Social Science* (Philadelphia: J. B. Lippincott & Co., 1858), p. 372 and *passim*. See also Luther L. Bernard and Jessie Bernard, *Origins of American Sociology* (New York: Thomas Y. Crowell Co., 1943), pp. 419—20.

9. These frequent social meetings at the Carey residence to discuss political economy and problems of the day were attended by such leading men as Joseph Wharton, William D. Lewis, Joseph Chandler, Morton McMichael, General U.S. Grant, Salmon P. Chase, Bayard Taylor, and Blaine. Green, *Carey, Nineteenth-Century Sociologist*, pp. 36—37. James G. Blaine, *Twenty Years in Congress* (Norwich, Connecticut: The Henry Bill Publishing Company, 1885).

10. Carey, *The Way to Outdo England*, p. 46.

11. Ibid., p. 95.

12. Ibid.

13. William Elder, *How the Western States Can Become the Imperial Power in the Union* (Philadelphia: Ringwalt and Brown, 1865), p. 1.

14. Ibid., p. 23.

15. Ibid., p. 18.

16. Ibid., p. 23.

17. Ibid., p. 18.

18. William Elder, *The American Farmer's Markets at Home and Abroad* (Philadelphia: Ringwalt and Brown, 1870).

19. James D. Richardson, *A Compilation of the Messages and Papers of the Presidents, 1789 — 1902*, Vol. VII (Washington: Bureau of National Literature and Art, 1905), p. 37.

20. For a discussion of Wells' commitment to economic expansion see Tom E. Terrill, "David A. Wells, The Democracy, and Tariff Reduction, 1877—1894," *Journal of American History* 56, 3 (December 1969), pp. 540—55.

21. Irwin Unger, *The Greenback Era. A Social and Political History of American Finance, 1865 — 1879* (Princeton, New Jersey: Princeton University Press, 1964), p. 51.

22. Quoted in Herbert R. Ferleger, *David A. Wells and the American Revenue System* (New York: Author, 1942), p. 154.

23. Ibid., p. 177.

24. *London Times*, September 2, 1867: *New York Times*, September 4, 1867.

25. *Report of the Special Commissioner of the Revenue for the Year 1867* (Washington: Government Printing Office, 1868), p. 48.

26. *Report of the Special Commissioner of the Revenue for the Year 1868* (Washington: Government Printing Office, 1869), pp. 80—81.

27. *New York Tribune*, January 5, 6, 1869.

28. Remarks of January 19, 1869, *Congressional Globe*, Part I, 1868—1869, p. 454 (hereinafter cited as *CG*, I: 1868—69: 454).

29. Ibid.

30. *New York Tribune*, May 23, 1869.

31. Ibid., June 8, 1869.

32. Fred B. Joyner, *David Ames Wells, Champion of Free Trade* (Cedar Rapids, Iowa: The Torch Press, 1939), p. 83.

33. *Report of the Special Commissioner of the Revenue for the Year 1869* (Washington: Government Printing Office, 1870), p. 31.

34. Remarks of January 11, 1870, CG, I: 1869—70:370.

35. Ibid., p. 371.

36. *Commerce of the United States with European Countries, 1790 — 1896* (Washington: Government Printing Office, 1896), p. 28.

37. Remarks of January 11, 1870, *CG*, I:1869—70:375.

38. Henry C. Carey, *Review of the Farmer's Question, as exhibited in the recent Report of the Hon. D. A. Wells, Special Commissioner of the Revenue* (Philadelphia: 1870).

39. *Examination of Statements in the Report of Special Commissioner of Revenue by Committee on Manufactures*, House Report 72, 41st Cong., 2nd Sess., 1869—70 (Washington: Government Printing Office, 1870), p. 65.

40. Quoted in remarks of John A. Griswold, July 9, 1866, *CG*, IV:1865—66:3689.

41. Wells to Garfield, July 21, 1868, in Ferleger, *Wells and Revenue System*, p. 208.

42. See remarks of James Brooks and James A. Garfield, January 20, 1870, *CG*, I:1869—70:621,624.

43. Duane M. Leach, "The Tariff and the Western Farmer: 1860—1890" (Ph. D. dissertation, University of Oklahoma, 1965), p. 115.

44. Ibid., p. 123.

45. James M. Swank, *British Efforts to Prevent the Development of American Industries* (Philadelphia: Tariff Tract No. 3, 1892).

46. James F. Tucker, "British Agriculture Under Protection and Free Trade, 1815–1895" (Ph. D. dissertation, University of Pennsylvania, 1957), p. 78.

47. Ibid., p. 79.

48. Ibid., p. 118. See also London *Economist,* November 26, 1893.

49. Leech, p. 159.

50. Remarks of May 25, 1876, *CR,* IV:4:3316.

51. Tom E. Terrill, "The Tariff and Foreign Policy 1880–1892" (Ph. D. dissertation, University of Wisconsin, 1966).

52. Thomas D. Worrall, *Direct Trade between Great Britain and the Mississippi Valley* (Manchester: North of England Co-op Printing Society, 1875).

53. *Examination of Statements by Committee on Manufactures,* p. 61.

54. In this tariff debate the West and South were defined as colonial areas. People were definitely aware that the Civil War resulted in the dominance of eastern capital and manufacturing elements over the economy. Charles A. Beard's view of the results and effects of the Civil War were not as far from the mark as recent critics contend.

55. John H. Allen, *The Tariff and Its Evils* (New York: G. P. Putnam, 1888), p. 49.

56. Ibid.

57. Sir Edward Thornton to Salisbury, Commercial No. 59, August 4, 1879, Foreign Office 115, Vol. 643, Public Record Office, London.

58. Ibid.

59. *New York Herald,* September 27, 1891.

60. William A. Dunning, *The British Empire and the United States* (New York: Charles Scribners Sons, 1916), p. 221.

61. Ibid.

The Search for Foreign Markets

They [Great Britain] complain of us that we are a forward, impatient nation, always getting into everybody's way. When do they ever hear of our mother country ever getting out of anybody's way?

William M. Evarts, 1879

We are in a position to contend for the markets of the world, fearing neither scarcity of food nor scarcity of raw material.

William M. Evarts, 1878

Through American enterprise England has not only lost her best customer, but that customer is competing with her in India, Brazil, and other markets . . . . England has not only lost an important market, but she has met with an active, shrewd, and powerful competitor, which produces as well as manufactures.

A. V. Dockery, 1877

The United States is now beginning to show itself restless and energetic to obtain foreign markets, and has a vision of becoming the greatest producer and manufacturer in the world.

Victor Drummond, 1878

The United States are running us hard in the race.

The Economist, 1880

The depression of the 1870s was one of the most acute economic collapses ever experienced in the United States. Throughout the decade the American people endured economic distress and dislocation unprecedented in the country's history. Precipitated by the Panic of 1873, the downturn continued for six years as the economy hit bottom in 1877–1878. While the terrible depression was felt throughout the land, it struck, as so often was the case, the farmer and the workingman particularly hard. The farmer confronted the twin calamities of inadequate prices and ever-mounting surpluses. Prices fell approximately 30 percent below the level of 1870–1873, while production of wheat jumped from 281.2 million bushels in 1873 to 420.1 million bushels in 1878 and that of cotton rose from 4.17 million bales in 1873 to 5.07 million bales in 1878.[1] Labor probably suffered even more than the farmer. The unemployed reached almost a million and those fortunate enough to hold jobs earned desperately low wages. Misery and squalor were the common lot of the industrial laboring class. The worker and his family were confined to the slums of the large cities which were infested with rats and vermin, filth, and garbage. To escape the urban hell people fled to the countryside and tramps, a sure sign of social and economic distress, were seen throughout the nation and became a prominent feature of the depression.

The general economic dislocation created a social powderkeg that momentarily threatened to explode into a serious and basic challenge to the existing system. Ultimately labor and farmer agitation erupted and culminated in the nationwide violence and destruction of 1877—the "year of violence." The labor outbursts and general strikes represented a widespread increase in lawlessness and disdain for the existing order, and conservatives believed that the turmoil and general dissatisfaction dramatically demonstrated the seriousness of the threat to the prevailing system. Graham Smith, an Englishman and friend of the American wealthy, found the American upper classes "pervaded by an uneasy feeling that they were living over a mine of social and industrial discontent, with which the power of Government, under American institutions, was wholly inadequate to deal: and that some day this mine would explode and blow society into the air."[2]

The new Republican administration headed by President

Rutherford B. Hayes and his secretary of state, William M. Evarts, intended to prevent the potentially destructive explosion. Having entered the White House as the result of an agreement with conservative southern cohorts, Hayes and his supporters did not hesitate to use federal troops to squelch labor unrest. Ironically, the understanding with the southern leaders called for the termination of federal rule in the South and an end to the use of federal troops to protect the rights of the Negro in the South. Despite their vigorous use of force in the urban North, Hayes and Evarts realized that federal intervention to break industrial and railroad strikes would merely restore order temporarily, and they understood that such an approach was at best only a stopgap measure. Both men knew that curing the malfunctioning of the system and preserving the established order would require a more sophisticated approach that offered long-range solutions for the nation's economic ills.

Hayes and Evarts, a pair of low-key but nonetheless determined economic nationalists, embraced the idea that the solution to the depression lay in expanding foreign markets for America's surplus. Those troubled and vexed leaders believed that overseas economic expansion was necessary, indeed essential, to stem further social unrest and disquiet, and they persistently sought ways to provide government aid and assistance to foster American commercial expansion. Secretary Evarts revealed the full scope of this analysis in an interview published by the *Northwestern Miller* shortly after he took over the State Department. Questioned about the importance of the tariff to the present economic dislocation, Evarts denounced any free trade scheme as pure folly, since it would mean sacrificing agriculture and "I cannot be willing to sacrifice the developing interests of my country to an abstract idea."[3] Although a protectionist, he dismissed the tariff as irrelevant in the crisis. He believed the more crucial issue was that "the vast resources of our country need an outlet, as we have recognized so disasterously during the past five years. Production is greater than our home demands, unless an outlet is found for the excess we must still continue to feel depressing effects." Evarts then sounded a theme that served as the policy guideline for his tenure in the State Department: in the pursuit of new markets and commercial expansion "it is the duty of the government to protect all classes, not only the manufacturers but the agriculturists, and the miners."[4] And as President Hayes and Secretary Evarts translated this rhet-

oric into action during their administration they thoroughly understood that Great Britain was the rival to beat in the race for
markets.[5]

Another expression of this analysis came during the 1877
banquet of the New York Chamber of Commerce. President Hayes
and Secretary Evarts attended, and they, as well as several members of the Democratic party, spoke to the importance of the expansion of the nation's trade.[6] Again, the new secretary declared
that "the vast resources of our country need an outlet" and assured
this gathering of businessmen and merchants as he previously had
assured the farmers, that the national government would play an
active role in the quest.[7] He intended "to make our representatives
to foreign nations . . . cooperators . . . in diffusing our commercial intercourse" and he hoped "through trade conventions with
foreign governments to further extend the markets for our
products."[8] Those were to be two positive aspects of the Republican
effort to expand foreign markets.

More important, Hayes and Evarts, in their speeches to the New
York Chamber of Commerce, explicitly stated their belief in the
importance of foreign markets and the pressing urgency of overseas
economic expansion to alleviate domestic turmoil and social
disorder. The depression of the 1870s forced those two men, along
with many other American leaders, to confront the economic mal-
adies of the American system. Their response was to externalize
the problem by defining foreign markets as the best remedy for
depression, and with the export solution they tied American
domestic prosperity directly to foreign policy.

Although President Hayes accepted the need for extended markets and directed his administration along that course, Secretary
Evarts actually implemented the policy. His selection to the first
place in the cabinet infuriated party regulars such as Roscoe
Conkling and troubled the likes of James G. Blaine and James A.
Garfield. Among other objections, Evarts' detractors scored his
political independence and questioned his loyalty to the Republican
party. To justify their concern they had only to recall the recent
presidential campaign in which Evarts wavered and failed to come
out for Hayes until a few days before the election. However, the
appointment did please important commercial interests,
particularly the New York mercantile and business community.
Evarts had close ties with a number of business and financial

leaders including Samuel B. Ruggles, Levi P. Morton, Thomas G. Sherman, and Clark Bell, and in 1874 the New York Produce Exchange made him an honorary member in recognition of "the deep interest manifested by him in whatever concerns the welfare and the commercial standing of this metropolis."[9] Support for the New Yorker among businessmen extended throughout the nation; they applauded his selection and heartily approved of his proposals to advance America's commercial interests.

It was Evarts' brilliance as an attorney that brought him to public notice, and his skillful handling of Hayes' legal case before the Electoral Commission probably was a decisive factor in his selection.[10] He had little diplomatic experience although he knew firsthand the problems of dealing with Great Britain. During the Civil War, Evarts had twice traveled to England to plead the cause of the Union. He also had served as the legal adviser and negotiator for the United States in the *Alabama* claims discussions which led to the Treaty of Washington. More important, Evarts was an economic nationalist who shared the president's sense of urgency about overseas commercial expansion. He advocated government encouragement of foreign commerce and was instrumental in making this the cornerstone of the Hayes administration's foreign policy.

Actually, the Hayes-Evarts analysis reflected the views of leaders of both major political parties. As a result there existed in foreign policy a bipartisan consensus on the importance of overseas expansion. The House Committee on Foreign Affairs, in its 1878 *Report* on the relations of the United States with Mexico, illustrated the bipartisan support for this ideology. The committee, Democratic by a seven-to-four ratio, asserted that the country had arrived at a "turning point" in its industrial and commercial development.[11] The United States was entering upon a new contest; the home market was no longer sufficient for the consumption of the products of American industry. The committee believed that because of the absence of foreign markets "our surplus products cannot be sold, and their production has to be restricted, throwing labor out of employment and causing widespread distress in the cities and manufacturing districts."[12]

The congressmen thought a rearrangement of relative occupations might eventually take place, at which time the unemployed industrial workers would embark upon agricultural pursuits. Yet such a change was not really desirable, and could not "be done on a very large scale without ruin to many and an enormous loss to the nation, while it would add to the over-production of our agriculturists and seriously curtail the home market for their produce."[13] To prevent this the committee urged that "we must find foreign markets for the productions of our manufacturers."[14] The analysis was concluded with the flat assertion that "the immense importance to us of foreign markets is therefore so clear that it is now universally admitted."[15]

The members of the committee agreed that American relations with Mexico should be conducted within the framework of that analysis. They advocated that the State Department vigorously support the protection of American citizens and property in Mexico, and informed the Hayes administration that there was "no good reason why we should not be the leading power in the markets of Mexico, as also in those of Central and South America."[16] This admonition revealed the committee members' deep concern over the imbalance in American trade with those nations whereby the United States purchased an annual average of over $100 million more than it sold to them. They bluntly complained in their report that "we buy from them, and other nations sell to them" and set as one of their objectives the increase in the volume of exports of manufactured goods to the Latin American nations. Great Britain presented the most formidable obstacle to expanded trade and was "our chief competitor" in great measure because that nation long recognized the need to support and protect its businessmen and citizens, a course of action the committee strongly recommended for the United States.[17]

Evarts and the State Department needed little prodding. One of their major programs was to expand trade with the nations of the Western Hemisphere, especially with Mexico and Brazil. American efforts to penetrate and dominate the markets of Brazil were unsuccessful during the late nineteenth century,[18] but the Hayes administration did prepare the groundwork for ultimate success in Mexico. After 1876, the United States began to dominate the Mexican market by displacing Great Britain as the chief supplier of Mexican imports. The annual value of exports from the United States exceeded the amount supplied by Britain after 1883; in 1900 the United States supplied 51.1 percent of Mexico's imports (compared with 17 percent for Great Britain), and by 1911 American trade with Mexico surpassed that of all the European nations combined.[19]

In July 1877, Evarts took one of the initial steps to expand overseas markets when he directed the State Department to issue a circular to all American diplomats and consular officers in Spanish America, Brazil, and Europe requesting information relative to the improvement of commercial intercourse between the United States and those countries. It was clear that the continued depression motivated the secretary's action and he confidently expected that the crisis could be turned to the country's advantage for a "favorable opportunity [was] now offered by the prevailing stagnation of business and depression of prices."[20] However, the plan was not entirely selfish, since mutual benefit would come from expanded trade. As Secretary Evarts explained, it was "desirable . . . for the United States that they should find markets for the export of their products and manufactures, and, on the other hand, it is advantageous to the people of those countries . . . to purchase at the present decreased valuation."[21]

His candid analysis serves to dramatize important consequences of the depression of the 1870s. While the domestic turmoil that erupted in 1877 frightened the administration and pointed up the importance and necessity of expanded markets, it also exposed a unique opportunity to establish the United States in the markets of the hemisphere and Europe. Necessity demanded, and at the same time fostered, American expansion. The administration understood that the economic stagnation had not damaged or diminished the nation's productive capacity, and Evarts' circular stressed that the "depression of prices" gave American products the required initial advantage to capture the market. After securing this foothold, the United States' position in the markets of the world was assured.

The depression years also brought, during the fiscal year 1876–1877, the turn of the corner after which the United States regularly maintained a favorable trade balance. To be sure, the United States remained a debtor nation in the overall international balance of payments account until World War I. Nonetheless, after 1877 it continually exported more than it imported. The most important aspect of this favorable balance of trade was the nation's newly acquired control and dominance in its home market. Great Britain was displaced as the country's primary supplier, while at the same time the United States retained its position as the leading exporter to the United Kingdom. Secretary Evarts proudly announced "that the United States maintains an indisputable lead in the imports into the United Kingdom, while in the exports there from the United States has fallen from a good first in 1872, to the fifth place in 1876."[22]

Economic nationalist that he was, Evarts gleefully noted this change in the trade between the two countries and observed that it was causing serious alarm among English newspapers and politicians. The aspect that received the greatest attention was the steady increase in Britain's imports and the alarming decrease in its exports.[23] The drop in British exports to the United States during the years 1872–1876 amounted to $124,298,000. Four items suffered the most—iron, cotton manufactures, woolen manufactures, and linen goods.[24] However, as Evarts quickly noted, "the decrease in the export of those articles is not attributed to any decrease in consumption in the United States, but is caused by the improvement and development of American manufactures, by which we are enabled to supply our own wants to the exclusion of so much foreign manufactures."[25]

Despite the favorable balance of trade, the overall condition of American commerce with Great Britain remained somewhat anomalous. American sales to the United Kingdom generally exceeded British shipments to the United States in the years after the close of the Civil War, yet Great Britain enjoyed the advantage in balance of payments with the United States.[26] Evarts hopefully believed that this unfortunate state of affairs—"where the more we sell the less we receive in return"—was beginning to correct itself. But for the present, and even with the tremendous advance in the country's exports, the United States lacked true economic and financial independence. The secretary of state explained America's "dependence" on Great Britain on the "fact that Great Britain is banker for the world."[27] Evidence of the dependency abounded, but Evarts cited only two principal items. First, the greater portion of

American debts abroad were paid in sterling exchange; second, the interest on American bonds went through the London exchange.

These, along with other factors, contributed to an unsatisfactory and psychologically irritating situation, and Evarts acknowledged that at best his review provided only a partial explanation of the trade and payments situation. He suggested a more thorough examination of the issue in the future. Some of the factors responsible for the American payment deficit not explored by the secretary of state included the following: dividends and interest on foreign investment in the United States, tourist expenditures, money sent abroad by the first and second generation immigrants, premiums paid to foreign shipping and fire insurance companies, and — perhaps most important — transportation costs.[28] On this last point Evarts did discuss the demise of the American merchant marine after the Civil War. In a lengthy analysis, Evarts outlined the disastrous results of the transfer of American shipping to the vessels of Great Britain in the period from 1860 to 1876. The net result was that "British tonnage increased in proportion to the decrease of our tonnage,"[25] and this contributed heavily to the unfavorable balance of payments.

Both Evarts and President Hayes advocated measures to revive the sagging fortunes of the American merchant marine and actively participated in the battle to grant a subsidy to the John Roach steamship line to Brazil. Hayes made various personal appearances to bolster Roach's campaign for federal aid. In a message to Congress on trade with South America he supported the subsidy idea and urged that "every element of aid to the introduction of the products of our soil and manufactures into new markets should be made available."[30] The president, sounding a theme striking in its similarity to the later Open Door precept, declared that "if we have equal commercial facilities we need not fear competition anywhere."[31] The scheme for federal aid to Roach's steamship line to Brazil as a first step to restore the American merchant marine found a good deal of congressional support, although the plan was ultimately defeated. (For a detailed discussion of the Roach subsidy bill and the ensuing congressional battle, see chapter 4.) Among those backing the measure were Representative Benjamin F. Butler of Massachusetts, Senators James G. Blaine of Maine, Roscoe Conkling of New York, Thomas W. Ferry of Michigan, and

Algeron Paddock of Nebraska. Future President James A. Garfield also strongly supported the subsidy.[32]

In a letter accompanying Hayes' message on South American trade, Evarts offered three observations on the issue of improving the postal and commercial facilities to South America. The secretary maintained that regular steamship service was essential, and cited the case of Great Britain as an example for the United States to follow, because that country had become commercially predominant in the Western Hemisphere through a program of government aid.[33] Second, he pointed out that other European countries had also overcome the geographical advantage enjoyed by the United States in competition for the markets of South America. Finally, he believed the plans for improved facilities had the support of the South American and Central American nations, since they desired direct trade with the United States. Evarts thus reiterated the idea that mutual benefit and prosperity would result from American overseas economic expansion.

The handicaps created by the predominance of Great Britain in the markets of South America, its control of the steamship service, and its role as banker for the world, did not dim the prospects for the United States in its drive for commercial preeminence. Evarts argued that America's position was assured, for one of the characteristics of world trade was the increased demand for breadstuffs, and these would be supplied principally from the United States. Manufactured exports were the extra benefit.

> As more than three-fourths of the export from the United States is composed of breadstuffs, and raw materials necessary to the manufacturers of Europe—exports which cannot be duplicated by any other country—it may be assumed that our actual export trade is at least assured of its present proportions. It may be further safely assumed that it must go on increasing with the increasing consumptive powers of Europe, and our own increasing agricultural capacity and carrying facilities. Any exportation of manufactures—and a few years hence must behold us successfully competing with the great manufacturing countries of Europe in the markets of the commercial world—will be so much added to our present export trade.[34]

This marvelous capacity to produce, and the versatility of its resources, were the strongest assets of the United States. Evarts, as well as other leaders—both American and British—understood that it would serve America well in its struggle with Great Britain for commercial hegemony. What the leaders of both countries also understood was that Great Britain's outstanding weakness was its inability to feed its population. Britain was dependent on other countries, especially the United States, for its food supply, and that vulnerability would in the end dictate an American triumph.

Evarts clearly expected a pattern to develop. In his view, agricultural exports penetrated foreign markets and opened the way for American manufactured goods in due course. Agriculture launched American economic expansion in two crucial areas: it supplied the necessary foreign exchange and capital to continue industrialization, and it provided the initial thrust into foreign markets. This actually happened in the three-year period 1879–1881. Agricultural exports, which accounted for 78.12 percent of all domestic exports in 1879, 83.3 percent in 1880, and 82.6 percent in 1881, played a major role in generating and sustaining recovery from the depression.[35] The experience reinforced the thinking of Evarts and dramatically verified President Hayes' earlier prediction in his first annual message that agricultural exports would be "the most important of all our resources for the revival of the depressed industries of the country."[36] The export boom had considerable impact and influenced and structured the thinking of a number of Americans who came to view expansion of foreign markets as crucial to the future success of the United States. Many leaders argued first that agricultural exports must be maintained and then stressed that industry's success also demanded foreign markets for its surplus. However, not all Americans shared this faith in the continued importance of agricultural exports and some, among them David A. Wells, worried that the boom was ephemeral and deceptive in its significance. They believed that improved crop years in Europe, European restrictions on the import of American meat products, and the increasing competition from Russia, India, Australia, and Argentina, seriously jeopardized the future importance of agricultural exports. Wells, for one, placed more emphasis on the need to expand markets for manufactured goods.[37]

Even in the midst of a great depression, Evarts remained basically optimistic and foresaw a bright future for the United States. He did fear the potential destructive features of continued labor disputes, and warned workingmen against this folly, in effect admonishing them to be patient and asking them to be, above all,

future-oriented. But government aid was the most important consideration in competing for the world's trade. Evarts explicitly
pointed to the example of Great Britain and other European nations; those countries had achieved supremacy through "the able
supervision, protection, and direction of their trade by their
governments."[38] That evidence made it clear that "the fostering,
the developing, and the directing of our commerce by the government" was "a necessity of the first importance."[39]

Several private organizations of merchants, businessmen, and
manufacturers applauded and further encouraged the active
participation of the national government in extending foreign markets for America's surplus. Two of the most enterprising groups
were the Associated Industries of the United States and the United
States Agency for Promoting Foreign Trade. The former became
the most important. It was based in Philadelphia and headed by
Henry C. Carey, that inveterate campaigner for American economic and financial independence. Lorin Blodget was secretary of the
group, and its Committee on Exports included Robert Patterson,
George Burnham, Thomas Potter, Charles Cramp, and Hamilton
Disston. In several letters to the State Department the Associated
Industries Organization urged the extension of markets for
American manufactured goods and recommended that the
diplomatic and consular officers "devote attention to the question
of methods by which trade with the United States can be most
judiciously fostered."[40] This group accepted the ideology of economic expansion and their dogma included a distinct distrust and
jealousy of Great Britain. They resented Great Britain's monopoly
of steamship service to Brazil and felt that this control inhibited
American manufactured exports to that market.

The Associated Industries informed the State Department in December 1877 of a plan to send two men to South America to promote trade. John W. Fralick and William M. Watts were the members of the proposed mission, and the organization requested that
Fralick be granted an appointment as bearer of dispatches. W. K.
Rogers, secretary to President Hayes, notified the State Department that the president gave his special endorsement to Fralick as
bearer of dispatches.[41] Rogers also noted the president was "impressed with the importance of the commercial enterprises" of the
Associated Industries group and desired "to extend to them, in ad-

dition to the recognition and support already given, such further encouragement and aid on the part of the Government as may be practicable."[42] This support was consistent with the continued and sustained efforts of the Hayes administration to expand markets in South America.

The organization also sent the State Department an instructional pamphlet describing the aims and objectives of the mission. It was to determine what effect British control of the steamship service played in the trade picture. The group suspected that British vessels were not simply passive carriers, but rather were examples of a pattern of discrimination against the interests of the United States. To overcome British domination of the trade of South America, the pamphlet outlined an ambitious program for Associated Industries and for the United States. They candidly announced that:

> Our mission to South America is not merely to sell a few goods and to obtain the small proceeds of irregular sales; it is to introduce into their entire social system the general features of our own social life, with its far greater production and consumption of the products of skill and industry.[43]

Here was a broad plan to reform the Latin Americans by changing their social fabric through the export of the American style of life. The Latins were to be converted into avid consumers who would guarantee and stimulate the market for American products.

Carlos Butterfield was another active lobbyist for the cause of expanded South American trade. He resided in Spanish America and constantly campaigned for improved commercial relations among the nations of the Western Hemisphere. Butterfield had initiated his activities during President Ulysses S. Grant's first term, but had achieved very little. He arrogantly informed President Hayes that there would not have been a serious depression if President Grant had followed his advice about opening new markets in South America.[44] Butterfield's analysis was wholly consistent with the intellectual climate of the 1870s, another expression of the rather widespread private concern and agitation for overseas commercial expansion.

He emphasized that the United States must displace Great Britain as the leading commercial nation in the markets of South America. If Americans expected to wrest the trade from the English and break their monopoly it was absolutely essential to pursue "the same commercial policy" and maintain "the same governmental support that Great Britain extends to private enterprise."[45] Butterfield boldly lectured the president (and admonished the administration): to beat the British it was necessary to play their game—an insight that Hayes and Evarts themselves expressed, accepted, and acted upon. As part of this strategy, Butterfield suggested improved steamship service, a policy of reciprocity, and the creation of a Bureau of American Republics. His advice was not lost upon the Republicans who, in the years between the Civil War and the end of the century, urged and fostered those proposals in their campaign for extended markets in the Western Hemisphere.

Throughout his years in the State Department, Evarts pursued a strong, nationalistic foreign policy and for his efforts received the plaudits of the press and the approval of the American business and industrial community.[46] And while Evarts was frequently lethargic and careless about the routine of departmental affairs, this disdain did not diminish his concern for market expansion as a way to ensure economic prosperity and domestic peace. He encouraged the extension of American influence by urging the navy to send warships on frequent visits to the coasts of Asia, Africa, and South America. This pattern was in keeping with the "trade follows the flag" dictum, or, as Evarts expressed it, "the National flag must be carried to such coasts before the merchant flag can be safely or profitably exhibited."[47]

Evarts also revamped the consular service and began the process of transforming it into an effective instrument for the extension of American commerce. The most important reform was the introduction of a new system of consular reports which were published monthly beginning in October 1880. These reports emphasized the role of the consular corps as a fact-finding agency for the use and convenience of American businessmen. In addition, Evarts took the initiative in having the department collect information from consular agents and send it to the Congress in the form of recommendations on how to increase trade with South America and other parts of the world.[48] And as part of this overall effort Evarts also concluded commercial treaties with China, Japan, and Samoa.

Evarts understood clearly the argument that exports and the extension of foreign markets would prevent future depressions (and their attendant social disorder and dislocation), and that analysis guided his conduct of foreign policy. As an economic nationalist he comprehended the role Great Britain played in the world and its meaning for American aspirations. Despite this awareness of British power and the obstacle it presented to the United States, during his service as secretary of state Evarts was not a rabid or blatant Anglophobe in the manner of his successor James Blaine. But he could pointedly remark at a banquet of the New England Society that the British "complain of us that we are a forward, impatient nation, always getting into everybody's way. When do they ever hear of our mother country ever getting out of anybody's way."[49] Later, during his career as senator from New York, Evarts became a more typically partisan politician and, perhaps reflecting a combination of frustration and political sagacity, developed a more emotionally heated negativism toward the English.

The intensity of Evarts' nationalism amused and mildly irritated the British. That was revealed in an anecdote related by Sir Edward Thornton, the British minister to the United States. Thornton wrote Lord Granville that Secretary Evarts was extremely angry over the notice that the Ottoman Empire planned to close several missions abroad, including the one in the United States. Evarts accused the British of influencing the decision and Thornton observed that "the irritation of course has its origin in petty jealousy, and in a desire that all the Nations of the World should acknowledge the United States to be one of the greatest and should worship her."[50] A man of tremendous ego and personal pride, Evarts displayed the same traits in his nationalism and deeply resented any affront to his country, no matter how slight.

The British response to the new economic situation arising from the depression of the 1870s transcended amusement and incidental irritation. As the American secretary of state had noted, London was more than slightly concerned about the deterioration of its commercial position in the world. Initially, however, the worry was mitigated by skepticism, complacency, and overconfidence. The British noted the alarming rise of imports over exports in their accounts for 1876 when imports exceeded exports by approximately £118.5 million, but generally shrugged it off with the assertion they could and would maintain their position.[51] Other spokesmen dismissed the situation as temporary and felt that, in any case, it represented the country's affluence rather than its vulnerability.

The reaction of the empire's foremost commercial and economic journal was typical of the early response. But the London *Economist* revealed an increasing concern about the nature of the American challenge to British commercial supremacy in little more than a year. The editors first noted "the determination of the American manufacturers to seek by all means to extend the foreign market for their goods, and the confidence they have in their ability to achieve success."[52] Then, in the summer of 1878, having analyzed the trade statistics for the period 1873–1877, the *Economist* warned its readers that the United States was "about to become our most formidable rival."[53] The competition would be felt particularly in the two leading industries of iron and cotton goods. The editors commented that the recent depression had forced American manufacturers to seek foreign markets and it had allowed them to sell at a lower price. They also realized that the failure of the United States to develop a merchant marine handicapped American efforts and worked to Britain's advantage in maintaining its supremacy.[54]

Victor Drummond, secretary to the British legation in Washington and firsthand observer of the American export phenomenon, commented in his reports to the Foreign Office on the American surge into world markets and the efforts to restore the United States merchant marine. Drummond was not alarmed about American plans for an improved merchant marine. In his discussion of President Hayes' message to Congress and the proposed United States subsidy for the Brazilian steamship line, the Englishman dismissed the efforts as offering any early threat to the British carrying trade. But with reference to American competition, Drummond warned English merchants of the determination "of the United States to push forward" with every means to extend American trade "not only with South America, but with every country with which they have commercial relations."[55]

It was time for England to "look to her own."[56] The United States was no longer dependent upon other countries, and when the depression lifted and capital was again available, employment would be restored and Great Britain "must then expect even still more serious competition to [its] trade and manufactures."[57] Contrary to the normally accepted view among historians that the United States did not offer a serious threat to British commercial supremacy until the 1890s, the testimony of Drummond, the editors of the *Economist,* and several other worried leaders, make it clear that there was a growing concern throughout the commercial and industrial centers of Great Britain.[58] It was the United States—not Germany—that first threatened British commercial hegemony in the world's markets. This challenge was neither accidental or inadvertent. It was planned and intentional.

Drummond believed that Britain's free trade policy allowed American manufacturers some success in the English market. Although fully cognizant of the American threat, he remained essentially optimistic. He continued alert to the danger of American competition throughout the next four years, however, and warned his countrymen that the United States was "restless and energetic to obtain foreign markets, and has a vision of becoming the greatest producer and manufacturer in the world."[59] The crucial consideration was the British working class. It held the key to the future success or failure of Britain in the world's markets. Both the British and American leaders openly expected the laboring forces in their respective countries to carry the long-run burden of capitalistic economic expansion for dominance in the markets of the world.

Other British expressions of concern about the challenge of the United States appeared in the 1870s. The most eminent spokesman was the Liberal leader, William E. Gladstone. He had recognized the potential of the American republic in 1878. In an article for the *North American Review,* he candidly stated that the United States posed a serious threat to the commercial preeminence of Great Britain. He predicted "that it is she alone who, at a coming time, can and probably will, wrest from us that commercial primacy."[60] The Liberal party leader labelled the United States and Great Britain as the two strongest nations in the world. The United States had tremendous resources and potential; Great Britain's future position was uncertain, and in the face of his nation's vulnerability Gladstone admonished his countrymen to reduce their "public burdens" in preparation for a day when the nation would have "less capacity than we have now to bear them."[61]

Such talk offended the national pride of many Englishmen, especially at a time when it appeared that Great Britain was supreme among the powers of the world. Gladstone's forthright statement particularly aroused the ire of public men and the press. The

London Economist was among those that took exception to the Liberal leader's views. The editors displayed a good deal of hostility for Gladstone and ridiculed his views through mockery and sarcasm. They agreed that the United States had succeeded in capturing its home market, but the editors explained that change by pointing out that it probably resulted from America's limited purchasing power during the depression. Not only did the depression curtail American consumption, but the economy also lacked an infusion of capital from Great Britain, which the editors believed contributed to the general business stagnation.[62] The *Economist* was mistaken in its belief that decreased purchasing power was responsible for the drop in British exports to the United States. There was not a decrease in American consumption, as Secretary of State Evarts made clear in his 1877 analysis of the nation's foreign commerce, but rather American manufactures were capturing the home market and displacing foreign, especially British, goods.[63]

In essence they pictured the situation as temporary, caused primarily by bad weather and poor European · harvests, and widespread depression. In addition, they argued, agricultural products accounted for most of the tremendous expansion of American exports. British manufacturing supremacy was not yet truly threatened. They did agree with Gladstone on one point; namely, that the United States would have to adopt free trade in order to expand its markets permanently. Only then would the United States have a real chance to overtake Britain; but on that basis the *Economist* believed the English could hold their own, especially in reasserting themselves in the American domestic market.[64] Two years later, however, the editors of the *Economist* more thoroughly understood Gladstone's prediction when they cried that "the United States are running us hard in the race."[65]

It was true that agricultural products accounted for the great American export boom, but that awareness brought little comfort to a number of Englishmen. In the late 1870s Britain was importing half its meat, dairy products, wool, and somewhat more than half its grain; it was wholly dependent on foreign sources for cotton to sustain its textile industries and the import of iron for conversion into steel rose noticeably. The impact of American food imports combined with a relatively stagnant export trade provoked the first serious reevaluation of the Cobdenite philosophy of free trade.[66]

American imports drove prices steadily downward as the average annual import of food increased from £79 million in 1867–1869 to £133 million for the years 1877–1879. As a result, England came face-to-face with the consequences of the repeal of the Corn Laws. A protectionist movement appeared in Great Britain and its fortunes were directly correlated to the business cycle. The nose dive in British exports from 1873 to 1879 prompted a rapid spread of protectionist sentiment that led to the formation in 1881 of the Fair Trade League. The unfavorable turn in trade continued in the 1880s but the Fair Trade movement floundered on the shoals of Irish home rule and Empire. Those issues diverted attention and created political complications unfavorable to the protectionist cause.[67] An additional difficulty for the protectionists was the inertia of the British agricultural community, some of whom were unwilling to accept the full extent to which British agriculture had been altered by the influx of food from America.[68]

However, the reality of the huge and ever-increasing American agricultural exports and its effects on British agriculture were generally appreciated. The English also encountered and understood the assertion of the economic expansionist ideology in several other areas. In the late 1870s the United States became more forceful in the Caribbean, and the British recognized the new vigor as a continuation of the push begun in the late 1850s. The Civil War had only delayed American imperialism, and in the 1870s the United States had again appeared directly across the path of Great Britain in the Western Hemisphere. When the Frenchman Ferdinand De Lesseps announced he intended to construct the Panama Canal, British diplomats sensed that his move would evolve into a dangerous and explosive diplomatic struggle with the United States over the Clayton-Bulwer Treaty.

The United States had long been fascinated by possible economic and strategic benefits of an interoceanic canal, and the appearance of De Lesseps in Panama in 1879 to begin work shocked Americans into action. The swiftness of the French enterprise greatly alarmed the Congress, the press, and the Hayes administration. After the government and the public recovered from their surprise, the majority came down on the side of an exclusively "American" canal. Americans had generally and confidently assumed that the project was strictly within their domain. As President Grant stated in 1869, any canal shall be "an American canal, on American soil, belonging to the American people."[69] He warned of the danger of European initiative, but to little practical avail; during his two terms public opinion lagged behind official government policy.

The De Lesseps project crystallized opinion and it rallied the public behind the Hayes administration in support of an American canal. The challenge was clear and apparent and it threw Washington into a frenzy. Both the Congress and the Executive acted immediately to guarantee America's vital and special interest in an isthmian canal. Congress quickly passed resolutions reaffirming the Monroe Doctrine and implicitly denouncing the French venture,[70] and the House established a committee to investigate the question of canal routes. To check the French project, the House recommended that the government promptly acquire naval stations on both coasts of Panama.[71]

The move to establish coaling stations at Chiriqui and Golfito in Central America signaled the administration's response at one level. Hayes acted at another level in March 1880 through a special message to Congress. He made it clear that "the policy of this country is a canal under American control. The United States can not consent to the surrender of this control to any European power or to any combination of European powers."[72] The president justified America's claim to primacy in the area with the logic that a completed canal would be an extension of America's coastline linking the country's Atlantic and Pacific shores.[73]

This blunt declaration of the country's position, coupled with the effort to establish coaling stations on the Caribbean and Pacific coasts of Panama, carried the issue to another level, one that led to a diplomatic bout with Great Britain. After France denied official auspices for the De Lesseps project and insisted that it was a private venture, England became the main adversary. This was made perfectly clear when, shortly after Hayes affirmed that any canal would have to be an American canal, the House of Representatives passed a resolution calling for the abrogation of the Clayton-Bulwer Treaty and recommending that Great Britain promptly be notified of this contingency.[74]

The administration declined to abrogate the Clayton-Bulwer Treaty, but congressional support for such action so soon after the administration's strong words about an "American canal" and its push to set up coaling stations alarmed and alerted the British to the seriousness of American designs. First, it became evident to the British government that American obstruction and the demand for American control had killed the De Lesseps project.[75] Second, the British marveled at the nationalism and excitement the incident had aroused. Some of the opposition Democratic newspapers took the lead in supporting a canal under American control, and the opposition editors strongly urged reaffirmation of the Monroe Doctrine.[76]

Further evidence of the bipartisan nature of the agitation came when Senator Thomas F. Bayard of Delaware wholeheartedly endorsed the claim that any isthmian canal had "to be under the control of the government of the United States."[77] Bayard's advocacy revealed that the talk was more than election year rhetoric. It was all too apparent that the policy had widespread national support. As Sir Edward Thornton worriedly commented, "that such language should have been used by so moderate, serious and intelligent a man as Mr. Bayard has caused some surprise and has made a great impression upon the public mind."[78] Once again the English leaders were forcefully reminded of the bipartisan support for the ideology of economic expansion that underpinned American imperial ambitions. Evarts' successor, James G. Blaine, brashly confirmed British fears with dispatches stoutly defending the concept that any canal must of necessity be an American canal.

The events of the late 1870s had awakened the British to the scope of the American challenge. And in the international marketplace a determined struggle for commercial hegemony began between Great Britain, the acknowledged leader, the United States, and Germany. The United States gained ground in 1876—1877 by establishing a favorable balance of trade, even though a balance-of-payments deficit remained. The balance-of-payments anomaly became a symbol of America's economic and financial dependence on Great Britain, and as such served as a psychological irritant that created a feeling of hostility, resentment, and jealousy. It was one of the more important facets of the widespread Anglophobia of the late nineteenth century.

American leaders at all levels realized after the export boom of 1879—1881 that prosperity was tied directly to foreign markets. The experience reinforced the economic expansionist ideology and enhanced the position of agrarians by giving them an added sense of importance. It also created a number of new problems for the farmers, and in the process reinforced their anti-British nationalism. During the next two decades the farmers and other interest groups continued their agitation in Washington for governmental support in the search for markets.

For other Americans, meanwhile, the export boom served to verify the existing hope and belief that the United States was a world power. But to become fully recognized as such, and to establish undisputed claim to commercial hegemony, the United States had to displace Great Britain. The export boom thus had the effect of intensifying old issues and creating new ones. Problems such as transportation, reciprocity, and the remonetization of silver all became distinctly political ramifications of foreign policy and Anglophobia during the 1880s and 1890s.

NOTES

1. Fred A. Shannon, *The Farmer's Last Frontier, 1860 − 1897* (New York: Farror and Rinehart, Inc., 1945), p. 415−17. Louis M. Hacker, *The Triumph of American Capitalism* (New York: Simon and Schuster, 1940), p. 404.

2. Quoted in Robert V. Bruce, *1877: Year of Violence* (Indianapolis: Bobbs-Merrill, 1959), p. 26.

3. *Northwestern Miller,* August 3, 1877.

4. Ibid.

5. For an expression of this awareness see James D. Richardson, *Messages and Papers of the Presidents 1789 − 1897* (Washington: Government Printing Office, 1898), Vol. VII, p. 613.

6. Chester L. Barrows, *William M. Evarts: Lawyer, Diplomat, Statesman* (Chapel Hill: The University of North Carolina Press, 1941), p. 375.

7. Ibid.

8. Ibid.

9. Resolution of the New York Produce Exchange, April 9, 1874, Vol. III, William M. Evarts Papers, Library of Congress.

10. Brainerd Dyer, *The Public Career of William M. Evarts* (Berkeley: University of California Press, 1933), p. 185.

11. The Democrats included Thomas Swann, Maryland; Samuel S. Cox, New York; Andrew H. Hamilton, Indiana; William H. Forney, Alabama; Gustave Schleicher, Texas; Samuel A. Briggs, Pennsylvania; and Benjamin Wilson, West Virginia. The Republicans were James Monroe, Ohio; Charles G. Williams, Wisconsin; William W. Crapo, Massachusetts, and John W. Killinger, Pennsylvania. *Report of the Committee on Foreign Affairs on the Relations of the United States with Mexico,* House Report No. 701, 45th Cong., 2nd Sess., 1878 (Washington: Government Printing Office, 1878), p. XXIV.

12. Ibid.

13. Ibid.

14. Ibid.

15. Ibid.

16. Ibid., p. XXXII.

17. Ibid., pp. XXV–XXVI.

18. Alan K. Manchester, *British Preeminence in Brazil, Its Rise and Decline* (Chapel Hill: The University of North Carolina Press, 1933), p. 332.

19. Alfred P. Tischendorf, *Great Britain and Mexico in the Era of Porfirio Diaz* (Durham: Duke University Press, 1961), pp. 129–31. David M. Pletcher, *Rails, Mines, and Progress: Seven American Promoters in Mexico, 1867 – 1911* (Ithaca: Cornell University Press, 1958), p. 3.

20. *Foreign Relations of the United States,* Appendix, 1877, p. 1.

21. Ibid.

22. *Report on the Commercial Relations of the United States with Foreign Countries for the year 1877,* House Exec. Doc. 102, 45th Cong., 2nd Sess., 1878 (Washington: Government Printing Office, 1878), p. 23.

23. Ibid., p. 22.

24. Ibid., pp. 29–30.

25. Ibid., p. 30.

26. Ibid.

27. Ibid., p. 31.

28. Harold V. Faulkner, *American Economic History* (New York: Harper and Row, 1960), p. 537.

29. *Commercial Relations, 1877,* p. 52.

30. *Message on Intercourse with South America,* Senate Exec. Doc. 7, 45th Cong., 3rd Sess. (Washington: Government Printing Office, 1878), p. 2.

31. Ibid.

32. Leonard A. Swann, Jr., *John Roach: Maritime Entrepreneur* (Annapolis: United States Naval Institute, 1965), p. 107.

33. *Message on Intercourse with South America,* p. 2.

34. *Commercial Relations, 1877,* p. 52.

35. *Report of the Commissioner of Labor,* House Exec. Doc. 1, Part 5, 49th Cong., 1st Sess., 1885 (Washington: Government Printing Office, 1886), pp. 248–49.

36. Richardson, *Messages and Papers,* Vol. VII, p. 477.

37. Tom E. Terrill, "David A. Wells, the Democracy, and Tariff Reduction, 1877–1894," *Journal of American History,* 56,3 (December 1969), p. 541.

38. *Commercial Relations, 1877,* p. 53.

39. Ibid.

40. Associated Industries of the United States to Wm. M. Evarts, September 6, 1877, Miscellaneous Letters, Department of State, National Archives, Record Group 59.

41. Ibid., Associated Industries to Evarts, December 3, 1877.

42. Ibid., W. K. Rogers to Evarts, December 8, 1877.

43. Ibid., Blodget to President Hayes, December 3, 1877.

44. Ibid., Carlos Butterfield to Wm. M. Evarts, August 13, 1877.

45. Ibid., Carlos Butterfield to President Hayes, November 27, 1877. Pamphlet included with letter entitled, "Value of Spanish-America to the United States," (New York: Metropolitan Job Printing, 1868).

46. Ibid., The comment of E. W. Fox of the St. Louis *Evening Dispatch* was typical: "Your efforts as Secretary of State to advance the commercial interests of our country deserve the thanks of the whole people, especially the Mississippi Valley." Fox to Evarts, October 31, 1877.

47. Dyer, *William M. Evarts*, p. 235.

48. Barrows, *Evarts*, p. 376.

49. Sherman Evarts, ed., *Arguments and Speeches of William Maxwell Evarts* (New York: The MacMillan Company, 1919), p. 402.

50. Thornton to Granville, May 10, 1880, in Paul Knaplund and Carolyn M. Clewes, *Private Letters From the British Embassy in Washington to the Foreign Secretary Lord Granville*, 1880—1885, Annual Report of the American Historical Association, Vol. I, 1941 (Washington: Government Printing Office, 1942), p. 94.

51. B. R. Mitchell, *Abstract of British Historical Statistics* (Cambridge: University Press, 1962), p. 283. As an example of this attitude see *Economist*, February 10, 1877 and March 31, 1877.

52. *Economist*, April 27, 1878, p. 490.

53. Ibid., July 27, 1878, pp. 883—84.

54. Ibid.

55. Parliamentary Papers, House of Commons, *Reports of Her Majesty's Secretaries of Embassy and Legation*, 1878, Commercial No. 17, Vol. 72, p. 455.

56. Ibid.

57. Ibid.

58. Stephen Bourne, *Trade, Population and Food, A Series of Papers on Economic Statistics* (London: George Bell & Sons, 1880). Benjamin H. Brown, *The Tariff Reform Movement in Great Britain 1881 — 1895* (New York: Columbia University Press, 1943).

59. Parliamentary Papers, *Reports of Embassy and Legation*, 1878, Commercial No. 23, Vol. 72, p. 686.

60. *North American Review*, September—October 1878, p. 180.

61. Ibid.

62. *Economist*, September 21, 1878.

63. *Commercial Relations, 1877*, p. 30.

64. *Economist*, September 21, 1878.

65. Ibid., May 15, 1880, p. 557.

66. Brown, *The Tariff Reform Movement*, p. 9. J. D. Chambers, *The Workshop of the World* (London: Oxford University Press, 1961), pp. 117—19.

67. Brown, *The Tariff Reform Movement*, pp. 85, 142—43.

68. Ibid., p. 146.

69. Lindley M. Keasbey, *The Nicaragua Canal and the Monroe Doctrine* (New York: G. P. Putnam's Sons, 1896), p. 315.

70. *Congressional Record*, Vol. 10, Part II, p. 1936. (Hereinafter cited as *CR*, 10:2:1936.) House Committee on Foreign Affairs papers, records of the United States House of Representatives, National Archives, Record Group 233.

71. Barrows, *Evarts*, p. 366. *CR*, 10:3:2324.

72. James D: Richardson, *Messages and Papers*, Vol. VII, p. 585.
73. Ibid.
74. *CR*, 10:2:1775.
75. Thornton to H. M. Principal Secretary of State for Foreign Affairs, No. 132, April 26, 1880, Foreign Office 115, Vol. 660, Public Record Office, London.
76. Thornton to Salisbury, No. 36, February 2, 1880, No. 45, February 16, 1880, No. 53, February 23, 1880, F. O. 115, Vol. 659, P.R.O., London.
77. Remarks of January 27, 1880, *CR*, 10:1:542.
78. Thornton to Salisbury, No. 36, February 2, 1880, F.O. 115, Vol. 659, P.R.O., London.

4

Blaine Challenges British Supremacy

We stand where we can defy her, and we are today the only power on the globe that can defy Great Britain, and we can do it with just as much dignity or with just as much insolence as we choose to employ. There is not a European power that can do it . . . .

There is no rival left to her in the commercial world, and if she can bluff us out, or buy us out, or bully us out of a tariff that shall protect American industries and any enterprise that shall stimulate lines of American steamships, she will have done all she desires to do for her factories and her commerce.

James G. Blaine, 1878

He is extremely impulsive and sensitive and whatever he may say to me to the contrary, he has evidently a strong feeling that we always endeavor to, and do, get the better of the United States in any discussion between us. The increasing growth and wonderful prosperity of the United States might well satisfy him that there is no ground of any other power; but still I feel that it is against us that he wishes to proclaim the superiority of his own country, and that it will therefore be well not to give him an opportunity of putting forward any just cause of complaint.

Sir Edward Thornton, 1881

He did indeed once remark to Sir Edward Thornton that England as against the United States was always wrong, but he also added that as against the rest of the world she was always right.

Gail Hamilton, 1895

Biographers and historians have generally stressed the Latin American policy of Secretary of State James Gillespie Blaine.[1] They invariably hail him as the man who initiated the modern Pan-American movement; the farsighted statesman who attempted, unsuccessfully, to create a community of nations in the Western Hemisphere. This view of Blaine is correct—as far as it goes. But it is incomplete and does not provide a full characterization of Blaine's importance as a key figure in the emerging American imperialism of the 1880s and 1890s. The standard interpretation fails to place his Pan-American policy in its proper context, as but one part of a comprehensive domestic and foreign program designed to transform the United States into the world's greatest power.

Blaine's *Weltanschauung* defined Great Britain as America's primary rival. The British thwarted and limited American aspirations for prestige at every turn; and, even more important, blocked the expansion of America's economic and political power. Consequently, Blaine believed that the United States should pursue a policy of economic nationalism that directly challenged Britain for world commercial and economic supremacy. His objective was to make the United States into *the* world power. As Blaine had pointed out in 1878, while still a senator from Maine, America was the "only power on the globe that [could] defy Great Britain."[2]

This definition of Great Britain as the most formidable obstacle to American dominance was not based on fantasy or distortion. Britain's influence and power were everywhere apparent. It ruled the sea. It possessed a global empire. It was the workshop of the world. It was the world's banker. And, as part of all these activities, it enjoyed important commercial and political power and influence in the Western Hemisphere. As a result, Britain was envied and resented by its former colony. However, a number of Americans conceded that Britain's unquestioned supremacy provided a clearcut example on which to pattern American national ambitions. This ambivalent attitude toward Great Britain—hostility and admiration—was a central characteristic of American leaders, including Blaine, during the years between the Civil War and the end of the century.

The United States did not confront British power and influence merely in its external push for world preeminence. England's dominance as the most mature industrial society, further strengthened by its surplus capital, placed the United States, still a developing country, in an economically dependent position. This was especially true for the trans-Mississippi West and South. Those areas needed investment capital, even though they disliked the power it gave the outsiders who supplied it. Great Britain also provided the major market for the agricultural exports of those regions: cotton, wheat, corn, and meat products. And they understood that their sections were not only colonial in relation to the northeastern American metropolis, but were also at the colonial end of an imperial relationship with Great Britain.

Blaine, and many other Americans, found this inferior relationship intolerable and they condemned it as an unwarranted restriction of the economic—and hence political—independence of the United States. An awareness of this relationship, and of the positive and negative reactions to it, provides a central insight into the persisting Anglophobia of these regions in the late nineteenth century. It also offers a basis for understanding a good deal of the politics of the period.

Republicans, especially that wing influenced by Henry C. Carey, relied on the protective tariff to overcome foreign domination of American economic development. Blaine realized, however, that protection alone would not secure the objective. To be sure, the tariff remained as the core of his beliefs, but he did not consider it a panacea, as did some of his fellow Republicans. In his view, protection had facilitated the rapid industrialization of the United States after the Civil War, and had enabled American manufacturers to capture a greater share of the home market. These gains had been made mainly at the expense of Great Britain. The United States was Britain's greatest market for exports in 1872, but by 1876 it had fallen to fifth.[3] This turn away from buying European—and particularly British—manufactures, while not accompanied by any decrease in consumption, was well along in the 1870s and the trend continued throughout the remainder of the century. The relative importance of manufactured goods declined and raw materials—crude rubber, wool, hides and skins, etc.—gained a position of unprecedented importance, jumping from approximately 6 percent of total imports in the mid-1870s to 13.6 percent in 1900.[4]

To a considerable extent, then, the protective tariff had served one of its major purposes by securing the home market for American manufactures, even though the promised benefits for the farmer remained elusive. This success did not prompt Blaine or the Republican party to abandon protection. Quite the contrary, they continually defended the principle, and in 1878 Blaine offered several Senate resolutions against any radical changes in the tariff. He maintained that "there is no more hurtful agitation today in this country than the agitation of the tariff."[5] In addition, Blaine and his fellow Republicans frequently employed the Careyite tactic of characterizing Democratic agitation to revise and lower duties as proof of their pro-British proclivities.

But the severe business dislocation and economic stress of the 1870s pushed Blaine beyond the routine approach to the tariff. The effects of depression dramatized for Blaine—as it did for other American leaders, including President Rutherford B. Hayes and Secretary of State Evarts—the problem of over-production and the need for new markets to absorb the surplus of America's farms, mines, and factories. Blaine readily grasped the eventual importance of agricultural exports in generating recovery from the depression and this perception structured and shaped his analysis about the role of exports in the future success of the United States. As secretary of state in 1881 he echoed Evarts, his predecessor: "We have reached the stage, after supplying our home demands, where we have a surplus left which must find consumption in foreign markets . . . ."[6]

And, in the depth of the depression during the winter of 1877—1878, Blaine's response was to make a study of "the resources, needs, aspirations and possibilities of the Southern hemisphere."[7] To be sure, this interest in South America was not solely the result of the depression. Blaine long had been an admirer of Henry Clay and he shared Clay's vision of making the United States the emporium of the Western Hemisphere.[8] During his early years he delighted in finding parallels between his career and that of Clay's. Clay's dogma of an "American System" provided the foundation for Blaine's dream of United States hegemony in the Western Hemisphere, and the doctrine was seemingly verified by the reality of the depression.

The first phase of Blaine's resulting Pan-American policy

emerged in the spring of 1878 during the second session of the Forty-fifth Congress, and it centered on his efforts to provide a federal subsidy for an American steamship line to Brazil. During the previous winter, when he had studied the resources of the Latin American republics with an eye to increasing American trade at the expense of Europe, Blaine had become especially interested in Brazil. That concern may have been initially influenced by John Roach, a political supporter of Blaine. But neither Blaine's ideas nor his program can be understood in terms of political jobbery or simple interest-group influence. In Blaine's analysis, Brazil presented a specific case in point to prove his general thesis: it offered an excellent market for American surplus agricultural products and manufactured goods. As he complained on the Senate floor, "they do not know in Brazil what we have to sell,—what we are able to manufacture and really offer them."[9] Consequently, the United States lost the market when Brazil bought its butter and cheese, boots and shoes, and its agricultural implements from Europe.

The prevailing trade balance between the two countries was highly unfavorable to the United States and reflected the general condition of American commerce with Latin America in the last third of the nineteenth century. The Brazilian pattern, in which the United States was a heavy importer of Brazilian goods while its exports to that country were negligible, presented one specific example of the deficits of American hemispheric commerce that a number of leaders recognized.[10] Blaine believed that there were several reasons for that unhappy state of affairs, but in the case of Brazil he stressed—and acted upon—the importance of the lack of steamship service between the two countries.

Not only were American shipping facilities to Brazil inadequate, but the situation was even more intolerable and embarassing because the United States depended to a great extent upon English lines for its communication with the South American country. This arrangement decidedly favored Great Britain. A triangular trade existed: Brazilian exports of coffee and sugar were carried in English bottoms to the eastern ports of the United States; after unloading the tropical products of Brazil (and perhaps taking on some American manufactured products and foodstuffs destined for Brazil) the vessel would depart for England; only after loading in an English port did the ship return to Brazil.

It was painfully obvious to Blaine that American interests suffered as a result of this trading pattern. On the one hand, American manufacturers had to pay the additional freight via England. On the other hand, they had somehow to remain competitive with British goods paying lower rates and being delivered with less elapsed time. The British thus possessed a decided advantage in the Brazilian market and also gained profits from American commerce with Brazil. Blaine argued the necessity of establishing an American steamship service in order to break the English monopoly, and as an initial step was willing to subsidize the Roach line to Brazil.

The Senate debate over the proposed subsidy revealed Blaine's thinking vis-à-vis Great Britain and his dreams for the United States. Breaking England's grip on Brazilian commerce was only the opening volley in a struggle for the carrying trade of the world. Hence, the subsidy for Roach was merely a stopgap while the major task of overcoming the deplorable condition of the American merchant marine was undertaken. If America failed in that task, Blaine warned, it would be tantamount to telling England to "take the seas; they are yours."[11] Blaine's worst fears then would be realized: the United States would "become tributary to Great Britain."[12]

To rebuild America's merchant marine, Blaine advocated reliance on the traditional navigation laws of the United States. He recommended a return to some of the mercantilist policies followed by President James Monroe. Blaine specifically referred to an 1817 law providing that no products could enter the United States except in American vessels or the vessels of the producing country. "I am radical on the question," he declared, and proclaimed that "these triangular voyages that sap the life out of our commerce could not be made under the law."[13]

Such mercantilist legislation would foster a broad program of economic nationalism based on America's right to control and carry its commerce. Blaine admonished Americans to alter their thinking and views on transportation, for in his view their conception was too narrow and too continental. Americans should view the route "from Chicago to Liverpool [as] one direct line," and not think that the job was done when the surpluses reached the coast.[14] It was an economic absurdity, Blaine argued, to operate only 1,000 miles of the Chicago-Liverpool route and "give three thousand miles to the foreigner."[15] If American agricultural exports to Europe went in American bottoms another link in Britain's chain of control would be shattered.

Blaine maintained that his program provided one path to increased financial independence for the United States. He illustrated that point with the statistics on the carrying trade in 1877. The United States furnished 13 million tons of ocean freight, and the profit on that cargo was $115 million. But, he pointed out, $89 million of that money went into the pockets of foreign shipowners.[16] Had the United States retained most of that cost, Blaine argued, "we should have no need, we should have been under no necessity 'of selling bonds to buy gold to resume specie payments."[17] Thus American control of transporting its exports on land and sea would end the need to borrow from abroad and would give America additional capital for economic development.

The Senate debate over the subsidy bill also revealed the ambivalence in Blaine's thinking about Great Britain. He was hostile and critical, but he nevertheless displayed a grudging admiration for the position the English had attained in the world. He viewed Great Britain's policy as a successful and proven course for the United States to follow, and frequently interpreted England's supremacy as the result of a strategy similar to his own program. He candidly pointed out that a nation could always learn from its enemies, and noted that the competition with Britain offered no exception to that historical rule.

The subsidy bill passed in the Senate as a rider to the Post Office appropriation bill under Blaine's persistent guidance. In the House, however, the subsidy advocates could not muster enough support and the amendment failed by a vote of 159 to 89 after long and acrimonious debate that was peppered with jeers of "jobbery for Roach" and cries of "corruption."[18] Many members of the House doubted the viability of government subsidies, particularly in the light of the failure of earlier efforts such as the Pacific Mail grant. Others, including Abram S. Hewitt of New York, dismissed the "trade follows the flag" argument of the proponents and offered different methods, such as tariff reduction and the negotiation of reciprocity treaties for increasing American trade to Latin America.[19] Perhaps the two strongest groups against the Roach bill were the free-ship people, who favored allowing foreign-built vessels under the American flag, and the Baltimore commercial community, who saw the Roach line as a serious threat to their existing trade with Brazil. The subsidy was anathema to Baltimore interests because, in a transparent effort to unite the northeastern and southwestern sections, the supporters of the Roach line had included Galveston as a port of call and bypassed Baltimore in favor of New York City.[20]

The Roach subsidy episode clearly illustrates the complexities of the politics of economic expansion in the last third of the nineteenth century. On the surface, the picture presents an image of a setback for the economic nationalists and their program for expanded trade in the hemisphere,—but that is not the full story. What marks the congressional debate on the issue is the universal bipartisan commitment to the export solution and the need for foreign markets. The defeat of the Roach subsidy was not a defeat for that analysis, it was merely an expression of dissent from that particular means and a preference for other tactics to the desired and shared end—expanded hemispheric trade. The opponents favored other means, such as free trade, free ships, and reciprocity treaties. As for Blaine, he remained undaunted; neither the defeat of the Roach subsidy bill nor the return of prosperity discouraged him in his efforts to establish hegemony in Latin America. Instead, he refined and extended his western hemispheric program into a more coherent and integrated set of policies.

In 1880 Blaine again was a leading contender for the Republican presidential nomination. A bitter convention fight ensued in which the Blaine forces denied former President Grant the nomination for a third term by throwing their support to James A. Garfield of Ohio. Garfield and Blaine were warm friends; both had supported the Roach subsidy and they were of one mind about the United States' future commercial role in South America and Asia. While a member of the House in 1876, Garfield had denounced a Democratic attempt to cut the diplomatic and consular appropriation. He reminded his colleagues that "by the addition of Alaska to our domain we have established relations most important for our commercial future" in China and Japan, and he declared that the proposed reduction would "abandon the field to Great Britain" not only in Asia, but in South America as well.[21]

After the Republican victory in 1880, and his appointment as Garfield's secretary of state, Blaine outlined his views and plans for American economic penetration of Latin America to Senator Lucius Q. C. Lamar of Mississippi. He first planned to call a peace congress of the states in the Western Hemisphere. Its purpose would be to control or possibly eliminate the constant eruptions of conflict and violence among Latin republics. Blaine feared that the all-too-frequent internal disruptions and petty border squabbles of the Latin states invited European intervention and meddling in hemispheric matters. To avoid this danger and to prevent further European encroachments, peace was essential. But that was not all, Blaine explained; control of violent outbreaks and the maintenance of stability would allow for the improved and extended commercial relations that were central in his dream of American preeminence.

The second project was a Pan-American railroad to connect all the nations of the two continents. Actually Hinton Rowan Helper, author of *The Impending Crisis,* former consul at Buenos Aires, and unflagging campaigner for increased Latin American trade, had initiated this scheme in 1880 by having a friend in the Senate introduce a bill calling for federal support of the Three Americas Railway.[22] Blaine understood the vital importance of transportation in the establishment of commercial supremacy, and his shift to the railway proposal was a way to avoid the opposition that had raised the cry of monopoly and special privilege against the Roach subsidy bill. He had not abandoned the fight for a merchant marine, but he was willing to move in another direction while the country adapted to his ideas.[23]

The third proposal Blaine outlined for Lamar involved reciprocity treaties with Latin America. Reciprocity was advocated as a means of driving a wedge into the South American markets. Bilateral agreements with the nations of South America would open markets for America's agricultural and manufactured surplus without endangering the principle of protection at home. It provided the means to overcome Britain's transportation and credit advantages in the hemisphere, and, Blaine argued, reciprocity would benefit the farmers of the South and West, open the way for the American manufacturer, including the southern cotton textile producer, and generally serve to establish American commercial hegemony in the Western Hemisphere.

The care and patience Blaine exercised in presenting his plans to Lamar and other southern senators in the months preceding the inauguration of General Garfield convincingly demonstrated the importance he attached to reestablishing the Republican party in the South. Although he would forego the use of the "bloody shirt" to woo southern protectionists, Blaine never conceded the South to the Democratic party, and he adroitly attempted to use foreign policy as a means of reasserting Republican influence among southerners.[24] He particularly directed his appeal to Senator Lamar as he "pictured to him how the commercial importance of the South could be increased through the development of this policy."[25] The southerners were also apprised of the importance of a Pan-American railroad as a link between their region and the countries of Central and South America.[26] One contemporary observer evaluated Blaine's southern policy as an appeal "to their self-interest, and through this self-interest to divide them" and thereby enhance the GOP's strength in the former Confederacy.[27]

The southerners did have such interests, but their latent Whiggism also drew them to Blaine's program. For his part, Blaine was following the pattern of his idol, Henry Clay, in attempting to convert the southerners with visions of economic and commercial expansion joined with internal transportation improvements. As secretary of state he continued his strategy through his strong support and participation in the 1881 Atlanta Cotton Exposition. His report, "The Cotton Goods Trade of the World," prepared for the exposition, was warmly received by southern leaders, especially John T. Morgan, Democrat of Alabama. Morgan praised the report and its author on the floor of the Senate, and it signaled the start of a long friendship that hinged on their mutual interest in an isthmian canal, a revived merchant marine, and overseas economic expansion.[28]

The *Atlanta Constitution* also applauded the secretary's report, happily noting the opportunities for exports of American cotton goods to Latin America. The editors felt that the United States could outdo Great Britain in those markets and that Blaine's program for commercial expansion was crucial to the South, for "the export of cotton goods has become almost indispensible to our prosperity."[29] While Blaine failed to win political converts in the South, he did win the sustained congressional support of many southern Democrats for his foreign policy. One of those Democrats who backed Blaine in the South was Washington C. Witthorne of Tennessee; he confidently expected that Blaine's vigorous foreign policy would serve to overcome sectionalism.[30]

Blaine also employed the idiom of Clay when he spoke of an "American system" in making clear his position on Hawaii.[31] To be sure, the disciple introduced changes into the system of the master, but they were more pragmatic than philosophical. They grew out of the changes in the economy during the last quarter of the nineteenth century, and the growing need for commercial expansion as a means of alleviating domestic economic dislocation and depression. Blaine's emphasis was on the need for Latin American markets for the nation's productions. Clay had given primary attention to the need to integrate the American economy through internal development. Blaine transposed that view to the Western Hemisphere and stressed transportation improvements as one method of extending and expanding American commerce.

As secretary of state, Blaine's immediate objective was to insure American hegemony in the Western Hemisphere. He saw the United States as the commercial center for North and South America, and as the successful republican model for emulation by the countries of Latin America. The United States would be the arbiter and mediator within the hemisphere. Blaine is often explained in terms of, and glorified as, a noble and far-sighted statesman because of his emphasis on peace in the Western Hemisphere. For Blaine himself, however, peace was not an end in and of itself. It was a means to attain the primary objective of American dominance in the trade patterns of the Latin countries. As one commentator has noted, the idea of union to promote peace "seems to have been secondary in his mind;" in reality "he desired to secure Latin-American tranquility first in order to obtain their trade."[32] In addition, harmony and tranquility among the Latin republics would serve to prevent European, and especially British, intervention in the internal affairs of those countries.

The unfavorable trade balance with Latin America was one of Blaine's chief concerns. When supporting the subsidy bill in the Senate, for example, he explained the problem and proposed an active policy to change the situation. One American observer, economist Jacob Schoenhof, demanded that "somebody ought to do something— invoke the Monroe Doctrine, to say the least—to make these republics acknowledge the solidarity of republican interest, and do their duty towards a sister republic—viz., buy more goods from us. We bought of them in 1880 $176,000,000 worth of goods . . . while they took only $58,000,000 from us."[33] This disparity earlier had troubled President Grant and Secretary of State Hamilton Fish and it continued to excite such influential Republicans as John Kasson and Hugh McCullough. For all of them the remedy appeared obvious: use the Latin American countries' dependence on the American market as a lever to increase United States exports to Central and South America.

All these factors were in Blaine's mind as he prepared the invitations for a Pan-American peace conference to assemble in Washington in 1882. Blaine intended to give the Monroe Doctrine an economic as well as a political interpretation. He heeded the advice of an old friend, Colonel Robert Ingersoll, who recommended that American foreign policy exhibit "a little less owl and a little more eagle."[34] That attitude was what prompted Edwin L. Godkin, editor of the *Nation* and one of Blaine's severest critics, to conclude that his conduct of the State Department was "rockety and journalistic."[35] But Godkin mistakenly equated vigor with recklessness. There was nothing original in Blaine's foreign policy. The interest in improving commercial relations and expanding trade with South America dated to the early nineteenth century, and increasingly penetrated the national consciousness as a result of the intellectual ferment produced by the Hayes administration's confrontation with the depression of the 1870s.

In a similar way, Blaine merely carried on the policy inherent in Hayes' assertion that the United States unilaterally would control any isthmian canal. He told James Russell Lowell, Garfield's Minister to Great Britain, that the president was concerned "that the great powers of Europe may possibly be considering the subject of jointly guaranteeing the neutrality of the interoceanic canal now projected across the Isthmus of Panama."[36] He reasserted that the canal was considered part of the American coastline, and then elaborated on Hayes' original statement in discussing the tremendous economic growth of the Pacific coast states. He argued that their expanded commerce with the rest of the Union meant that "the projected canal at Panama will form a part and be as truly a channel of communication between the Eastern and far Western States as our own trans-continental railways."[37]

This was ingenious logic, but it was not new. Blaine was simply more direct and forceful. Granted the assumption that the canal would form a part of the American coastline, it followed that the demand for complete control of the area was justified. The Gladstone ministry refused to accept the crucial assumption. Lord Granville, the British foreign minister, simply referred the American secretary to the Clayton-Bulwer Treaty, a document Blaine conveniently ignored in raising the issue.

Regardless of the validity of Blaine's argument, his message was clear to the foreign as well as the domestic audience. A particularly revealing expression of the favorable response came from Andrew Carnegie:

> You are exactly right about Clayton Treaty. America is going to control anything & everything on this Continent—that's settled. The more this is argued against the stronger the determination of the American people will be. No joint arrangements . . . America will take this Continent in hand alone—but your personal intercourse with certain people over there will do much good—never fear your reception. It will be grand—The highest authority, the Spectator has agreed with your claim. No American party could take ground against it.[38]

Carnegie's reference to the *Spectator* 's acceptance of Blaine's stance was accurate. Its editors did not find anything in his action on the canal (or in the Chile-Peru conflict) that was "in the least inconsistent with European diplomacy."[39] America's interest in the Western Hemisphere was similar to Great Britain's position in Egypt, or Germany's preoccupation with Trieste. They dismissed the anxiety of some of their countrymen and frankly asserted that the United States was "not exceeding the rights which would be recognized in Europe."[40] They accepted Blaine's logic even though they were nettled by his haughty tone and "bad-tempered rhetoric." It was not in Britain's best interest to challenge the American position, if only because in time of war such a claim might rebound to jeopardize British claims to the Suez Canal.[41]

Another noted British publication, the *Saturday Review,* was more cynical about Blaine's motives and less sympathetic to his argument. Its editors described his note as a bold attempt by the United States to claim "political supremacy in the Western

Hemisphere."[42] At first, they dismissed the commercial aspects of the correspondence as superfluous. Then, as the Blaine argument became clearer with the publication of the last note to Lowell in December 1881, they declared that "the political pretensions now advanced by the United States are not improbably preferred with the ulterior purpose of establishing a commercial monopoly." The editors were further concerned because they concluded—quite correctly, as it turned out—that Blaine's successor in the State Department, Frederick Frelinghuysen, would follow a similar course.[43]

The British minister at Washington, Sir Edward Thornton, noted his concern about Blaine's vigorous policy in his private correspondence with Lord Granville. In a letter to Granville in February 1881 Thornton at first expressed relief that the Republicans had remained in power, since the pretensions and demands of the Irish bloc would have been more difficult for the Democrats to ignore. He believed the Republicans were not dependent on the Irish vote and thus would pander less to their whims.[44] Despite this appreciation of the Irish issue, Thornton nevertheless distrusted Blaine. He had warned Granville in May 1880, before the Republican National Convention, that "Blaine is a noisy mischievous demagogue and most unscrupulous; he hesitates at no falsehood."[45]

Although the British minister eventually gained more respect for Blaine as secretary of state, he initially entertained doubts and expected the American might be "a very difficult man to deal with."[46] Thornton realized that Blaine distrusted the British and resented their power and position in the world. Even before the American secretary jolted the Gladstone ministry with his brash notes on the interoceanic canal, Thornton detected in Blaine a rankling at any suggestion of cooperation with Great Britain because it implied subservience and humiliation. America was the adolescent power, Thornton felt, and hence unable to view any joint action with Great Britain as a partnership of equals. He not only sensed this in Blaine, but also perceived "a feeling of dislike entertained by all Americans to do anything in conjunction with us."[47] This psychological factor was a part of the American attitude, but the antagonism toward Great Britain was based on very real conflicts, grievances, and ambitions.

The interoceanic canal controversy revealed only one aspect of Blaine's diplomacy. By the time all its ramifications had been displayed (even in the little more than six months he held office), the true nature of his challenge became increasingly apparent to the British leaders. Blaine was ever on the alert for British transgressions in what he defined as the American sphere of influence. He made this very clear to New York banker Levi Morton in September 1881: "The interests, commercial and political of the United States, on this continent, transcend in extent and importance those of any other power, and where those immense interests are deeply involved this government must preserve a position where its influence will be most independent and efficient."[48]

The same attitude became apparent when Venezuela requested American support in its long-standing dispute with England over the boundary with British Guiana. Thornton reported to Granville that Blaine minced no words: "as long as he was in the State Department, he would do his utmost to prevent Great Britain from gaining a foot of ground upon this Continent."[49] Territorial acquisition was not the only British threat that worried Blaine. As his whole Pan-American scheme indicated, the commercial predominance of Great Britain had to be destroyed and replaced by American hegemony.

When Chile, victorious in the War of the Pacific, demanded a territorial settlement and a cash indemnity from prostrate and humbled Peru, Blaine interpreted the action as further evidence of English meddling and influence. Although he suspected that British material and money were largely responsible for the success of Chile, he replied to a reporter's query about whether he considered England as the instigator with the remark that "to blame England would be childish."[50] But he was ambivalent as well as subtle in his analysis of the war and his jealousy became apparent: "England is always bold, energetic and vigilant in spreading her commercial power. I admire her ceaseless activity, but I do not believe in having it exercised at the expense of the United States. Especially do I dislike to see England winning great commercial triumphs in a field that legitimately belongs to the United States, and which the United States could readily command if she would."[51]

During Blaine's brief tenure as secretary of state the Hawaiian Islands also served as a diplomatic battleground between the United States and Great Britain. The conflict grew out of a reciprocity treaty negotiated between the United States and Hawaii in 1875. Great Britain had immediately complained that the preferential treatment accorded the United States violated the "most-favored nation" clause of their own treaty with the island kingdom. The American government ignored these protests until, in 1881, the English demanded that the Hawaiians grant them refunds on all customs duties greater than paid by Americans since the reciprocity treaty took effect.

Secretary Blaine responded to this English pressure on the Hawaiian government in a note to James Comly, the American minister to the islands. He instructed Comly to make it clear to the Hawaiian authorities that the extension of the privileges in the reciprocity treaty to any power under a "most-favored nation clause" would be considered a flagrant violation of the 1875 treaty. The United States held that stipulation to be the "essence of the treaty." The note further directed Comly to "add that if any other power should deem it proper to employ undue influence upon the Hawaiian government to persuade or compel action in derogation of this treaty, the government of the United States will not be unobservant of its rights and interests and will be neither unwilling nor unprepared to support the Hawaiian government in the faithful discharge of its treaty obligations."[52]

Prime Minister Gladstone acknowledged the seriousness of the American challenge to the "most-favored nation" clause as a successful tool of British commercial policy. He bluntly complained to Granville about the inability of Great Britain to make the clause "a reality."[53] The prime minister underscored the necessity of providing some sort of "remedy" or "safeguard" against the persistent leaks in the "most-favored nation" clause.[54] The British not only failed in the Hawaiian episode, however, they never successfully countered the reciprocity tactic, and their repeated public and private complaints during the next decade bore witness to their concern about the effectiveness of the measure throughout Latin America.

When the English realized they had been out-manuevered by Blaine in the fight over reciprocity, they employed other tactics in an effort to neutralize American influence in Hawaii. That prompted Blaine to make one of his most comprehensive statements on the nature of his "American system." Blaine received word from Comly that the British planned to arrange a scheme with the

Hawaiian government for the importation of Indian coolies from the subcontinent of Asia. These laborers were to be granted a separate and special status, amounting to extraterritoriality. Blaine feared that such an arrangement would eventually subvert the independent position of Hawaii and replace American influence with British control.

Using the idiom of Clay to define the limits of the American commercial empire, Blaine outlined his "American system" and clarified Hawaii's place in that grand scheme. To begin with, he reviewed the enormous growth and development of the Pacific states, and maintained that the Pacific was "little inferior in extent, and superior in natural wealth to the Atlantic seaboard." The purchase of Alaska had further added to the value and extent of the Pacific domain.[55] The limits of the commercial domain of the western coast, Blaine explained, were defined in the following manner:

> taking San Francisco as the commercial center on the western slope, a line drawn northwestwardly to the Aleutian group, marks our Pacific border almost to the confines of Asia. A corresponding line drawn south-westwardly from San Francisco to Honolulu marks the natural limit of the ocean belt within which our trade with the oriental countries must flow.[56]

Blaine then tied his Panama canal policy to Hawaii with the argument that "the extension of commercial empire westward from those states is no less vitally important to their development than is their communication with the Eastern coast by the Isthmian channel."[57] The strategic control possessed by the Hawaiian Islands over the North Pacific "brings their possession within the range of questions of purely American policy, as much as that of the Isthmus itself."[58] There was to be no doubt that America was to have a Pacific empire; Hawaii and the Panama Canal were crucial to the realization of that vision.

But Blaine went still further in explaining his plans for creating an empire second to none on the earth, and in so doing foreshadowed the informal empire that was to become a reality in the twentieth century. First the secretary, who had once defined the North Atlantic as an "English mill pond," asserted that America's Pacific policy was "the natural complement to our Atlantic policy."[59] Although the North Atlantic was an English lake, the Gulf of Mexico would be the door, with Cuba as the key, to American control and domination of the Western Hemisphere. The analogy Blaine constructed was as follows: "Hawaii, although much farther from the Californian coast than is Cuba from the Floridan peninsula, holds in the western sea much the same position as Cuba in the Atlantic. It is the key to the maritime dominion of the Pacific states, as Cuba is the key to the Gulf trade."[60]

While Cuba and Hawaii were included in the "American commercial system," Blaine disavowed any intention on the part of the United States government to annex either of these territories. One may question the sincerity of Blaine's denial of annexationist aspirations, since in a subsequent private conversation with Thornton's successor, Sackville-West, "he frankly admitted that the only acquisition of territory which he desired was the island of Cuba."[61] The American secretary did clarify his position to the British minister when he added that the United States would not go to war to gain Cuba, but fully expected "annexation would be brought about by the inevitable result of bad government."[62] In 1881 what the American government would not contemplate was the transfer of those territories to any other power, particularly not the national rival, Great Britain. Although Cuba belonged to Spain, in Blaine's framework that island was part of the "American system"; Hawaii, while nominally independent, also formed "part of the American system of states." What was demanded of the Hawaiian Islands was their "neutrality." The United States under no circumstances could allow a change in territorial control "which would cut it adrift from the American system, whereto they both indispensably belong."[63]

In addition to the dispatch to Comly outlining the American position which demanded Hawaiian neutrality, Blaine also explained the policy to Thornton. The American secretary suspected the king of Hawaii was trying to arrange a deal for the sale of the islands to a European power, and informed Thornton that he saw it as "his duty to say plainly that the United States Government would not allow such a transfer of the Islands."[64] Blaine's bluntness reinforced the British conclusion that he was "dangerous" and a real threat to their overseas interests, for his program directly challenged their economic and commercial supremacy.

While the Liberal Gladstone ministry was favorably inclined toward the United States, they did not allow their admiration for the republic to blind them to the threat the United States posed to England's position in the world. Blaine's brief tenure at the State Department dramatically revealed the full magnitude and extent of American aspirations. The British realized that Blaine had fired the American imagination with his vision of national power and glory. As the new British minister, Sir Lionel Sackville-West, observed: "both Frelinghuysen and Bancroft Davis (the new men) are of course reticent on the subject, for whatever they may think of the course pursued by Mr. Blaine, they are well aware that *he* has touched a national prejudice which *they* cannot disregard."[65]

And despite their frequent, formal expression of confidence in Britain's continued commercial supremacy, many English leaders recognized the threat implicit in the stupendous economic growth of the United States, and its more aggressive posture on the world scene. The drop in the volume of British exports in the 1870s and early 1880s increased their apprehension.[66] Above all, they feared for the future if James G. Blaine became president. As early as December 1881, Sackville-West apprehensively viewed the 1884 election. He confided to his chief that "the Democrats [will] elect for Civil Service Reform and it may be that the Republicans are preparing theirs by propounding the policy of sole supremacy over South America—a policy which certainly is likely to be popular among their Constituencies."[67] Shortly thereafter, Sackville-West again wrote Granville speculating that even in retirement from public life Blaine would keep the British bugbear alive and before the people.[68] Finally, in June of 1884, he remarked that "there is no doubt that if the nomination of Mr. Blaine results in his election to the Presidency in November next, our relations may become uneasy. Blaine is a personal friend of mine, and I know that he might become dangerous."[69]

British preoccupation with the challenge represented by Blaine, even after he left the State Department, stemmed from his conduct of foreign policy. Their anxiety did not arise as the result of his vocal flaying of the British lion in his attempts to capture the Irish vote for the Republican party. To be sure, Blaine aroused Irish pride and emotion by standing up to the traditional enemy. However, the English realized that Blaine's hostility for their country ran deeper than mere posturing to secure Irish support in an attempt to undermine the important source of Democratic strength. He was "dangerous" to England because he posed a challenge and threat to their economic supremacy in the world marketplace. In terms of petty diplomatic irritations, Sir Edward Thornton believed that the Democrats were actually more dependent on Irish support and thereby might cause England some difficulty in order to placate and retain the Irish vote.

British fears were confirmed when Blaine received the Republican presidential nomination in 1884. John Hay had jokingly written Blaine in June that "England would consider your nomination as a declaration of war."[70] The Blaine forces capitalized on this feeling as Republican newspapers reprinted numerous articles from British journals which expressed their apprehension and misgivings over his candidacy. The GOP editors, in particular Whitelaw Reid of the *New York Tribune,* concluded that English objections to Blaine hinged on their fear that his foreign policy threatened their commercial supremacy.[71] The campaign was waged chiefly on the issues of the tariff, Blaine's vigorous foreign policy, his program for South America, and the demand for an end to the abuses of alien land ownership. The tariff controversy was cast in the typical anti-British mold; the Republicans labelled Grover Cleveland a free trader who served the interests of England. The GOP employed slogans such as "British Gold can't shine in this crowd" and "America for Americans," a cry that on the one hand applied primarily to the alien land issue while on the other hand conveniently served to unite all the issues.[72]

In his speeches to Irish audiences during the campaign, Blaine appealed to their Anglophobia and expressed his chagrin and disappointment at the fact that they predominately supported the Democratic party. How, he rhetorically asked, could they justify their allegiance to a party that subscribed to the pro-British policy of free trade and truckled to every English whim and desire? Their continued support for Democrats aided their traditional enemy and served to retard America's bid for world primacy. The solution, Blaine argued, was to vote Republican and guarantee an end to American subservience to John Bull. Although unsuccessful in the bid for the presidency, Blaine drew the support of a great many Irish voters on the basis of his foreign policy and his strong stand with Great Britain.[73]

It was Blaine's policy of economic nationalism and overseas economic expansion that prompted English diplomats to label him "dangerous", not his political speeches to throngs of Irish-Americans in the urban centers of the United States. Actually, the Irish question was somewhat irrelevant, for its influence on foreign policy in the 1880s was barely discernible.[74] To be sure, the two major parties attempted to capitalize on the issue politically, and campaign orators frequently "twisted the lion's tail," but this remains an inadequate explanation of the persistent Anglophobia of the period. Anti-British nationalism was not simply a campaign phenomenon. It represented a fairly widespread emotional and psychological response to Great Britain as the nation that presented most of the obstacles and frustrations encountered by the United States in its drive for marketplace hegemony.

James G. Blaine the economic nationalist epitomized this hostility and resentment for British power. His sustained support for the protective tariff served to limit and exclude the British from their most valuable market, and his 1884 demand for restrictions on alien land ownership threatened to curtail and possibly eliminate British capital from a lucrative field of investment in the underdeveloped West. Perhaps most alarming, however, was Blaine's aggressive foreign policy which directly challenged Great Britain's primacy in the markets of the Western Hemisphere and the Pacific.

NOTES

1. See, for example, David S. Muzzey, *James G. Blaine: A Political Idol of Other Days* (New York: Dodd, Mead and Company, 1934), and Alice Felt Tyler, *The Foreign Policy of James G. Blaine* (Minneapolis: The University of Minnesota Press, 1927). For a more perceptive view of Blaine's influence on American imperialism see William Spence Roberston, "The Pan-American Policy of James G. Blaine," (Master's thesis, University of Wisconsin, 1900), Edward Stanwood, *James Gillespie Blaine* (New York: Houghton Mifflin Company, 1905), and Gail Hamilton (Mary Abigail Dodge), *Biography of James G. Blaine* (Norwich, Connecticut: Henry Bill Publishing Company, 1895).

2. Remarks of June 5, 1878: *Congressional Record*, VII, Part 5, p. 4134 (hereinafter cited as *CR*, 7:5:4134).

3. *Report on the Commercial Relations of the United States with Foreign Countries for the year 1877*, House Exec. Doc. 102, 45th Cong., 2nd Sess., 1878 (Washington: Government Printing Office, 1878), p. 23.

4. L. C. Ford and Thomas F. Ford, *The Foreign Trade of the United States* (New York: Charles Scribner's Sons, 1921), p. 18.

5. Remarks of May 1, 1878, *CR*, 7:3:2996.

6. "The Cotton Goods Trade of the World," *Special Consular Report*, No. 12, Vol. 4 (1881) (Washington: Government Printing Office, 1881), p. 8.

7. Hamilton, *Biography of Blaine*, p. 439.

8. Theron C. Crawford, *James G. Blaine, A Study of His Life and Career* (Philadelphia: Edgewood Publishing Company, 1893), p. 60.

9. Remarks of June 5, 1878, *CR*, 7:5:4134.

10. An example is the "Latin American Circular" of Hamilton Fish in *Foreign Relations of the United States, 1870* (Washington: Government Printing Office, 1871). See also Thomas F. McGann, *Argentina, the United States, and the Inter-American System 1880 — 1914* (Cambridge: Harvard University Press, 1957), and Robert G. Albion, "British Shipping and Latin America," *Journal of Economic History*, XI (1951), pp. 361—77.

11. Remarks of June 5, 1878, *CR*, 7:5:4134.

12. Ibid., p. 4131.

13. Walter S. Vail, *The Words of James G. Blaine on the Issues of the Day* (Boston: D. L. Guernsey Company, 1884), p. 150.

14. Ibid., p. 144.

15. Ibid.

16. Ibid.

17. Ibid.

18. For a complete discussion of the subsidy bill see Leonard Alexander Swann, Jr., *John Roach: Maritime Entrepreneur* (Annapolis: United States Naval Institute, 1965), pp. 98—119.

19. Remarks of Hewitt and others of February 28, 1879, *CR*, 8:3:2113—2132.

20. Swann, *John Roach*, p. 109.

21. Remarks of February 7, 1876, *CR*, 4:1:926.

22. McGann, *Argentina*, p. 108.

23. *Official Proceedings of the Republican National Conventions, 1884 — 1888* (Minneapolis: Charles W. Johnson, Publisher, 1903), p. 194.

24. The two monographs dealing with the Republican party's efforts to reestablish itself in the South during this period ignore Blaine's use of foreign policy to appeal to the latent Whiggism of Southern whites. See Vincent P. De Santis, *Republicans Face the Southern Question: The New Departure Years, 1877 — 1897* (Baltimore: John Hopkins Press, 1959), and Stanley P. Hirshson, *Farewell to the Bloody Shirt* (Bloomington: Indiana University Press, 1962).

25. Crawford, *Blaine*, p. 491.

26. Ibid.

27. Ibid.

28. Remarks of October 17, 1881, *CR*, 12:SS:524.

29. *Atlanta Constitution*, February 25, 1882.

30. Remarks of March 2, 1882, *CR*, 13:2:1555.

31. *Foreign Relations of the United States, 1881* (Washington: Government Printing Office, 1882), p. 637.

32. Alva Curtis Wilgus, "James G. Blaine and the Pan-American Movement," (Master's Thesis, University of Wisconsin, 1921), p. 12.

33. Quoted in Sydney J. Chapman, *The History of Trade Between the United Kingdom and the United States* (London: Swan, Sonnenschein and Company, 1899), p. 63.

34. *Chicago Times*, December 14, 1881, p. 3.

35. *The Nation,* December 15, 1881, p. 461.

36. *Foreign Relations,* 1881, pp. 537–40.

37. Ibid.

38. Andrew Carnegie to Blaine, January 14, 1882, James G. Blaine Papers, Library of Congress.

39. *The Spectator,* December 17, 1881, p. 1599.

40. Ibid.

41. Ibid.

42. *Saturday Review,* October 29, 1881, p. 528.

43. Ibid., December 24, 1881, pp. 778–79.

44. Thornton to Granville, February 22, 1881, in Paul Knaplund and Carolyn M. Clewes, *Private Letters from the British Embassy in Washington to the Foreign Secretary Lord Granville, 1880 – 1885,* Annual Report of the American Historical Association, Vol. I, 1941 (Washington: Government Printing Office, 1942), p. 118.

45. Ibid., May 4, 1880, p. 93.

46. Ibid., May 10, 1881, p. 131.

47. Ibid., March 14, 1881, p. 121.

48. Blaine to Levi Morton, September 5, 1881, *Chile—Peru,* House Report No. 1790, House, 47th Cong., 1st Sess. (Washington: Government Printing Office, 1882), p. 229.

49. Thornton to Granville, June 14, 1881, Knaplund and Clewes, *Private Letters,* p. 137.

50. *New York Tribune,* January 30, 1882, p. 1.

51. Ibid.

52. *Foreign Relations,* 1881, p. 635.

53. Gladstone to Granville, June 22, 1881, in Agatha Ramm, *The Political Correspondence of Mr. Gladstone and Lord Granville, 1876 – 1886* (Oxford: Clarendon Press, 1962), p. 282.

54. Ibid.

55. *Foreign Relations,* 1881, p. 636.

56. Ibid.

57. Ibid.

58. Ibid.

59. Ibid., p. 637.

60. Ibid., p. 638.

61. Sackville-West to Granville, No. 355, Confidential, December 8, 1881, Foreign Office 115, Vol. 681, Public Record Office, London.

62. Ibid.

63. *Foreign Relations,* 1881, p. 638.

64. Thornton to Granville, April 12, 1881, Knaplund and Clewes, *Private Letters,* p. 128.

65. Ibid., December 28, 1881, p. 160.

66. For evidence of this concern see *The Spectator,* 1881, and *The Economist,* 1880; also Stephen Bourne, *Trade Population and Food, A Series of Papers on Economic Statistics* (London: George Bell and Sons, 1880).

67. Sackville-West to Granville, December 28, 1881, Knaplund and Clewes, *Private Letters,* p. 161.

68. Ibid., January 31, 1882, p. 163.

69. Ibid., June 10, 1884, p. 178.

70. Hay to Blaine, June 7, 1884, Blaine Papers.

71. For a fine analysis of the campaign and election see David M. Pletcher, *The Awkward Years, American Foreign Policy Under Garfield and Arthur* (Columbia: University of Missouri Press, 1962), pp. 257−69.

72. Swann, *John Roach,* p. 196. William Turrentine Jackson, "British Interests in the Range Cattle Industry, 1878−1951," *When Grass Was King* (Boulder: University of Colorado Press, 1956), p. 191.

73. Hamilton, *Biography of Blaine,* p. 584.

74. Joseph Patrick O'Grady, "Irish-Americans and Anglo-American Relations 1880−1888," (Ph. D. dissertation, University of Pennsylvania, 1965), p. 273.

5

The Campaign Against Alien Ownership

American soil is for Americans, and should be exclusively owned and controlled by American citizens.

> Joint resolution of the
> New Hampshire Legislature,
> 1885.

America for Americans will meet a response in every soldier's heart.

> G.A.R. Journal, 1884

We believe that our land, our industries, and our mines should be held sacred to American capital and American industry.

> Washington State Grange,
> 1889

I stand sir by the principle—keep every source of wealth the God of nations has blessed us with to be developed by Americans for Americans only.
I mean America for Americans!

> Lewis E. Payson, 1890

Anglophobia in the United States during the late nineteenth century was shaped and intensified by an increasing popular awareness of the dominant role played by Great Britain in American economic and political life. To be sure, long-standing national prejudices as well as existing opinions and preconceptions about England's historic policy of stymieing the nation's aspirations provided fertile grounds for such a response among millions of Americans. However, to dismiss American hostility and resentment toward Britain as merely a senseless, irrational "hunt for devils" is misleading and inaccurate. The grievances undoubtedly were magnified and distorted, but the complaints were neither totally unfounded nor the handiwork of a capricious imagination. Deep-seated abuses were inherent in the American economy of the 1880s and 1890s, and the sustained agrarian protest and fierce anti-British nationalism of those decades were symptomatic of the prevailing inequities.

One specific source of antagonism among Americans, particularly those connected with the land, was the prevalence of British capital in such enterprises as cattle ranches, grain elevators, farms, cotton plantations, irrigation projects, railroads, stockyards, mines, and land companies. While the role of British investment in the overall development of the American economy was not crucial, it was substantial, particularly in cattle ranching and mining ventures. During the last half of the nineteenth century there were approximately 1,500 British companies doing business in the trans-Mississippi West, and by 1899 the total British investment in the United States reached approximately $2,625 million.[1] These speculative activities were focused primarily on the developing West but also included considerable outlays in the old Northwest and the South.[2] Understandably, anti-British sentiment flourished in those areas, especially in the region between the Mississippi River and the Rocky Mountains.

The settler of the western plains suffered from a variety of existing afflictions that intensified his reaction to the alien corporations. Such environmental handicaps as scarce water and timber resources and the all-too-frequent devastating attacks of grasshoppers, coupled with a distorted economic scene in which railroads and markets were monopolistically controlled, all contributed to the farmer's anxiety and resentment. He suspected and distrusted outside corporations, and when the enterprise or large landholder was labelled alien, or more commonly British, the response was even more bitter, bringing outraged cries of exploitation and domination.[3]

But concern over the extensive landholdings of foreigners was not restricted to the actual pioneers in the regions where the British corporations prevailed. In the 1880s the idea that available public land was disappearing and the frontier soon would be closed pervaded the national consciousness. This fear was not based on the simplistic notion that the public domain had vanished completely, and later critics, who assert that an abundance of unsettled territory remained, essentially miss the point. What troubled that generation of Americans, many of whom were familiar with the writings of Henry George and his thesis that abundant cheap land was the basis of the United States' institutions and greatness,[4] was the recognition that the frontier as a positive social force shaping American life was rapidly coming to an end. Hence, the disposition of the remaining public land became a major issue to the farmer and settler, the industrial laborer, and the former Union soldier.

Americans were also concerned about the increased concentration of economic power in fewer and fewer hands which led to an alarming growth of trusts and monopolies. The trend to concentration increased tenancy and speeded the disappearance of the small farm owner, and deepened the general dissatisfaction with government land policy. Scores of concerned citizens petitioned the Congress to correct the abuses by reclaiming the unearned grants of the railroads. That would return vast acres to the people, delay the demise of the frontier, and preserve the American dream. Some critics of government land policy even charged that the evil of alien ownership had originated in the congressional acts granting large acreages of the public domain to the railroads. They contended that speculators, including a number of aliens, quickly purchased large tracts from the roads, or that alien corporations later bought the land from such profiteers. Government construction of the railroads would have prevented the evil, and in the 1880s the remedy promoted by reformers included legislation to return the unused railroad grants to the public domain and to restrict and curtail alien ownership of land.[5]

The fight to preserve the public domain for the actual settler became a multi-issue campaign with a call for the repeal of the timber culture, preemption, and desert land acts, the organization of the Oklahoma territory, and the demand that the great Sioux reservation be opened for settlement. According to the petitioners it was strictly a matter of legal rights and priorities: corporations had been given preference long enough, and it was now the turn of the people.[6] This legislative program would check further economic concentration, for "nothing can be a surer safeguard in a free community against the dominating influence of powerful corporations and combinations of capital than a body of independent small land owners living upon their own freeholds."[7]

A psychology of scarcity possessed many Americans who were nagged by the fear that free or cheap land would shortly become unavailable to the settler and the pioneer. To the actual homesteader these apprehensions were dramatically confirmed when he confronted the fences surrounding the vast holdings of British noblemen and their corporations. Such encounters frequently provoked impassioned denunciations of alien and absentee ownership and demands that foreign control of American land be terminated immediately. The ever-mounting evidence that federal land was dwindling made the disposition of the public lands an urgent, vital issue for Americans in the 1880s. The question transcended regional and sectional interests and a typical nationalist response came from the New Hampshire legislature in a joint resolution passed in 1885; "American soil is for Americans, and should be exclusively owned and controlled by American citizens."[8]

Perhaps more than any other, the one venture in the early 1880s that aroused public attention, and a certain disquiet, was the conspicuous role of the British investor in the burgeoning American livestock industry. Cattle-raising became a lucrative enterprise in the late 1870s when United States exports of live animals increased enormously. What had been an insignificant and minor aspect of American agricultural exports to Great Britain and continental Europe developed in a few short years into an important aspect of the nation's commerce. In 1877 some 50,000 head of cattle were shipped abroad; two years later American shipments increased to 137,000 head, 60 percent of which entered Great Britain.

In conjunction with the growth in the live cattle trade, a technological innovation—which allowed the principle of the refrigerated railway car to be incorporated into ocean-going vessels—produced similar results in the exports of fresh, or dressed, beef. Great Britain was also the largest importer of this item. The United

Kingdom purchased some 1,732 tons of fresh beef in 1876; with
the aid of refrigeration, the totals for the years 1878—1880 soared
to an annual average exceeding 30,000 tons. A multimillion dollar
business had emerged virtually overnight. The sudden expansion of
trade, in which the United States provided 80 to 90 percent of the
British foreign supply of fresh beef and almost two-thirds of its
live cattle imports, greatly stimulated the development of the trans-
Mississippi livestock industry.[9]

This cattle bonanza greatly intensified the interest of Scottish
and English capitalists in the possibilities of profitable investment
in the American West. One Englishman enthusiastically told his
countrymen that

> you or I can to-day start for any of the . . . territories, pick out for our
> stock a good range for grazing, as yet unoccupied, drive on to it a herd
> of ten thousand cattle, select a suitable spot near to a convenient creek, and
> there build our ranche or farmhouse, fence in fifty or a hundred acres for
> hayland, and . . . make ourselves entirely at home, disporting ourselves as
> virtual owners of the land, without paying one penny for it or outstepping
> any territorial or United States statute, or doing what is not perfectly
> lawful.[10]

Then he reassured his readers that "there is no trouble about title,
deeds, surveyors and lawyers,"[11] an observation that surely pleased
and encouraged his fellow Englishmen. But the free use of the
public domain by alien capitalists infuriated and outraged
Americans.

During the heady years of the early 1880s, Scottish and English
cattle companies were rapidly organized in Edinburgh and London
to participate in the newest American boom. Ten major British-
American companies were incorporated in 1882 alone, with a
subscribed capital of nearly $11 million, and 70 percent of the funds
were actually used to purchase land and cattle in the West. If the
investments of the earlier Prairie Cattle Company and Texas Land
and Cattle Company are included, the total subscribed capital
amounted to $15 million (of which $10.25 million were spent).[12]

All of this activity occurred in the three-year period between
1879 and 1882; yet it proved only the beginning, even though the
boom was short-lived. To be sure, cattle prices continued to rise
in 1882 and early 1883, with the early profits being quite

phenomenal, but the rapid entrance of foreign, and some domestic, capital into the ranch and range industry soon resulted in overexpansion and overcapitalization. To aggravate the situation further, exports of live cattle declined sharply in 1882, the result in part of an 1879 act of the British Parliament which placed the importation of American cattle under stringent regulations.[13] By the autumn of 1883 cattle prices began to slump and continued downward throughout 1884 and 1885. British investors moved with greater caution after the initial surge tapered off, but their enthusiasm remained unabated; by 1888 a total of 33 cattle companies with a capital structure of more than $37 million had registered in Great Britain.[14]

In addition to the storm signals of overcapitalization and overexpansion another cloud darkened the British investor's financial sky in the American West. Amid rosy predictions by a leader of the Powder River Cattle Company, one of the early British corporations, that they need not fear that "we western graziers will be taxed in return for the free use we make of government lands," American homesteaders and farmers began exploding in a nationalistic frenzy demanding the ouster of all alien landowners.[15] One congressman, James B. Belford of Colorado, rhetorically caught the mood of the people when he asked: "Are we the servile and supple tools of foreign capitalists or are we going to preserve this country for our own people?"[16] What emerged from the widespread discontent was a national campaign against alien corporations and alien land ownership that, since the term alien was nearly synonymous with the term British, bore a strong imprint of Anglophobia.

Numerous petitions and complaints protesting the abuses of foreign and domestic corporations in the trans-Mississippi West flooded Congress and the General Land Office of the Interior Department during 1883–1884.[17] The major grievance against the cattle companies was the enormous size of their holdings, and the petitioners called for legislation preventing the further aggregation of the public lands into their hands. The settlers also condemned the fraudulent manner in which the corporations had secured their holdings and protested their illegal fencing of public domain — practices at which native and alien companies were equally adept.[18] All of the abuses impeded the extension of settlement and threatened to subvert the American dream of open economic opportunity. The elimination of such transgressions thus became the first objective of the campaign to save the public domain for actual homesteaders.

Veterans groups, labor organizations, and major political parties were aroused at the prospect of a vanishing frontier; periodicals throughout the country expressed their misgivings about the development and published lists of alien holdings and recent acquisitions to reveal the extent and nature of this evil. A Nebraska Alliance chapter, comparing the situation in the West to conditions in Ireland, asserted that "the great mission of our government is to see that all classes have an equal chance in the great race."[19]

Knights of Labor groups were particularly active in sending demands to Congress for legislation to curb alien landowners. The Grand Master Workman, Terence V. Powderly, almost singlehandedly aroused workers to the danger and was the most outspoken leader of that wing of the movement. Powderly, while addressing the general assembly of the Knights at Pittsburgh in 1880, informed the delegates that "millions of acres have been stolen from the people" and he apocalyptically warned that "for every acre of the land which God designed for man's use and benefit that is stolen, another link is riveted in the chain which the land bond lords hope to finally encircle us."[20] Clearly, Powderly was upset because he accepted the frontier philosophy and a theory of upward mobility, a view of American society that held that every man could still be an entrepreneur. His outlook demanded the opportunity of the frontier and the concept of public domain. Powderly had not yet abandoned the laborer to a lifetime of toil and permanent membership in the working class. In 1883, when noting that seven English noblemen owned 8.9 million acres of American land, and their goal was "to have absolute control of the soil, and can thus exact such terms as pleases them," he emphasized his fear that such a pattern would recreate Ireland in America.[21] Powderly vowed to "fight to remove the alien oppressor from our lands" as one means of realizing his dream for the American worker.[22]

Union Army veterans were also interested in maintaining the public domain by restricting alien corporations and landowners. Their concern was perhaps motivated more by self-interest and economic gain than any national crusade, since the Grand Army of the Republic campaigned for a program of individual land warrants for veterans. The Commander-in-Chief, Paul Van Der Voort, predicted in 1884 that "unless land warrants are given soon the public domain will largely fall into the hands of foreign syndicates, alien to our soil and leave the Union soldier homeless and landless."[23] Some veterans opposed the land-warrant scheme because of a vested interest in pensions. They also cast their argument in an anti-British, antiaristocratic tone by denouncing and labelling opponents of pensions as upper-class bondholders, bankers and moneylenders "who aped English manners" and "wished the lower classes treated as in Britain."[24]

Congress responded to the public demand for action by investigating the problem during the latter part of President Chester A. Arthur's administration. The Senate, under the leadership of Charles H. Van Wyck of Nebraska, directed the Committee on Public Lands "to inquire in what manner large quantities of public lands became transferred to, or possessed by, foreign corporations or syndicates, and what, if any, legislation is advisable to prevent such transfers or possessions."[25] As congressional concern mounted, several bills were offered in both houses to check further foreign acquisitions and reserve the remaining public lands for bona fide settlers. In the House of Representatives, Newton W. Nutting of New York and Charles B. Lore of Delaware presented lists of recent purchases of land by foreigners in the United States. Their evidence purported to show that nearly 20 million acres were owned by aliens who were members of the nobility (and chiefly from England). The totals included holdings in Florida, Mississippi, Texas, Arkansas, Kansas, and West Virginia. The sums may have been exaggerated, but the problem was real.

As part of the alien land question, Congress also investigated the validity of the numerous complaints concerning unauthorized fencing of public lands. A report by the Department of the Interior verified that millions of acres of the public domain were illegally enclosed throughout the grazing regions and thereby prevented settlement and obstructed public travel and intercourse.[26] Domestic corporations participated in the illegal activity, but among the most flagrant violators cited by the commissioner of public lands were the Prairie Cattle Company, a Scottish organization, and the Ar-

kansas Valley Land and Cattle Company, an English firm. Each
company reportedly had illegally enclosed 1 million acres in
Colorado alone. Two other British firms, the Carlisle Cattle Company and the Wyoming Cattle Company, were also listed as
offenders.[27]

The various attempts to pass laws against alien ownership were
temporarily stymied during the first session of the Forty-eighth
Congress, and the issue naturally played a prominent role in the
1884 presidential election campaign between Grover Cleveland and
James G. Blaine. Both parties included a plank in their platforms
calling for a curb on alien holdings and the restriction of further
acquisitions. Blaine declared in his letter accepting the Republican
nomination that "it is but fair that the public land should be disposed of only to actual settlers and to those who are citizens of
the Republic, or willing to become so."[28] One of Blaine's campaign
slogans was "America for Americans," a direct appeal to anti-
British nationalism on the basis of the alien land question.[29]

The *Democratic Campaign Book* contained a list of alien
holdings to bolster their demand for restriction, a list nearly identical to that previously presented in the House of Representatives
by Democratic Congressman Lore of Delaware.[30] Each party emphasized in its campaign rhetoric that it would endeavor to reserve
the public lands as far as possible for small holdings by actual
settlers. The Republicans offered the stronger plank, however, and
advocated legislation "to correct this evil." They also claimed the
Democrats merely promised to prevent further acquisitions of large
holdings by alien absentees.[31]

Political agitation of the issue continued until the passage of an
Alien Land Law in March 1887. Most Americans subscribed to
the logic of the frontier as a transmuting force in preserving the
American dream, and that outlook was intensified by the economic
depression of the mid-1880s. The abuses of the railroads, domestic
corporations, and alien landowners were flagrant and open, as
revealed by the congressional investigations. And in the winter of
1884–1885, before the inauguration of the victorious Cleveland,
the last session of the Forty-eighth Congress was besieged with
appeals for legislation to correct the abuses of the British
corporations in the Great Plains region. Some settlers refused to
wait for official action by the federal government and, as in Texas,

began to cut the fences. The *Dallas Daily Herald* explained these outbreaks of frontier lawlessness as arising out of "the conviction that the great bulk of West and Northwest Texas, was alarmingly passing into the control of a few wealthy men and corporations, largely non-resident, and materially alien to the United States."[32]

The violence on the Texas frontier and the flood of petitions impressed Congress with the urgency of the situation and the need for some positive action. It responded by passing a law on February 25, 1885, which prohibited enclosures on the public domain in any state or territory which prevented a person "from peacefully entering upon or establishing a settlement or residence on any tract of public land."[33] President Cleveland issued a proclamation on August 7, 1885, which ordered all unlawful fences to be removed and forbade any threats or intimidation against actual settlers on the public lands.[34] This federal legislation and the ensuing executive order curtailed the abuses. Most cattle companies, especially the British, readily complied. Some firms attempted to circumvent the law by diverting streams, but most fences had disappeared by 1889, and settlers had claimed much of the land.[35]

The push to eliminate unauthorized fencing was a corollary to the campaign to restrict alien ownership of land. Before the passage of the fencing act, the House received a favorable report from the Committee on Public Lands concerning a bill to prevent aliens from holding any land in the United States.[36] The committee, under the chairmanship of William Oates of Alabama, expressed all the existing objections and fears in connection with alien ownership. The members asserted that certain noblemen—principally English—owned in the aggregate about 21 million acres of land in the United States. This vast empire under alien control provided the foundation for a system of landlordism in the western states and territories that was incompatible with the best interests and free institutions of the nation.[37] The committee proposed to squelch the growth of this insidious landlordism, and to guarantee that "American soil should be owned exclusively by American citizens."[38]

The feature of alien absentee landlordism that aroused the greatest apprehension among Americans was the tenantry system, believed by many to be an integral and most repressive aspect of the evil. And what they feared above all was that tenantry as practiced by the English would inevitably lead to the deplorable conditions that existed in Ireland.[39] The analogy to Ireland was especially pertinent to the agrarians in the trans-Mississippi West. They identified with Irish efforts to secure home rule because they felt—not without reason—that the West was in the same relative colonial position vis à vis the Northeast.[40]

The tenantry and absentee landlord issues linked various rather amorphous aspects of the rampant antiforeignism and xenophobia that marked late nineteenth century American life. The urban anti-immigration groups of the East and the anti-Chinese forces of the West Coast joined with the antialien ownership cadres in demanding protection for native Americans, and they all freely employed the slogan "America for Americans." At least one attempt was made to unite these diverse strands of neonativism in Philadelphia in September 1887. The ephemeral American party, organized to coincide with the centennial celebration of the Constitutional Convention, was dedicated to maintaining "the power and supremacy of American born citizens," to guaranteeing "that American lands should be reserved for American citizens," and to pursuing "a firm and consistent foreign policy and vigorous assertion of our national dignity and respect to our flag on land and sea."[41] Certainly one shared fear among these groups was the belief that the frontier was disappearing and there no longer existed unbounded economic opportunity and unlimited public domain for "true" Americans.

The spread of tenantry and the conviction that a "considerable number of the immigrants annually arriving in this country are to become tenants and herdsmen on the vast possessions of these foreign lords under contracts made and entered into before they sail for our shores" challenged fundamental American beliefs.[42] Tenantry was the antithesis of the American dream; it was European in origin and it typified to Americans all the evils of the Old World. The 1880 census was the first to include figures on farm ownership and tenantry, and the findings jolted the American populace and appeared to give the lie to many cherished American ideals and traditions dating to the Founding Fathers. Of the 4,008,907 farms in the United States in 1880, 1,024,601, or one in four, were cultivated by tenants who paid rent either by cash or a share of the product.[43] Thus about 74 percent of American farms were operated by owners and 26 percent by tenants.[44] The trend continued unabated through the decade, and by 1890 tenants accounted for 34.08 percent (an increase of 8.52 percent).[45]

In the eyes of a majority of Americans the most notorious practitioner of the tenant system was William Scully, resident of London and son of an Irish landed family, who by 1900 held 220,000 acres in Nebraska, Kansas, Missouri, and Illinois.[46] Scully's career as an Irish landlord had been unsavory, and his Irish policies in the late 1860s had given a "decisive impulse to public opinion" for passage of the Reform Land Act of 1870.[47] On his American holdings, "Lord" Scully established a permanent tenant system that, at least to many frustrated farmers, smacked of European landlordism. Tenants were required to pay all taxes and make all improvements above the ground, i.e., on houses, barns, fences, and other buildings. His rental system differed sharply from that of most other frontier landlords, but even so it did not include all the worst features of the Irish policy.[48] Scully had 300 tenant farms in Illinois; during the depression of the 1870s, when prices were low, he was not inclined to be lenient.[49] The harshness of his terms aroused the tenants and they held several mass protest meetings and drew the by then inevitable comparison to "the tyranny of the absentee landlords of Ireland." A bill was introduced in the Illinois legislature attacking Scullyism and calling for an extraordinary tax on absentee and alien owners of land.[50]

In the 1880s Scully and his practices came to symbolize all the evils of alien landlordism and tenantry, and reinforced all the fears and anxieties of Americans. Widespread hostility for Scully existed because, among other things, he exacted a cash rent and refused to improve his land. Consequently, the quality of tenant improvements was low. He was an alien who apparently contributed little to the development of the states in which he owned land while withdrawing a huge tribute. He became a favorite target of Anglophobes, and from 1883 to 1887 numerous western newspapers condemned his reign. They stressed the un-American character of tenancy and identified his cash rent policy with rackrenting in Ireland.[51]

Despite the mounting case against alien corporations and alien ownership, two features of the Oates bill troubled some Americans. First, the critics doubted the constitutionality of the measure and seriously questioned the federal government's authority to apply the law to the states. Second, others, especially in areas where mining was an important feature of the economy, feared that such legislation would drive much-needed British capital to other countries. Even among the doubters, however, there prevailed an awareness of the problem and a realization that the bill had merit and "should be carefully considered."[52] Most Americans felt it was desirable to keep Dakota wheat fields and Colorado cattle ranges out of the hands of the British aristocracy, but the law as proposed was too sweeping; it should only apply to the western regions of the country and not the thickly populated East.[53]

Representative Oates anticipated the unconstitutional charge by defining his bill as a "part of the foreign policy of this country."[54] The law would "operate only prospectively, and therefore, not harshly, to prevent absolutely the citizens or subjects of other nations . . . from acquiring the ownership of American soil within the jurisdiction of the United States."[55] Oates' logic failed to convince the opponents of the bill and it did not pass. A basic ambivalence was apparent among Americans who generally admitted the need for some form of corrective legislation. They denounced the evils of British investment while simultaneously responding to the benefits it provided. The attitude delayed passage of an alien land law until the spring of 1887. One state, Indiana, preceded federal action when it passed an alien land act in 1885.[56]

President Grover Cleveland moved cautiously in response to the mounting public clamor for restrictive legislation. His series of executive proclamations issued during the early months after he took office evicted ranchers and their herds from Indian lands in the Dakota Territory and from the Cheyenne and Arapahoe Reservation.[57] Those actions, combined with the executive order directing federal officers to destroy unauthorized fencing, incensed cattlemen and influential eastern investors and united them against the administration. His fear of arousing further opposition prevented the president from offering active and sustained support for alien land legislation. The tariff and silver issues were destroying party unity and a full-scale administrative campaign for an alien land law might further decimate the Democratic party.

But another mass petition campaign began in 1886, when local chapters of the Knights of Labor, the Alliance, Grange, and the Grand Army of the Republic bombarded legislators in behalf of an eight-step program to save the public domain and renew the American dream.[58] The effort was spearheaded by the national organization of the Knights which, in a special session of the general assembly in May 1886, invited the Grange to support the petition drive and to help in the "efforts to restore to the public domain all land wrongfully held by alien non-resident owners and cattle syndicates." Also, the Knights appointed a three-man committee to lobby in Washington in behalf of alien land legislation, and to urge the Democrats, who had a majority of some forty votes in the House, to honor their 1884 campaign pledge.[59]

The volume of signatures was tremendous, and came from all sections of the nation. The Senate Committee on Finance and the Senate and House Committees on Public Land received petitions with approximately 100,000 to 150,000 signatures demanding among other things a "bill prohibiting aliens from holding land in the United States."[60] The bulk of the petitions arrived in June and July 1886, and this tremendous public pressure induced Congress to act. In addition, newspapers throughout the country, but especially in Kansas and Illinois, conducted a sustained campaign against William Scully, the symbol of all that was evil in alien landlordism and tenantry.[61]

The major impetus for the bill as finally passed came from the Senate where Preston Plumb of Kansas provided the leadership. The Senate passed its bill on June 24, 1886, and the House approved its version, framed by Representative Lewis E. Payson of Illinois, on July 31, 1886, by a margin of 210 to 6.[62] The Senate, under Plumb's direction, amended the Payson bill and passed it on August 7, 1886, at the close of the first session of the Forty-ninth Congress. When the second session convened in December 1886, however, the House did not concur with the Senate version and a conference was appointed to arrange a compromise. The Senate agreed to the conference version on February 26, 1887; the House followed on February 28, 1887, and the bill became law when President Cleveland signed it on March 3, 1887.[63]

The Alien Land Law prohibited for the future all aliens or foreign corporations from holding real estate in the territories and the District of Columbia except by inheritance or the lawful collection of debts. A similar provision was placed upon any syndicate or corporation in which more than 20 percent of the stock was held by aliens. Finally, no companies, domestic or foreign, other than those organized for the construction of canals, turnpikes, or railroads, could obtain or hold more than 5,000 acres in the territories. All property acquired, held, or owned in violation of the act was to be forfeited to the United States government.[64] Existing titles were not affected. The law did nothing, therefore, to remedy existing monopolistic aggregations.[65]

Public opinion generally favored the law, although it was frequently condemned as being too mild because it left untouched the existing foreign holdings in both the states and territories. Demands for a stronger measure appeared almost immediately, and since the law applied only to the territories, a number of states enacted alien land laws to overcome the existing abuses not covered by the federal legislation. With the passage of the 1887 national law the battle against alien ownership entered a second stage. It slowly emerged as a regional issue with a sustained and heightened agitation appearing in the Midwest and the trans-Mississippi West. National support gradually faded after 1887 because the urban East was relatively satisfied with the federal law applying to the territories. Some journalistic support for a stronger law continued until 1890; but many, if not most, easterners felt the law adequately rectified the existing injustices.

Two other characteristics appeared along with the more pronounced regional base in the agitation for stronger measures against alien landowners. First, the campaign became identified almost totally with the agrarian protest movement of the late 1880s and the 1890s. Second, the tenor of the campaign became exclusively anti-British, a vocal and outward manifestation of the rabid Anglophobia of the Populists. And in their frequent denunciations of English investors some of the Populists' literature demanding a more extensive federal alien land law was tinged with anticapitalist logic. But generally it coincided with the agitation of the mid-1880s, which was not markedly anticapitalist. Quite the contrary, for the argument for curbs on alien participation in the economy explicitly accepted the capitalist framework. The agrarian reformers glorified and defended the homestead tradition as the basis of a prosperous yeomanry that constituted the backbone of the republic.

Nebraska, Minnesota, and Illinois passed their own versions of an alien land law in 1887; Iowa followed their lead a year later.[66] The state bills were similar, and in each case the legislation was tougher than the federal act. The Nebraska law, which had been hastily prepared, stipulated that all lands belonging to nonresident aliens be forfeited, and it barred nonresident aliens and foreign corporations from acquiring or inheriting land in the state.[67] The Illinois law reflected the same lack of thorough study, and it was declared unconstitutional by the United States Supreme Court. The people of Illinois and Nebraska, anxious to curtail the activities of the likes of William Scully—if they could not eliminate him—quickly amended their laws to conform to the court ruling while still providing strong antialien legislation.[68]

Wisconsin and Colorado also passed alien land acts in 1887. The Wisconsin statute prohibited aliens and corporations with more than 20 percent of their stock held by aliens from acquiring or holding more than 320 acres of land in the state.[69] The Colorado law restricted alien ownership but excluded mining enterprises.[70]

Kansas, a state with a sizeable Irish population and no shortage of Anglophobes, enacted its alien land law in 1889. The voters had given the legislature a virtual mandate the previous November when they recommended legislation by a tally of 220,419 to 16,611.[71] British noblemen, according to the legislators, owned 500,000 acres in Kansas; the largest single landholder was Scully, who in 1889 controlled 80,000 acres. Scullyism was the main target; a select committee of the legislature had, in a report issued that year, warned that his system of tenantry "would tend to degrade and pauperize its victims, and retard the prosperity of these sections afflicted with this un-American system of landlordism, which if not checked will do for these sections what it has done for Ireland."[72] To Kansans the threat of alien absentee landlordism was real enough—many of the more recent Irish immigrants previously had experienced tenantry, rackrenting, the firebrand in the night, and wanted no more of it.[73]

The hostility of agrarians to alien ownership continued unabated during the 1890s. A number of states, including Texas,[74] Missouri,[75] Idaho,[76] and Washington passed alien land laws, while others, such as Mississippi,[77] restricted the operations of foreign corporations. By the beginning of the twentieth century only 15 of the 45 states in the Union made no distinction between alien and domestic owners.[78] State legislation against aliens was prompted by the all-too-evident inadequacies of the federal law, which by 1890 lost even more of its limited effectiveness when North Dakota and South Dakota, Montana, Washington, Wyoming, and Idaho entered the Union.

Quite naturally British investors, especially the Scottish capitalists who were undoubtedly the most heavily involved, closely watched the buildup of pressure demanding restrictions on alien holdings in the United States. At the start of the decade William Mackenzie of the Dundee Mortgage and Trust Company appealed to the Foreign Office to negotiate a treaty with the United States granting recognition and protection to the foreign investor. Mackenzie charged that "Americans are extremely jealous of foreign corporations if they are doing a profitable business" and readily disposed to handicap them with restrictions and heavy taxes. Since state legislatures were particularly hostile and dangerous, Mackenzie favored an agreement which provided federal safeguards against state interference with British investments, and he went so far as to suggest an arrangement for dual citizenship. To strengthen his case, Mackenzie pointed out that Great Britain already had treaties with France, Germany, Italy, and Belgium that provided mutual protection for investors. Equally important, such a move would be consistent with the Gladstone government's efforts "to cultivate friendly relations with the United States, and to obliterate, as far as possible, all feelings of jealousy between the two nations."[79]

Nothing came of Mackenzie's initial request after Secretary of State Blaine rejected a Foreign Office overture on the grounds that such an agreement would violate the rights of individual states.[80] Five years later, in 1886, when the antialien campaign was cresting and some form of federal legislation appeared certain, Mackenzie renewed his efforts to secure treaty protection for British joint stock companies. For the next year and a half he badgered a rather indifferent Foreign Office in behalf of the British investor by urging, in letter after letter, that the government link the issue of immunity for British corporations to the existing negotiations for the renewal of the North Atlantic Fisheries Treaty. Why not, Mackenzie persisted, offer the United States favorable terms in regard to the fisheries in return for some guarantees for British companies doing business in America.[81]

In response to Mackenzie's correspondence, the Foreign Office sought advice from the British minister in Washington, Sir Lionel Sackville-West. Again the reply was negative, as Sackville-West contended that the Cleveland administration would be even less likely to countenance a proposal which clearly transgressed the issue of state's rights, especially when the recent actions of Congress had "been decidedly opposed to all alien enterprise and the employment of alien capital in this country."[82] This rebuff failed to deter Mackenzie and his allies, Samuel Smith and Edmund Robertson, both members of Parliament. Just after President Cleveland signed the Alien Land Law in March 1887, Robertson, who earlier had prompted the Foreign Office to investigate the status of aliens and alien corporations in the United States,[83] led a deputation of worried Scotch investors in an interview with Parliamentary Undersecretary of State Sir James Fergusson. They expressed their concern about the impact the new law might have on British companies and arranged with Fergusson to submit their demands in a formal memorial to the government.

In a matter of a few weeks the entire financial and business community of Dundee, claiming to represent interests that exceeded "the capital affected by the present Fisheries' question," petitioned Lord Salisbury for protection against the "caprice" of America's "multitudinous legislators" and its unpredictable courts of law. The Dundee memorial, which closely paralleled the arguments of William Mackenzie, outlined the precarious position of foreign capital in America and emphasized the necessity of a treaty with the United States similar to existing conventions with France, Germany, Italy, and Belgium that "secured the British corporations all the privileges and advantages of domestic corporations." The petitioners also strongly endorsed the strategy of incorporating the issue with the fisheries negotiations because they were convinced "that there is no time so favourable for getting something from the Americans as the time when they themselves are very anxious to get something."[84]

After rather thoughtful consideration of the Dundee proposal the Salisbury government declined to include the question in the Fishery Commission's agenda regretting "the inconvenience to which British corporations in the United States are occasionally subjected." Salisbury believed his government had no power to expand the scope of the fishery negotiations "without fresh negotiations and a fresh agreement."[85] Perhaps Sir Charles M. Kennedy, senior clerk in the Commercial Department, summed up the feelings of the Foreign Office when he caustically wrote in regard to the Dundee petition: "British subjects who invest in foreign countries must take the laws of these countries as they are, and not seek to dictate alterations in them."[86] The decision not to mix the question of security for British investors with the fishery discussions proved diplomatically sound, but even that did not salvage the treaty arrived at by Joseph Chamberlain and the American secretary of state, Thomas F. Bayard. It was rejected by the Republican-dominated Senate in August 1888 in a burst of preelection anti-British nationalism designed, in part at least, to oust the Cleveland administration.[87]

Mackenzie, who was in the American West on a business trip in late 1887, reluctantly but graciously accepted defeat. And, judging by the flurry of British investment at the end of the decade and in the early 1890s, he and a host of others learned to live with the legislation and found it did not inhibit their activities to any measurable degree. However, the continued activity of English and Scottish investors in the United States added fuel to the fire of anti-British feeling raging in the western states and temporarily reignited the nation's subsiding fears of alien landlordism. Americans daily confronted newspaper accounts of the renewed onslaught of the British investor. British capital increasingly entered semimanufacturing enterprises and the processing industries; and the magnitude and frequency of the invasion appeared to numerous critics to forecast the complete domination of the American economy by foreign capital. One observer wrote reformer Henry Demarst Lloyd that "your 'free' citizens are fast becoming the bond slaves of rich men in London. What would Washington have thought of this kind of independence."[88] Indeed, such alien control was defined by many as being "inimical to the interests of every class of Americans" as it would greatly enrich foreign countries at America's expense.[89]

In 1888 and 1889 two widely publicized acquisitions by English companies triggered a roar of protest among westerners. The sale of Chicago's Union Stockyards through Chauncey M. Depew to a London syndicate for $19 million alarmed farmers, cattlemen, and meat packers alike, and their outraged protests were heard immediately.[90] News of the formation in London of the Pillsbury-Washburn Mill Company, Ltd., dramatized how the British moved in to control one segment of a vital processing industry. A regional quasi monopoly was created that controlled three Pillsbury mills, two Washburn elevators, two water power companies; it dominated St. Anthony Falls and included great elevator capacity in Minnesota and North Dakota.[91]

Agrarians were becoming increasingly preoccupied with the economic power of monopolistic corporations and trusts, and the role of the British investor in those two gigantic sales confirmed their highly exaggerated suspicions that the actions signalled the first phase of England's modern plan of conquest.[92] British investment was seen as quickening the pace of the formation of trusts and monopolies, and opening a sustained drain on the nation's economy. British corporations, in the two-year period from 1888 to 1890, invested over $100 million; by 1890 the British investment in the United States of roughly $2 billion was approximately 25 percent of England's total overseas investment. Assuming no more than a modest five-and-one-half percent profit, the annual "tribute" to Great Britain amounted to $110 million.[93]

American cattlemen defined the alien land issue in terms of the depression that plagued the livestock industry in the late 1880s. The English in western cattle ranches were retroactively accused of having been one of the key factors in bringing on the depression. The federal government had been an unwitting accomplice by allowing the British companies to occupy the western plains without cost, which led to increasing the surplus or overproduction of cattle. These cattle were then dumped on the Chicago market, lowering the price and helping to ruin the American farmer and jeopardizing American capital. Cattlemen and their journalistic spokesmen, ignoring American participation in the earlier boom, charged that the greed of British investors for quick and huge profits had caused overproduction and depression in the cattle industry.[94]

The American livestock industry jumped on the antialien bandwagon later than most agrarian groups. They first passively accepted the entry of British capital into the cattle trade as beneficial, but with the depression and their increasing reliance on an export solution they ultimately agreed that Great Britain presented the major obstacle to recovery. Many western Americans were pleased that English investors also were suffering heavy losses in the depressed state of the market, for the nation would profit considerably by discouraging ranching "at arm's length and by proxy, with the profit going abroad."[95] When American cattlemen did join the antialien campaign to eliminate the English from the western lands they did so with a vengeance. They demanded that Congress restrict all alien landlordism, collect rents for herds grazing on public lands, declare forfeit all public lands illegally acquired, and compel ranches to pay taxes.[96] Their opposition was not a flash-in-the-pan response; members of the industry remained adamant in their demands for more stringent federal legislation into the 1890s.

The renewed burst of British capital investment in real estate, and more frequently in industry, led to demands for stricter federal legislation that would apply to the states as well as to the remaining territories. Among the supporters of the move to extend federal legislation to include the states was a broad spectrum of the American press.[97] They frequently levelled the charge that English capital represented "a standing menace to our liberties."[98] But, paradoxically, the same federal-state separation that vexed British investors like William Mackenzie also frustrated Americans demanding stronger federal legislation that would apply to the individual states.

The frustration was particularly evident in the congressional debates over a bill introduced by Congressman Oates of Alabama and an attempt by Far West representatives to amend the 1887 law to exempt mining operations in the territories. The Oates measure, which was an obvious response to the public clamor for stronger controls, would prohibit aliens from acquiring title to lands anywhere in the United States. Once again the advocates of nationwide restrictions on alien ownership felt constrained by the Constitution, and while Oates searched for a solution in the Judiciary Committee, other long-standing proponents of alien land legislation waged the floor fight against the mining exemption amendment. Representatives Payson of Illinois and Holman of Indiana deplored any move, no matter how small, to weaken the 1887 statute which, they made clear, would have applied to the territories and the several states from its inception, had they not been stymied by the constitutional limitation. Payson, particularly outspoken in his opposition to the amendment, emotionally declared to the House that "not an acre of real estate, not a dollar's worth of real property under the flag that floats over you and me should be under the ownership of a foreigner . . . I mean," he concluded, "America for Americans."[99]

Payson's patriotic outburst succeeded in having the amendment tabled by a 50-27 vote.[100] The drive to exempt mineral lands, which ultimately triumphed in 1897, exposed the ambivalence of certain western groups who generally favored restrictions on alien ownership but who also recognized that outside capital was essential for the economic development of their territories. However, the supporters of a more inclusive alien land law suffered a general defeat when the Oates bill, after receiving a favorable report from the House Committee on the Judiciary, languished and died on the floor of the House.[101] By 1890 Congress was preoccupied with silver and the tariff; those issues unquestionably had superseded the alien land question in the United States.

However, an active and organized campaign against alien ownership continued during the 1890s under the aegis of the agrarian groups that eventually formed the Populist party. Their broad goal was to eliminate British capital and influence from American economic life; they defined the English land system as a "monster" that had "seized upon the fresh energy of America and is steadily fixing its fangs into our social life."[102] The Southern Alliance, which originated in Texas and then spread to Arkansas, Louisiana, Alabama, and North Carolina, stated its demands jointly with the Knights of Labor in 1889. This labor-farmer coalition asked Congress to pass "laws prohibiting the alien ownership of land," and urged the legislators to take "early steps to devise some plan to obtain all lands now owned by aliens and foreign syndicates."[103] The Northern Alliance also advocated legislation restricting alien ownership, and with the formation of the People's party in 1892 the issue was dealt with in a plank in the Populist national platform.[104]

The agrarians who agitated for alien land legislation throughout the 1880s and 1890s held to the thesis expressed so eloquently in 1893 by the historian Frederick Jackson Turner. They acted upon an acceptance of the frontier thesis by demanding that foreigners be eliminated from the public domain and the frontier be opened to the actual settler. Their petitions to Congress revealed their anxiety about restricted economic opportunity and social unrest in the cities. What they feared most was the closed frontier; what they deemed essential was free or cheap land as the safety valve that guaranteed social stability and economic opportunity.

Anglophobia in the United States reached its zenith with the Populist movement. The alien land issue became fused as one alloy in the Populists' multi-issue campaign against Great Britain. The British were identified in the farmer's mind with subjugation of other peoples, with aristocratic institutions, and with financial and economic power. All of those themes were present in the issue of alien landlordism. The compounded evil of alien ownership was that the rent went to a foreign country and thus contracted domestic monetary circulation.[105] This tribute to the foreign investor added to the nation's balance of payments deficit which in turn sustained the country's financial bondage to England.

Populism was a revolt against a progressively more oppressive financial imperialism centered in the East and directly linked to England. Silver became the all-encompassing issue for the agrarians in the 1890s because in their mind gold monometallism represented and symbolized American financial servitude to Great Britain. Western discontent was directed against the forces that were identified as suppressing the farmer in his struggle for economic equity. In that view, the shackles that America had most to fear were those of "interest, earnings, rents, and profits."[106] Alien ownership as an issue remained, but it was increasingly overshadowed by the silver question, which became the Populist panacea to end America's dependence upon Great Britain.

NOTES

1. J. Fred Rippy, "British Investments in Texas Lands and Livestock," *The Southwestern Historical Quarterly* LVIII (January 1955), p. 332. Oscar O. Winther, "The English and the Far West," *The Westerners Brand Book* 11:8, pp. 57–59. Roger V. Clements, "The Farmers Attitude Toward British Investment in American Industry," *Journal of Economic History* Vol. 15 (March 1955), pp. 151–59. See also Clark C. Spence, *British Investments and the American Mining Frontier, 1860 – 1901 (Ithaca: Cornell University Press, 1958)*.

2. Alfred Tischendorf, "North Carolina and the British Investor, 1880–1910,"

North Carolina Historical Review XXXII (October 1955), p. 512. London *Times,*
August 15, 1883, p. 3. Letter to editor from Phillips, Marshal, & Co. stated they
had 1.3 million acres in the United States. It was spread throughout 18 counties
with 800,000 acres in the "great cotton belt" and the rest in the long-leaf yellow
pine region of Mississippi. Also E. J. Reed, in a letter to the editor in the *Times,*
August 17, 1883, commented that his syndicate, the Florida Land and Mortgage
Co., Ltd., composed of British, Dutch, and American speculators, owned 2.3 million
acres in Florida.

3. Roger V. Clements, "British Investment and American Legislative Restrictions in the Trans-Mississippi West, 1880–1900," *Mississippi Valley Historical
Review* XLII, (September 1955), p. 207. Clements lends to disparage and
deemphasize agrarian reaction to alien ownership as simply a "hunt for devils," I
believe he underestimates the nature and intensity of their hostility and resentment,
which went far beyond a mere search for a scapegoat.

4. Henry George, *Progress and Poverty* (New York: Robert Schalkenbach Foundation, 1948), p. 390.

5. A. J. Desmond, "America's Land Question," *The North American Review*
CXLII (February 1886), p. 154, *The National Economist,* August 31, 1889.

6. Mass petitions to the House Committee on Public Lands, 49th Cong., records
of the United States House of Representatives, National Archives, Record Group
233.

7. *Report of the Secretary of the Interior,* 1887 (Washington: Government Printing Office, 1887), p. 3.

8. The analysis of the problem expressed by the New Hampshire legislature was
virtually identical to scores of other appeals that flooded Congress in 1885: "Whereas, more than twenty million acres of the Lands of the United States are now held
by non-resident aliens and in great measure by the titled and governing class of
Great Britain; . . . and,

Whereas, this non-resident ownership of Lands in the United States may eventually lead to a system of alien landlordism, of which the unhappy condition of Ireland
is a lamentable example . . . ." Contained in the file of the Senate Committee
on Public Lands, 49th Cong., records of the United States Senate, NA,RG 46.

9. William Turrentine Jackson, "British Interests in the Range Cattle Industry
1878–1951," *When Grass Was King* (Boulder: University of Colorado Press, 1956),
pp. 138–39.

10. W. Baille Grohman, "Cattle Ranches in the Far West," *Fortnightly Review*
Vol. 34 (1880), p. 441.

11. Ibid.

12. Jackson, "British Interests" p. 160.

13. Ibid., p. 193. The British order stipulated that American cattle had to be
slaughtered at port of entry within ten days. The presence of pleuropneumonia in
the eastern United States prompted the British action. This restriction offers another
possible explanation for the rapid growth in shipments of dressed beef.

14. Ibid., p. 223.

15. Remarks of Moreton Frewen in "Free Grazing, A Report to the Shareholders
of The Powder River Cattle Co., Ltd." (London, 1883), p. 4.

16. Remarks of June 3, 1884, *Congressional Record,* XV, Part 5, 4778 (hereafter
cited as *CR,* 15:5:4778).

17. Harold H. Dunham, *Government Handout: A Study in the Administration of the Public Lands 1875 — 1891* (Ann Arbor: Edwards Brothers, Inc., 1941), p. 297.

18. *John Clay, My Life on the Range* (New York: Antiquarian Press, Ltd., 1961), pp. 128—29.

19. Dunham, *Government Handout,* p. 296. *Western Rural,* January 16, 1886.

20. Record of the Proceedings of the Fourth Regular Session of the General Assembly, held at Pittsburgh, September 7—11, 1880.

21. Terence V. Powderly, *Thirty Years of Labor, 1859 to 1889* (Columbus: Excelsior Publishing House, 1889), p. 341.

22. Ibid., p. 342.

23. Wallace Evan Davis, *Patriotism on Parade* (Cambridge: Harvard University Press, 1955), p. 148.

24. Ibid., p. 162

25. Remarks of March 17, 1884 *CR,* 15:2:1960.

26. *Report on Unauthorized Fencing of Public Lands,* Senate Exec. Doc. 127, 48th Cong., 1st Sess., 1883—1884 (Washington: Government Printing Office, 1884), p.2.

27. Ibid.

28. *Official Proceedings of the Republican National Conventions, 1884 — 1888* (Minneapolis: Charles W. Johnson, Publisher, 1903), p. 194.

29. Jackson, "British Interests" p. 191.

30. *Democratic Campaign Book, 1884* (New York: National Democratic Committee, 1884), pp. 3—4.

31. *Republican Campaign Text Book,* p. 171.

32. Lester F. Sheffy, *The Life and Times of Timothy Dwight Hobart* (Canyon, Texas: The Panhandle-Plains Historical Society, 1950), p. 76.

33. Jackson, "British Interests," p. 228.

34. James D. Richardson, *Messages and Papers of the Presidents, 1789 — 1897* (Washington: Government Printing Office, 1898), Vol. VIII, p. 309.

35. Louis Pelzer, *The Cattleman's Frontier* (Glendale, California: Arthur H. Clark Co., 1936), p. 184.

36. *Report on Land Titles to Aliens in the United States.*

37. Ibid.

38. Ibid.

39. *Western Rural,* March 22, 1884, January 16, 1886. *New York Sun,* May 22, 1886.

40. *Western Rural,* January 30, 1886. See also Henry Cohen, "Vicissitudes of an Absentee Landlord: A Case Study," in David M. Ellis, ed., *The Frontier in American Development* (Ithaca: Cornell University Press, 1969), pp. 192—216.

41. *Appleton's Annual Cyclopoedia, 1887,* New Series, Vol. XII (New York: D. Appleton & Co., 1891), pp. 659—60.

42. *Report on Land Titles to Aliens in the United States,* p. 1.

43. *Tenth Census of the United States,* Report on the Productions of Agriculture, Vol. III (Washington: Government Printing Office, 1883), p. XIII.

44. Ibid.

45. *Eleventh Census of the United States,* Report on Farms and Homes, (Washington: Government Printing Office, 1896), p. 25.

46. Homer E. Socolofsky, "The Scully Land System in Marion County," *Kansas Historical Quarterly* XVIII (November 1950), p. 338.

47. Paul W. Gates, "Frontier Landlords and Pioneer Tenants," *Journal of the Illinois State Historical Society* 38, (June 1945), p. 177.

48. Ibid., p. 185.

49. Ibid.

50. Ibid., p. 192.

51. Ibid., p. 196.

52. *New York Times,* January 22, 1885, p. 4.

53. Ibid.

54. *Report on Land Titles to Aliens in the United States,* p. 4.

55. Ibid.

56. Gates, "Frontier Landlords," p. 201.

57. Dunham, *Government Handout,* p. 177.

58. See the mass petitions to the Senate and House Committees on Public Lands and the Senate Committee on Finance, 49th Cong., records of the United States House of Representatives, and of the United States Senate, National Archives, Record Groups 233 and 46.

59. Record of the Proceedings of the General Assembly of the Knights of Labor of America, Richmond, Virginia, October 4—20, 1886.

60. See petitions and memorials to Senate and House Committees on Public Lands and the Senate Committee on Finance, 49th Cong., records of the House of Representatives and the Senate, *NA,* RG 233, 46. The Knights of Labor claimed to have 500,000 signatures to present to the House of Representatives; see Ibid., Ralph Beaumont and John J. McCartney to Hon. John G. Carlisle, June 25, 1886, Report of the Legislative Committee.

61. Gates, "Frontier Landlords," p. 196.

62. *CR,* 17:7:7834.

63. Ibid., 18:3:2755.

64. *United States Statutes at Large,* 49th Cong., Vol. 24 (Washington: Government Printing Office, 1887) p. 476.

65. Another difficulty appeared with the provision of the law applying to the District of Columbia. In 1888 a bill exempting legations and residences of representatives of foreign governments passed both Houses of Congress. See *CR,* 19:2:1519.

66. Jackson, "British Interests," p. 255, Herman C. Nixon, "The Populist Movement in Iowa," *Iowa Journal of History and Politics* 24 (January 1926), p. 38.

67. Addison E. Sheldon, *Land Systems and Land Policies in Nebraska,* Publications of the Nebraska State Historical Society, Vol. XXII (Lincoln: Nebraska Historical Society, 1936), p. 324.

68. Ibid.

69. *Laws of Wisconsin,* 1887, Vol. I (Madison: Democrat Printing Co., 1887), p. 536.

70. Gates, "Frontier Landlords," p. 201.

71. Kansas Legislature, House Journal, 1889 (Topeka: Kansas Publishing House, 1889), p. 382.

72. Ibid.

73. James C. Malin, *Confounded Rot About Napoleon, Reflections Upon Science and Technology, Nationalism, World Depression of the Eighteen Nineties, and Afterwards* (Lawrence, Kansas: Author, 1961), passim.

74. Texas passed an Alien Land Law in 1891; it was declared unconstitutional and the following year a modified version was again passed by the legislature. Robert C. Cotner, ed., *Addresses and State Papers of James Stephen Hogg* (Austin: University of Texas Press, 1951), pp. 180, 549.

75. Gates, "Frontier Landlords," p. 201.

76. Ibid.

77. *The Official and Statistical Register of the State of Mississippi* (Nashville, Tennessee: Brandon Printing Co., 1908), p. 1235.

78. London *Times,* October 3, 1901, p. 5. For a detailed state by state analysis, see Parliamentary Papers, House of Commons, *Report on the Purchase and Holdings of Lands by Aliens, 1901* Misc. Series No. 567. Vol. 103.

79. William Mackenzie to Lord Granville, January 7, 1881, Foreign Office 5, Vol. 1763, Public Record Office, London, (hereinafter cited as F.O. 5/1763 P.R.O.).

80. Foreign Office to Mackenzie, July 11, 1881, F.O. 5/1763 P.R.O., Granville to Thornton, July 14, 1881, F.O. 115/676 P.R.O.

81. Mackenzie to Rosbery, June 17, July 20, 1886, F.O. 5/1953 P.R.O.

82. Sackville-West to Foreign Office, July 3, 1886, in Foreign Office memo, May 20, 1887, F.O. 5/2002 P.R.O.

83. Robertson to Foreign Office, August 7, 1886, F.O. 5/1953, Report on the Status of Aliens and Foreign Companies in the United States, 1888, F.O. 5/2043 P.R.O.

84. Memorial to the Most Noble The Marquis of Salisbury, K.G., on behalf of the Town and Trade of Dundee, in Respect of British Corporations Doing Business in the United States of America, March 28, 1887, F.O. 5/2002 P.R.O.

85. Fergusson to Mackenzie, June 30, 1887, F.O. 5/2002, Salisbury minute on Mackenzie to Fergusson, October 18, 1887, F.O. 5/2003 P.R.O.

86. Note by Kennedy on Dundee memorial, March 30, 1887, F.O. 5/2002 P.R.O.

87. For a thorough discussion of the Fisheries Treaty and its rejection by the Senate see Charles C. Tansill, *The Foreign Policy of Thomas F. Bayard* (New York: Fordham University Press, 1940), pp. 298–323.

88. W. Clark to H.D. Lloyd, June 28, 1890, Henry D. Lloyd Papers, Wisconsin State Historical Society.

89. *National Stockman and Farmer,* June 26, 1890. *Public Opinion,* Vol. 8, 1889–90, p. 46.

90. Jackson, "British Interests" p. 253.

91. *London Times* October 30, 1889, p. 5.

92. *National Economist,* August 17, 1889. *Bedford's Magazine,* February, 1890.

93. Bruce M. Russett, *Community and Contention* (Cambridge, Mass.: The M.I.T. Press, 1963), p. 229.

94. *Breeder's Gazette,* January 30, 1889, August 6, 1889.

95. *National Stockman and Farmer,* December 20, 1888.

96. Ibid., June 26, 1890.

97. See the editorial comments from newspapers throughout the nation in *Public Opinion,* Vols. 8–9, 1889–1890.

98. Ibid., Vol. 8, p. 46.

99. Remarks of August 20, 1890, *CR*, 21:9:8879.

100. Ibid.

101. *CR*, 21:6:5879.

102. *National Economist*, June 29, 1889.

103. John D. Hicks, *The Populist Revolt* (Lincoln: University of Nebraska Press, 1961), p. 428.

104. The Populist plank demanded that "all land now held by railroads and other corporations in excess of their actual needs and all lands now owned by aliens, should be reclaimed by the government and held for actual settlers only." The People's party maintained this demand against alien ownership in its platform until the 1908 campaign. See Kirk H. Porter and Donald B. Johnson, eds., *National Party Platforms 1840 – 1964* (Urbana: University of Illinois Press, 1966).

105. See the comments of ex-Congressman John Davis in *The Land Question from Various Points of View* (Philadelphia: C. F. Taylor, 1898).

106. *National Economist*, July 6, 1889.

6

The Struggle for Latin America

It is simply a question whether the United States shall curtail its production or seek new markets for its products. There is no field in the world so inviting as that to be found in Central and South America.

Report From the Central
and South American
Commissioners, 1885

That we are to be a competitor with Great Britain in foreign markets, especially in the markets of the South American States, is as certain as anything in the future can be.

Hugh McCullough, 1884

We can beat the English in various lines of manufacture, even in the markets of Great Britain and why is it we can't largely increase our exports of products of manufacture so as to give vent as will at once relieve our glutted markets, and our stagnant industries?

Hugh McCullough, 1885

When [the United States] pushes its enormous natural products into every country, underselling the local market, and is increasing its exports of manufactured goods until they are found in all parts of the earth, competing with the long established factories of Europe, it cannot expect to hold aloof from the rest of the world, and cannot consider itself isolated, either politically or commercially.

Frederick Frelinghuysen, 1884

American foreign policy in the 1880s reflected the country's expanding power and its awakening national consciousness. In the minds of the economic expansionists, the slogan "America for Americans" applied to and encompassed the entire hemisphere.[1] A new aggressiveness marked American diplomacy as the nation, acting on this belief, directly challenged Britain's commercial and economic supremacy in the Western Hemisphere. The ensuing confrontation with British power and influence evoked a mixed emotional response among Americans that in some ways resembled a love-hate, or more accurately hate-love, relationship: jealousy and distrust for the national rival were intermingled with a grudging admiration that inspired a desire to emulate the obvious and phenomenal success of England. Thus, Anglophobia—with all its ambivalent features— not only emerged as a corollary to America's dynamic economic nationalism, it also went hand-in-hand with the nation's heightened sense of power and influence.

President Chester A. Arthur's sudden withdrawal of the invitations to the Latin American countries to attend the Pan-American conference—at the insistence of his new secretary of state, Frederick Frelinghuysen, in 1882—appeared to doom the vigorous diplomacy of James G. Blaine. The change was more apparent than real. What seemed to be a drastic overhaul of foreign policy proved instead to be a change in means. Despite the intense party factionalism and acrimonious political debate that characterized the period, the ideology of economic expansion pervaded intraparty feuds and crossed party lines. The bipartisan support for that commercial strategy, which had developed earlier as a response to the depression of the 1870s, remained undisturbed. Frelinghuysen, who was not opposed to the goals of a Pan-American conference per se,[2] modified the tactics of American economic expansion without altering the basic nature of the challenge to British dominance in the markets of Central America and South America.

The Arthur administration clearly and unhesitantly revealed its intention to sustain the American push into the world arena. In his 1881 message to Congress, the president strongly supported government programs to rebuild the merchant marine and to create an enlarged and powerful navy.[3] The concern for a major navy reflected a crucial change in the definition of national security from the continental limits of the United States to an analysis of security now dependent upon the maintenance of American commercial empire and the protection of American citizens and property overseas.[4] A navy was deemed essential to enforce American foreign policy and to protect and stimulate trade. The theme of government support for overseas economic expansion, which had been steadily pushed in the previous administrations of Hayes and Garfield, guided Frelinghuysen's strategy throughout his tenure at the State Department. Both he and President Arthur defined the Western Hemisphere, and Japan and China as well, as the most promising areas into which to extend American influence and power.

Hayes and Evarts had adopted the ideology of overseas economic expansion as a response to the depression of the 1870s, and government encouragement to trade and business abroad became a crucial segment of their policy. Another turn of the business cycle in 1882 increased the sense of urgency and necessity connected with expanding foreign markets. The depression of 1882−1885 came within five years after the prolonged and severe crisis of 1873−1879, and the timing intensified its impact upon the thinking and policies of American leaders. President Arthur, Secretary Frelinghuysen, and numerous congressional and administration leaders reinforced this pattern of response by diagnosing the crisis in the same way that Hayes and Evarts had analyzed the depression of the 1870s. Overseas economic expansion was recommended as the remedy for the country's business distress and as a means to preserve the existing system. Once again an economic downturn shaped American diplomacy.[5]

Although Arthur and Frelinghuysen accepted the ideology of economic expansion, they were less sanguine than Evarts about the continued importance of agricultural exports. Frelinghuysen did not abandon the farmer, but he believed that a transition in the nature of American commerce was evident. Agricultural exports could no longer be expected to shoulder the burden of the nation's foreign trade; the dominance of American farm products, particularly wheat, was threatened by the rising competition of India and Russia.[6] By the mid-1880s, for example, American journals constantly discussed the Indian challenge to American wheat exports, and India became a veritable bugbear to such spokesmen. Frelinghuysen's awareness of the shift caused him to stress the need to acquire foreign markets for manufactures, although he did labor to get American meat products readmitted to European markets.[7] The increased emphasis on markets for manufactures aroused many westerners, and one farm journal typically complained that Frelinghuysen was too "respectable" and "conservative" in his diplomacy. A "strong diplomacy" was needed to protect the "vast interests" of the American farmer.[8]

Despite agrarian dissatisfaction, the administration did develop a positive program to expand markets for the nation's agricultural surplus. Frelinghuysen rejected the tactic of economic retaliation against the offending European nations, and that clearly irritated many in the agricultural sector. He preferred to use the tariff as a more subtle weapon: bilateral reciprocity treaties with the Latin American countries became the crucial aspect of his foreign policy. The Arthur administration also pursued trade expansion through the appointment of a commercial commission to Central and South America, participated in an international conference on the Congo, devoted its attention to securing unilateral control of an isthmian canal, opened treaty relations with Korea, and began negotiations for a naval base at Pearl Harbor.

Frelinghuysen was virtually obsessed with the need to further hemispheric trade, talking "by the hour about all this" in 1882–1883 to his colleagues in the State Department.[9] He reasoned that the native buyer needed three facilities: those to order goods promptly, those to obtain the goods cheaply and promptly, and the ability to pay for the products at a reasonable and steady rate of exchange. His answers to these needs included direct and speedy postal service, direct lines of communications (including subsidies for the streamship service), and a "stability of government, a sound system of banking, so correlated between the several states of the American hemisphere as to constitute in some degree a financial solidarity."[10] Frelinghuysen believed the last requirement to be most important, and he envisioned a parent intercontinental bank in New York with associated banks in the various South American countries. Capital for each branch bank would be supplied by American stockholders with "the majority of the stock of each to be held by a holding company in the United States, whereby the whole system could be harmoniously controlled."[11] The capital of each bank might be determined by the volume of trade of each country.

American leaders recognized that Great Britain was the main obstacle in expanding trade to Central and South America. Their concern was intensified by another potential threat. England's leaders were uneasy about Britain's dependence on American food-stuffs. In an effort to replace the United States as the chief source of food and fiber, they were busy attempting to develop India, Egypt, and Australia as alternate sources of such raw materials. The threat at one level made a solution of the other problem even more urgent. Confronted with the British effort to overcome their reliance on American wheat and meat products, the Arthur administration stressed increased exports of manufactured products to Latin America to take up the anticipated slack in the nation's trade. Their program was designed to continue the Blaine policy of making the Monroe Doctrine a reality by extending the nation's economic—and hence political—control in the Western Hemisphere.

Amid this concern for the establishment of American dominance in the Western Hemisphere, some Americans made an explicit analogy to the English commercial model as they confidently predicted that Latin America was to be to the United States what India was to Britain.[12] "These countries represent twenty American Indias," argued one typical enthusiast, "whose unsupplied and inviting trade fields we will find most profitable to occupy with our surplus energy, skill, products, and manufactures."[13] This "India to the South" would open sufficient new markets to "keep every loom, and every anvil, and every manufactory of this country in motion."[14] Several congressmen saw a complete, first-class navy as crucial to America's commercial success in these "Indias," and Senator George Vest of Missouri dogmatically announced that "commercial supremacy and naval power are inseparable."[15] Another plan designed to convert Latin America into the nation's India was the Three Americas Railway scheme proposed by Hinton Helper.[16]

One member of the administration, Secretary of the Treasury

Hugh McCullough, who had seen exports as the key to American welfare as early as the late 1860s, was perplexed by the nation's inability to displace England quickly. He was in a hurry to grasp the markets of South America. "We can beat the English in various lines of manufactures even in the markets of Great Britain and why is it," he impatiently lamented to Joseph Nimmo, "we can't largely increase our exports of products of manufactures so as to give vent as will at once relieve our glutted markets, and our stagnant industries?"[17] Nimmo explained the apparent paradox by pointing out that the two crucial factors were wages of labor and wages of capital (or rates of interest). Labor was cheaper in Great Britain, as was capital, "the latter being in great measure the result of almost perfection in the finance of British commerce," and Nimmo admitted "generally they beat us in foreign markets."[18] The British had "strong weaknesses" however, and Nimmo expected the United States to succeed through its inventive and innovative spirit. The nation would be able to meet foreign competition in the markets of the world as "our list of exports of products of manufacture is somewhat more than a suggestion of the whole story."[19]

Frelinghuysen and Arthur, who were nearly as anxious as McCullough to accelerate the extension of the American commercial empire while simultaneously displacing Great Britain in the Western Hemisphere, relied principally on a comprehensive program of reciprocity treaties with Latin American nations. As explained by Secretary Frelinghuysen, such treaties were to be a weapon of national economic expansion. And he campaigned long and hard trying to educate legislators about the efficacy of that strategy. He worked closely with Senator John F. Miller of California, who as chairman of the Foreign Relations Committee was the crucial link between the Senate and the Executive. Miller was a strong economic expansionist who favored reciprocity and ardently pushed for an isthmian canal.[20]

Frelinghuysen outlined the strategy in a long letter to Miller that was in every sense a position paper on the grand conception of the American empire. The "true plan" was to make a series of reciprocity treaties with the Latin American states, "taking care that those manufactures and as far as is practicable those products which would come into competition with our own manufactures and products should not be admitted to the free list."[21] The reduction of duties had to be confined to nations that were willing to negotiate treaties, but in this way the American government would "cheapen these products for our own people and at the same time gain the control of those markets for the products of our fields and factories."[22]

Frelinghuysen also recommended a silver monetary union between the United States and the South American and Central American nations. The United States was a large producer of silver, and any market would be of direct advantage to the nation. The other nations of the hemisphere were also silver producers, however, and hence it would be mutually advantageous "to agree upon a common silver coin" and thereby "value would be given to our silver products, and commerce with these countries would be aided."[23] Frelinghuysen realized that such a plan would meet stiff opposition from the national rival, for "Great Britain on the other hand strives to disparage and exclude silver as means of exchange for its use in this way depreciates her wealth and works to her disadvantage."[24]

President Arthur, in his annual message to Congress in December 1884, neatly summarized his administration's program for opening markets in Latin America. Top priority was given to negotiating reciprocity treaties with the countries of America. The diplomatic and consular service required more support, and the consular service needed to be placed on a salaried footing, to provide the efficient and careful study of the markets that was needed to aid American businessmen. His third suggestion was to enact legislation "to favor the construction and maintenance of a steam carrying marine under the flag of the United States."[25] Finally, the president proposed the creation of a uniform currency basis for the American countries through a monetary union.[26] He also stressed that the policies need not be confined to the countries of the Western Hemisphere, but could be employed for "the healthful enlargement of our trade with Europe, Asia, and Africa."[27]

However much Arthur may have desired to implement these various proposals, the rhetoric of his administration far exceeded its actual, concrete achievements. And in reality reciprocity became virtually the only tactic to be employed, and then with little success. Secretary of State Frelinghuysen ultimately negotiated treaties with Mexico, Cuba, Puerto Rico, Santo Domingo, El Salvador, and Colombia. Discussions with the English government for a reciprocity agreement for the British West Indies also were inaugurated. None of the efforts succeeded. Negotiations for the West Indies treaty collapsed when the Gladstone ministry balked at the American definition of the most-favored-nation clause in existing treaties. The Arthur administration insisted upon the traditional American interpretation of conditional most-favored-nation clauses that prevented Britain or other European nations from claiming an equal share of the benefits of a reciprocity treaty. For example, if a country with which the United States had a reciprocity agreement (such as Mexico) extended the same advantages to Great Britain via a most-favored-nation clause, the United States could automatically suspend the treaty. This prevented any British effort to gain advantages for its exports to Latin American countries at the expense of the American tariff system.

The other treaties did not win congressional approval, were withdrawn by President Cleveland after March 1885, or fell victim to the lassitude and partisanship implicit in the change of administrations.[28] Frelinghuysen did have one secondary success. Negotiations for the renewal of the Hawaiian Reciprocity Treaty began during his tenure, and in 1887 the new version of the treaty included an amendment ceding the use of Pearl Harbor as a naval base.[29]

When the lame-duck Arthur administration in 1884 presented the Senate with the treaty calling for reciprocity with Cuba and Puerto Rico, a storm of controversy erupted. Reactions were mixed, sometimes contradictory, and heavily influenced by the short-run calculations of various special interests; the episode provides some insight into why, even when widespread support for overseas economic expansion may have existed, specific proposals were defeated. The issue split the New York mercantile community, for example, with the heaviest fire coming from New York sugar refiners (and their allies) and the Louisiana sugar growers. Cigarmakers and their unions opposed the Cuban treaty and tobacco manufacturers split on the issue, for some feared the 50 percent reduction of the duty on manufactured tobacco would deal a death-blow to their business. Others, especially cigar-manufacturing firms, anticipated a tremendous boom in business. The San Francisco Board of Trade opposed the treaty on the ground that it would not substantially boost exports, particularly manufactured goods. The Philadelphia Board of Trade doubted the constitutionality of the treaty and viewed it as a ploy to delay serious revision of the tariff. The Philadelphia merchants had little faith in reciprocity treaties and preferred "one set of revenue laws which should apply to all nations in their dealings with the United States." The St. Louis Merchants' Exchange reluctantly urged rejection of the Spanish treaty claiming "that the advantages to be gained by its adoption are not by any means commensurate with the concessions it is proposed to make."[30]

But it was the reaction of the New York City organized business community that revealed the entire controversy in microcosm. The city's Chamber of Commerce petitioned Congress in favor of the treaty claiming it would secure for the United States "the substantial control of the markets of the Spanish Colonies for our coal, flour, rice, corn, lard, cotton goods, lumber, petroleum, hardware, furniture, and the many other articles which we manufacture."[31] The Chamber expected increased American imports of Cuban sugar to "add to the capacity of the inhabitants of these Colonies to take and pay for our commodities," and at the same time to eliminate "the commission of the London banker" by decreasing American imports of sugar "from Europe and from the East."[32] Then, to allay the fears of Americans who suspected the policy of reciprocity would lead to overseas territorial expansion, the Chamber of Commerce noted that "our tradition and the policy of our institutions are alike opposed to Colonies. Yet trade with the outer world is as important to us as it ever was in England, or as it is to Germany at this moment. Our sole resource is, through treaties of this character, to open new markets to our people."[33]

But the petition unmistakably demonstrated the division within the New York mercantile community by including two minority reports opposing the treaty. The critics doubted the veracity of the claims made by the advocates and generally felt that American concessions, which were particularly devastating to sugar refiners and the tobacco industry, outweighed any advantages to be gained. The authors of the minority reports suggested other alternatives for developing trade with Latin America, such as providing more efficient communication with the nations of the hemisphere.[34] Then, early in 1885, a petition from 600 New York merchants opposed the treaty. That group denied that the Chamber of Commerce truly represented the feeling of city businessmen, and urged rejection on the basis that the overall results of the treaty would not be beneficial for American economic interests.[35] The varied opinions of the New York business community fairly revealed the national division, and illustrated the judgment that any reciprocity treaty could be rejected on the ground that it was unfair to the United States.[36] While the debate revealed little criticism of the ultimate goal of expanded hemispheric trade, wide disagreement arose as to the means to that end.

Administration spokesmen stressed a more long-range view of the advantages of the treaty. They contended it offered the first step in the creation of a Caribbean reciprocity system that the United States would dominate as part of extending commercial hegemony over the hemisphere. Representatives of American industry supported this analysis and favored the treaty: it would be "the entering wedge for the United States in obtaining her share of the thousand millions of imports into the West Indies and South American countries every year."[37] Maritime interest also supported the treaty, seeing the provision granting American vessels equal status with Spanish ships as a tremendous boon to the merchant marine. A memorial to Congress from the shipbuilding center of Bath, Maine, for example, enthusiastically approved the treaty and suggested "it could be much improved if it could be amended so that the Philippine Islands might be included in its scope."[38]

Spokesmen for the American farmer also favored the treaty and the idea of reciprocity. A resolution of the New York Produce Exchange recommended approval of the treaty and urged that free flour be included in its provisions. Merchants of St. Paul spoke for the farmer when they supported ratification because it "shall open these important markets, to the products of our country, on fair and equitable terms." Another advocate of American agriculture, Representative Frank H. Hurd of Ohio, flatly asserted that "there is absolutely no relief to the American farmer except in the making of foreign markets for him." One way to extend foreign markets, was "with wise reciprocity treaties negotiated between this country and other nations" which, Hurd argued, would "open the markets of 150,000,000 people to the grain of the farmers of this country."[39]

Secretary Frelinghuysen and his top negotiator, John Foster, understood that reciprocity was more than a means of promoting commercial expansion. They knew it also offered a way to gain an economic and political foothold in the Latin American countries. Some opponents missed the point when they charged that the Cuban treaty was the first step toward annexation. As Frelinghuysen explained, annexation "would be unwise . . . for even could it be accomplished by general consent our institutions would be endangered by the beginning of a colonial system or by an incorporation into our body politic of a large population not in entire sympathy with our government's aims and methods."[40] Reciprocity was preferable because it removed "the causes of complaint as to the treatment of our citizens and their property in Cuba and Porto Rico [sic]," and because it would bring the islands into a close commercial connection with the United States that "confers upon us and upon them all benefits which would result from annexation were that possible."[41]

Foster, a career diplomat who negotiated the treaty with Spain, shared Frelinghuysen's optimistic appraisal of the results of reciprocity. He wrote his friend Walter Q. Gresham that he was "quite confident it will result in giving us the almost complete commercial monopoly of the commerce of Cuba . . . . It will be annexing Cuba in the most desirable way."[42] Or, as an American sugar planter in Cuba wrote Senator George F. Edmunds of Vermont, the treaty "will give every practical advantage of 'Annexation' without the inconveniences of governing."[43]

When he assumed office in 1885, President Cleveland withdrew the Spanish treaty for reexamination in the belief that the reciprocity tactic kept protection with all its evils intact and thus delayed general tariff reform. He explained in December that further study had convinced him "of the inexpediency of entering into engagements of this character not covering the entire traffic."[44] Reciprocity treaties surrendered "large revenues for inadequate consideration," and additionally failed to amply aid the consumer since they only partially covered total importation of a product such as sugar. He was also troubled because, in his view, the treaties violated the most-favored-nation principle. On this point Cleveland sided with the British by accepting their analysis of the most-favored-nation clause and rejecting the Arthur administration's argument of conditional clauses. Finally, the president argued, the treaty would create a large drain on the treasury by circumventing the traditional practice whereby the government enjoyed independent control of the revenue.[45]

The Senate debate over the treaty concerning Cuba and Puerto Rico was closely watched by English diplomats serving in the Caribbean and Central America. Their consul general in Havana informed the Foreign Office that the treaty was very popular in Cuba, and—not incidentally—that it would extend American influence over the island economy.[46] British West Indian sugar interests, alarmed at the prospect of being shut out of the American market, implored the home government to seek a comparable treaty with the United States. Frelinghuysen offered negotiations and the British representative in the United States, Sir Lionel Sackville-West, advised his government to accept the American offer. Otherwise "the British colonies will indeed be left out in the cold."[47] Foreign Minister Granville, having failed to get an American concession on most-favored-nation status for the British West Indies through the Spanish treaty, agreed to negotiations for the reciprocity treaty.

Minister Sackville-West and Neville Lubbock, a representative of the West Indian planters, met with the key American bureaucrat, Alvey Adee, in Washington in an attempt to reach an agreement. The British offered, in turn for free entry of sugar into the United States market, a duty-free list that extended basically to agricultural products. Adee gladly accepted the British concessions on agricultural goods and countered with a list that authorized duty-free status to coal, wood products, lumber, machinery of all kinds, and certain textile fabrics. As part of the American proposal the Arthur administration insisted upon a conditional most-favored-nation clause that disallowed the transfer of benefits of the treaty without an equivalent concession from the third nation. There were also several quasi-mercantilistic articles that reserved the United States—British West Indies trade exclusively to American vessels and those of Great Britain. Despite these objectionable features, which were an obvious extension of economic nationalism to the foreign sphere, Minister Sackville-West and Lubbock urged Lord Granville to accept the American revision.

The Foreign Office gave serious consideration to the American offer soliciting opinions and observations from its own staff, the Colonial Office, and the Board of Trade. Granville received conflicting advice from the other departments as Lord Derby, the colonial secretary, echoed the arguments of the West Indian planters in favoring adoption while the Board of Trade raised numerous objections and counseled a policy of delay. Lord Derby acknowledged that acceptance "would be at variance with the general commercial policy of Great Britain," but claimed the West Indian colonies were on the edge of ruin because of European sugar bounties, and if their entry into the American market was restricted or closed they faced certain disaster. In pushing Granville to accept, Derby noted that similar differential provisions had been allowed in the 1854 treaty with the United States for Canada.[48]

Granville ultimately chose to reject the American version because, in his view, it emasculated the most-favored-nation clause and its shipping provisions were termed a throwback to the navigation laws.[49] The foreign secretary appears to have been swayed by the arguments of the Board of Trade presented in a memo by T. H. Farver, and those of his assistant under secretary, Lord Edmond Fitzmaurice. The most-favored-nation clause, Farver maintained, was "one of the most valuable parts of commercial treaties and leads to universal freedom of trade"; however, "with the limitation which the United States seek to put upon it, it becomes a snare, which is calculated to lead to endless disputes" and "tends to fetter instead of liberating trade." The whole tendency of the American proposal was "to strengthen the connection—political as well as economical—of the West Indian Colonies with the United States, and pro tanto, to weaken their connection with the British Empire."[50] Lord Fitzmaurice agreed with the Board of Trade analysis and warned his chief that the American scheme was "the application of a sort of Monroe Doctrine to commerce."[51] The British rejection, coming in the eleventh hour of the Arthur administration, effectively killed any hope of further negotiation for a treaty.

Similar tensions arose between the two rivals over the question of control of a future isthmian canal, especially since it was an integral part of the American drive for economic expansion in the Western Hemisphere. The major obstacle to American ambitions was Great Britain, and the particular difficulty was the Clayton-Bulwer Treaty of 1850. James G. Blaine had tried, through a series of peppery notes, to coax and cajole the British into modifying the treaty. Frelinghuysen, far less flamboyant than his predecessor but sharing his desire for an American-controlled canal, pursued a stronger line with Great Britain and tried to abrogate the agreement.[52] After being rebuffed, Frelinghuysen moved to outflank the British by negotiating a separate arrangement with Nicaragua. The Frelinghuysen-Zavala treaty was an effort to trade American protection of Nicaragua for a canal route outside the British sphere. Presented to the Senate in December 1884, the treaty failed to receive the required two-thirds majority.[53] Any hope of reconsideration was dashed when President Grover Cleveland withdrew the treaty shortly after he took office.[54]

Although unsuccessful either in the Clayton-Bulwer squabble or the Nicaraguan treaty ploy, Frelinghuysen emerged as a zealous and militant advocate of American dominance in the Caribbean who did not hesitate to challenge the national nemesis, Great Britain. The administration argument in support of the Frelinghuysen-Zavala treaty hinged upon the logic of extended markets on the west coast of South America and Asia.[55] In addition to the formal attempt to establish a protectorate over Nicaragua, moreover, Frelinghuysen's strategy of reciprocity furthered American efforts to control an isthmian canal. Each nation in the Caribbean with which he negotiated a bilateral treaty controlled a crucial sector of the strategic approach to the canal. His maneuver was two-pronged: it proposed to extend American markets and then, through that acquired economic dominance, intended to exercise the necessary control over the entire canal area without cumbersome political obligations.[56]

The appointment of the Central and South American Commission, admittedly a last-minute attempt to foster the strategy of economic expansion, further verifies this analysis of the Arthur administration. The commission, consisting of George H. Sharpe, Thomas C. Reynolds, Solon O. Thatcher, and William E. Curtis, as secretary, solicited the views of businessmen and merchants in several countries of the hemisphere on improving trade. They filed an

extensive   report including suggestions on how to capture Latin
American markets. But Cleveland scuttled their efforts and refused
to support a positive program based on the commission's findings.
Arthur and Frelinghuysen, who undoubtedly realized the commission would never complete its task before they left office, had been
far too sanguine about the nature and extent of the   bipartisan
congressional support for *their* particular strategy of overseas economic expansion.

The commission had taken the pulse of the nation's business
community vis à vis Latin American trade and, as a leading commercial journal recognized, the entire purpose and rationale of the
mission was to plot a course for the United States to overtake
Great Britain in the markets of Central and South America.[57] The
most   enthusiastic   receptions given the commission were in the
mercantile communities of New Orleans, San   Francisco,   New
York, and Philadelphia. In the midst of an acute economic depression, American business leaders had "become   absorbed   by   a
realization   that   the   internal development of this country has
reached a point where an external commerce is necessary for its
prosperity . . . and that markets must somewhere be found for the
disposition of the surplus."[58] It became clear to the commissioners
that countless American political, business, industrial, and
agricultural leaders had, through a variety of mental processes,
accepted the notion that the United States needed overseas markets
to prevent economic and social disaster.

All seemed to agree that the "natural" market for America's
surplus agricultural and manufactured products was Central and
South America, and the commission in its report suggested the
United States adopt a series of "measures which have won the commercial glory of our rivals." It recommended regular and direct
steamship   communications,   a   system   of reciprocity treaties,
simplification of customs regulations, and an increase in size and
improvement in performance of the consular service. It also called
for the establishment of American mercantile houses, a more thorough survey of the wants of South American customers, a network
of banking connections, a common standard of values, more liberal
credits by American merchants, and finally, the introduction of a
bonded warehouse system.[59] The recommendations provided little
that was new, for all the proposals had been offered earlier by the

Hayes and Garfield administrations. Even President Arthur had outlined a similar program in his fourth annual message in December 1884. However, the report of the South American Commission did substantiate the original analysis and reinforce the thinking of many American economic expansionists.

The commission defined two areas of concern as crucial — Britain's monopoly of the South American carrying trade, and its grip on the credit and exchange facilities of the region. British control of the steamship service crippled any American effort to capture the markets of the hemisphere and reverse the pattern of buying more from the South Americans than it sold in return. The existing triangular trade definitely benefited Great Britain. The first leg carried South American exports, such as coffee and sugar, to the eastern ports of the United States. The second leg began after the tropical products had been unloaded and a cargo of American manufactured products and foodstuffs destined for South America had been taken on for the voyage to England. Then the ship loaded British goods in an English port for the final leg to South or Central America.[60]

The absence of banking facilities for American businessmen was "a great drawback," especially because the notes of the Bank of England were the only measure of value recognized throughout South America. That was "a standing disgrace to American statesmen" and another form of tribute that "produced an annual profit of $1,000,000 for English bankers."[61] Banking via London humiliated Americans by exposing their nation's financial and commercial inferiority, and the whole process aroused anti-British feelings. As the commission complained, "it is somewhat mortifying for an American who proposes to travel in the countries so adjacent to our own to be compelled to convert the money of his own Government into notes of the Bank of England."[62] Long-term credit facilities were the key to British success in South America. As a mature economy, the English had enormous capital reserves and a banking structure suitable to the market. American merchants lacked capital and American banks were "prevented from loaning money on merchandise by their charters."[63] The commission urged the creation of banking facilities and favored a uniform monetary system employing silver to penetrate the British commercial empire. It cited President Arthur's scheme for a monetary union as further support for their recommendations.

All of the commission's proposals demanded substantial government aid and encouragement. Arguing that such massive government support was not at variance with America's traditions, the commissioners drew an analogy to the internal development of the nation. "The same agency that developed our own Great West—government aid and encouragement" should now foster overseas economic expansion.[64] That broad "earth-ocean" that lay between "the Mississippi Valley and the Pacific slope would have been an insurmountable obstacle" even to American enterprise, had not the "Government by gifts of lands and guarantees of bonds laid a foundation upon which private capital was secure."[65] That theme pervaded the report, and numerous businessmen who testified before the group urged such support for commercial expansion. But it was just that feature of the report—the strong and constant appeal for federal aid— that engendered the most hostile opposition. Critics, many of whom might be in sympathy with the commission's overall objectives, worried that such a program promoted special interests, created monopolies, and damaged the domestic fabric of society.[66]

Clearly, Frelinghuysen and Arthur, who undeniably tasted little actual success, sustained the policy of the previous Republican administrations by attempting to establish the commercial hegemony of the United States in the Western Hemisphere. Despite some differences over means with the Blaine wing of the party, they were active economic nationalists who honored the Monroe Doctrine and acted on the options for American empire implicit in that policy. As their British rivals well understood, the Monroe Doctrine and the slogan "America for Americans" meant in truth nothing less than "America for the United States."[67] One area of disagreement among Republicans arose over American participation in the Congo Conference. Blaine and his faction vehemently opposed that action. He confided to Sir Lionel Sackville-West: "How can we maintain the Monroe Doctrine when we take part in conferences on the internal affairs of other continents?" Blaine feared such a course invited British and general European involvement in the Western Hemisphere.[68]

Frelinghuysen, frequently cast as being more prudent and conservative than Blaine, was actually less inhibited by the Monroe

Doctrine. Perhaps he understood that it was a two-edged sword: freeing the United States in the Western Hemisphere while restricting it in the rest of the world.[69] More important, Frelinghuysen had no illusions about the full implications of America's outward economic thrust that his policy was designed to encourage when he commented about the United States: "when it pushes its enormous natural products into every country, underselling the local market, and is increasing its exports of manufactured goods until they are found in all parts of the earth, competing with the long established factories of Europe, it cannot expect to hold aloof from the rest of the world, and cannot consider itself isolated, either politically or commercially."[70] The market restrictions placed on American agricultural exports by European nations were evidence of this, for "this invasion of foreign markets is not patiently regarded by foreign nations."[71]

Other Americans also realized that the nation's economic expansion prompted European hostility, and that European imperialism in turn threatened the future success of the United States. One observer, John W. Bookwalter, noted that Europe's imperialism, by integrating the various underdeveloped areas as colonies, "has been daily drawing toward a position in which it will be, in a sense most injurious to our financial and industrial interests, independent of the United States."[72] Great Britain provided only the most blatant example of the danger since it was integrating its empire toward "an imperial policy in the most effectual meaning of the word" by grooming India to replace the United States as its major source of wheat and cotton.[73] It also encouraged Canada to challenge the United States in western South America and the Pacific. In this perspective the Canadian Pacific Railroad was construed as a design to capture "the Canadian and trans-continental traffic" and to "secure the trade to and from China and Japan, and the chief cities of the United States, east of the Rocky Mountains."[74] A number of Americans feared and resented that British effort to finesse them out of the Asian trade and denounced the Canadian Pacific "as a scheme for enhancing British power upon the North American continent."[75]

The foreign policy of Frelinghuysen and Arthur sustained the challenge to British primacy in the Western Hemisphere. They accepted the broad strategy enunciated by earlier American economic expansionists who recommended the opening of foreign markets for the country's surplus as the solution to recurrent economic depression. Frelinghuysen emphasized reciprocity treaties as the initial requisite for a comprehensive system of mutual trade for the entire hemisphere. Although unsuccessful in the immediate sense, the Arthur administration's efforts set the pattern for America's unceasing outward thrust in the late 1880s and 1890s. They personally dramatized the need for foreign markets, and espoused a policy of economic nationalism that awakened the country to the reality of England's power and presence in Latin America. Anti-British feelings frequently appeared as a psychological response to the frustration and jealousy inherent in such explicitly economic confrontations with the existing king of the marketplace.

NOTES

1. The slogan appears in the late 1870s in response to the De Lesseps project and prevailed until the turn of the century. See House Select Committee on the Interoceanic Ship Canal papers, records of the United States House of Representatives, National Archives, Record Group 233 (hereinafter cited as NA, RG 233). Alfred Williams, *The Inter-Oceanic Canal and the Monroe Doctrine* (New York: G. P. Putnam's Sons, 1889). *New York Tribune,* 1889–1890. *Public Opinion,* 1890–1891. For the response of British diplomats to the slogan see comments in V. G. Kiernan, "Foreign Interests in the War of the Pacific," *Hispanic American Historical Review* 35 (February 1955), pp. 14–36.

2. Frelinghuysen, in several letters to John F. Miller, Chairman of the Senate Foreign Relations Committee, stressed that the timing for a conference was inappropriate since the United States required additional opportunities to organize and consolidate its influence among the Central and South American nations to guarantee their votes. See Frelinghuysen to Miller, July 24, 1882 and March 26, 1884, House Committee on Commerce papers, records of the United States House of Representatives, NA RG 233.

3. James D. Richardson, *Messages and Papers of the Presidents* Vol. VIII (Washington: Government Printing Office, 1902), p. 63.

4. In the 1880s American leaders began developing the historical thesis of the influence of sea power, and the idea that only nations that possessed a powerful navy flourished was taking hold. Robert Seager II, "Ten Years before Mahan: The Unofficial Case for the New Navy, 1880–1890," *Mississippi Valley Historical Review,* 40 (1953–1954), pp. 491–512, and John A. S. Grenville and George B. Young, *Politics, Strategy, and American Diplomacy* (New Haven: Yale University Press, 1966), Chap. I.

5. See, as an example, the remarks of Abram Hewitt, March 30, 1882: *Congressional Record* XIII, Part 3, 2435 (hereinafter cited as *CR,* 13:2:2435); Edward Younger, *John A. Kasson: Politics and Diplomacy from Lincoln to McKinley*

(Iowa City: State Historical Society of Iowa, 1955), p. 295; and Hugh McCullough in *Annual Report of the Secretary of the Treasury, 1884,* House Executive Doc. No. 2, 48th Cong., 2nd Sess., (Washington: Government Printing Office, 1884), p. XI. For Arthur's view on the desirability of Latin American markets see Richardson, *Messages and Papers,* Vol. VIII, pp. 251–52.

6. See United States State Department, *Consular Reports,* No. 19 (May 1882) (Washington: Government Printing Office, 1882), pp. 156–57, No. 22 (August 1882), p. 672: *Bradstreets,* May 27, 1882: John W. Bookwalter, "America's Danger," *Bradstreets,* December 12, 1885; *The First Annual Report of the Commissioner of Labor,* March 1887 (Washington: Government Printing Office, 1886), pp. 247–48; and Morton Rothstein, "America in the International Rivalry for the British Wheat Market, 1860-1914," *Mississippi Valley Historical Review,* 47 (1960–1961), pp. 401–18.

7. For a lucid discussion of Frelinghuysen's efforts to have the market restrictions inflicted by Germany and France removed, see James L. Erlenborn, "The American Meat and Livestock Industry and American Foreign Policy 1880–1896," (Master's thesis, University of Wisconsin, 1966).

8. *Western Rural,* February 9, 1884.

9. See remarks of Alvey Adee to Elihu Root, November 24, 1906, file (1906–1910) 1700/5, records of the Department of State, NA, RG 59.

10. Ibid.

11. Ibid.

12. Another expression of patterning American visions for dominance in Latin America after the English model was contained in an 1884 presidential election tract for James G. Blaine in which the author defined Mexico as "America's Egypt." See James Morris Morgan, *America's Egypt, Mr. Blaine's Foreign Policy* (New York: Herman Bartock, Printer, 1884).

13. Testimony of Alexander D. Anderson, representative of the World's Industrial Exposition of New Orleans, in *Report From the Central and South American Commissioners.* House Exec. Doc. No. 226, 48th Cong., 2nd Sess., 1885 (Washington: Government Printing Office, 1885), p. 49.

14. Remarks of John F. Miller urging a first-class navy, February 28, 1884, *CR,* 15:2:1564.

15. Ibid., 3:2763.

16. Helper and his supporters saw railway communication as a more viable alternative in the face of British control of South America's carrying trade. See resolution of James B. Belford, February 6, 1882, *CR.,* 13:1:922; Hinton R. Helper, *The Three Americas Railway* (St. Louis: W. S. Bryan Company, 1881).

17. See Nimmo to Hon. Hugh McCullough (n.d., 1885), in Edward Atkinson Paper, Massachusetts Historical Society. I am indebted to my friend Howard Schonberger for bringing this letter to my attention.

18. Ibid.

19. Ibid.

20. Perhaps Frelinghuysen's lack of success with the Senate arose from the fact that he worked too closely with the Foreign Relations Committee, erroneously assuming it represented the views of the Senate, which it did not. The Committee

was far more expansionist-minded than the Senate per se. For an expression of this view see Allen Lawrence Burnette, Jr., "The Senate Foreign Relations Committee and the Diplomacy of Garfield, Arthur, and Cleveland," (Ph. D. dissertation, University of Virginia, 1952).

21. Frelinghuysen to John F. Miller, March 26, 1884, House Committee on Commerce papers, records of the United States House of Representatives, NA, RG 233.

22. Ibid.

23. Ibid.

24. Ibid.

25. Richardson, *Messages and Papers,* Vol. VIII, p. 251.

26. Ibid.

27. Ibid., p. 252.

28. See David M. Pletcher, *The Awkward Years, American Foreign Policy Under Garfield and Arthur* (Columbia: University of Missouri Press, 1962), p. 103.

29. Ibid.

30. See the petitions and memorials to Senate Committee on Foreign Relations, 48th Cong., 2nd Sess., records of the United States Senate, NA, RG 46.

31. Ibid., Petition of Chamber of Commerce of New York, December 28, 1884.

32. Ibid.

33. Ibid.

34. Ibid.

35. Ibid.

36. James Laughlin and W. Parker Willis, *Reciprocity* (New York: The Baker and Taylor Co., 1903), p. 109.

37. Memorial of Jarvis Engineering Company, December 5, 1884. Petitions of Pioneer Iron Works, December 10, 1884, and Motley and Sterling, Railway, Steamship and Contractors' Supplies, December 15, 1884, Senate Committee on Foreign Relations papers, records of United States Senate, NA, RG 46.

38. Ibid., Memorial from Bath Board of Trade, February 23, 1885.

39. Ibid., Resolution of New York Produce Exchange, December 29, 1884. Petition of St. Paul Chamber of Commerce, January 20, 1885. Remarks of Representative Hurd, April 29, 1884, *CR* 15:4:3551.

40. Frelinghuysen to Andrew G. Curtin, chairman, House Committee on Foreign Affairs, December 26, 1884 in House Committee on Foreign Affairs paper, records of the United States House of Representatives, NA, RG 233.

41. Ibid.

42. Foster to Gresham, September 28, October 26, 1884, Gresham Papers, Library of Congress.

43. George K. Thorndike to Edmunds, January 19, 1885, Senate Committee on Foreign Relations papers, records of the United States Senate, NA, RG 46.

44. Richardson, *Messages and Papers,* Vol. VIII, p. 333.

45. Ibid.

46. Consul General A. Crowe to Granville, November 29, 1884, Commercial No. 3, Foreign Office 115, Vol. 755, Public Record Office, London, (hereinafter cited as F.O. 115/755 P.R.O.).

47. Sackville-West to Granville, December 8, 1884, in Paul Knaplund and

Carolyn M. Clewes, *Private Letters From the British Embassy in Washington to the Foreign Secretary Lord Granville, 1880 – 1885,* Annual Report of the American Historical Association, Vol. I, 1941 (Washington: Government Printing Office, 1942), p. 180.

48. Colonial Office Memo on Reciprocity treaty between British West Indies and the United States of America, January 6, 1885, F.O. 115/755, P.R.O, and Granville to West, February 12, 1885, F.O. 115/756, P.R.O. See also Colonial Office to Foreign Office, January 15, 1885, F.O. 5/1917 P.R.O.

49. Granville to West, February 12, 1885, F.O. 115/755 P.R.O.

50. Board of Trade memo by T. H. Farver, January 13, 1885, F.O. 5/1917 P.R.O.

51. Ibid., Memo of Sir Edmond Fitzmaurice, January 22, 1885.

52. Pletcher, *Awkward Years,* pp. 103, 257.

53. The vote was 32 ayes, 23 nays, indicating a majority of senators favored Frelinghuysen's efforts to establish a protectorate over Nicaragua. See Lindley M. Keasbey, *The Nicaragua Canal and the Monroe Doctrine* (New York: G. P. Putnam's Sons, 1896), p. 435, and George F. Howe, *Chester A. Arthur, A Quarter Century of Machine Politics* (New York: Frederick Ungar Publishing Co., 1935), p. 274.

54. Pletcher, *Awkward Years,* p. 337.

55. Frelinghuysen to Curtin, December 26, 1884, House Committee on Foreign Affairs papers, records of the United States House of Representatives, NA, RG 233.

56. Walter LaFeber, *The New Empire, An Interpretation of American Expansion, 1860 – 1898* (Ithaca: Cornell University Press, 1963, pp. 48–50.

57. *Bradstreets,* January 3, 1885.

58. *Report From the Central and South American Commissioners,* p. 3.

59. Ibid., p. 4 and passim. ˙

60. Ibid., pp. 16, 24, 72. For Frelinghuysen's analysis of the effects of the triangular trade on American commerce and shipping see *Foreign Trade of Mexico and Other Countries.* Senate Exec. Doc. No. 39, 48th Cong., 2nd Sess., 1885 (Washington: Government Printing Office, 1885), p. 4.

61. *Report from the Central and South American Commissioners,* p. 11.

62. Ibid.

63. Ibid., p. 161.

64. Ibid., p. 26.

65. Ibid.

66. For a discussion of the contemporary response to the commissioners' report see Pletcher, *Awkward Years,* pp. 340–42.

67. See comments of R. Graham to Granville, May 18, 1882 in dispatch from Pauncefote to West, July 15, 1882, F.O. 115/696, P.R.O.

68. Quoted in David S. Muzzey, *James G. Blaine: A Political Idol of Other Days* (New York: Dodd, Mead and Co., 1934), p. 425.

69. For an example of this analysis see *Bradstreets,* December 13, 1884.

70. Frelinghuysen to Arthur, April 26, 1884, in *Support of the Diplomatic and Consular Service.* House Exec. Doc. No. 146, 48th Cong., 2nd Sess., 1884 (Washington: Government Printing Office, 1884), p. 3.

71. Ibid.

72. Bookwalter, "America's Danger," *Bradstreets,* December 12, 1885, pp. 376—79.

73. Ibid.

74. Comments of Canadian Pacific President Van Horne to Sir John MacDonald, October 25, 1885, Letterbook 14, Van Horne Papers, Canadian National Archives, Ottawa. Again, I am indebted to Howard Schonberger for bringing this correspondence to my attention.

75. Rosemary L. Savage, "American Concern Over Canadian Railway Competition in the North-West, 1885—1890," Annual Report of the Canadian Historical Association, 1942 (Toronto: Canadian Historical Association, 1942), pp. 82—93.

7

Cleveland Sustains the Outward Thrust

Republican rule and policy have managed to surrender to Great Britain, along with our commerce, the control of the markets of the world.

Instead of the Republican party's British policy, we demand on ·behalf of the American Democracy, an American policy.

Democratic Party platform,
1884

A great and powerful and wealthy Nation like ours, with its active, aggressive people, ought not to allow England to monopolize the trade of our neighbors, upon our own continent.

Thomas J. Jarvis, 1885

What England needs in commerce and finance America does not need. What England recommends to America, America had better reject. English policy has been selfish for centuries, and has never favored the development of this country. It has been consistent in its regard for strictly English interests. Can we not have an American policy?

Senator Thomas M. Bowen, 1886

They [Samoan Islands] lie in a pathway of a commerce that is just being developed. The opening of the west coast of North

America to civilization and commerce by means of the trans-conti-
nental railways had given to this group of islands an interest which
they never had before.

Thomas F. Bayard, 1887

The election of Grover Cleveland in 1884 signaled a temporary change in the tone, pace, and to some degree the direction, of American foreign policy in the late nineteenth century. To be sure, the nation's outward thrust continued under the first Democratic administration since the Civil War. Cleveland and his secretary of state, Thomas F. Bayard, safeguarded and extended American interests, most notably in the Pacific. However, the Cleveland-Bayard years possessed a decidedly different character from that of preceding Republican administrations. While both men accepted the logic of overseas economic expansion and the necessity of foreign markets, their foreign policy denigrated overt government involvement and generally rejected entangling commitments and overseas territorial expansion. By and large, the Democratic brand of economic expansion reflected the laissez-faire philosophy of Cleveland and his secretary of state. It was devoid of government aid and subsidy, and was less stridently anti-British, less clamorous and chauvinistic, than that of the Republicans.

Domestic political considerations, as well as ideology, prompted this shift in American diplomacy. Members of the Cleveland administration hoped to utilize tariff reform to overcome an intra-party split and in the process forge a national following for reelection. Lower tariff duties, in addition to aiding the consumer and preventing further concentrations of industrial power, would bring expanded markets and increased trade. That in turn, it was argued, would thwart the silverite attempt to dominate the party and unite Democrats behind Cleveland. The comprehensive programs for economic expansion favored by Republicans and embodied in the report of the South American Commission were rejected as transgressions of the laissez-faire faith. Such proposals were politically dangerous, particularly the GOP tactic of reciprocity, which threatened Cleveland's domestic and foreign policies. As employed by Republicans, reciprocity preserved protection and allowed for the evasion of tariff reform. Given the limitations of ideology and the exigencies of domestic politics, it was little won-der that the foreign policy of Cleveland and Bayard was distinctly more reserved and perhaps almost lethargic.

Of course, no one in the administration openly denied the general accuracy of the observations of Perry Belmont, a Democratic representative from New York, member of the House Foreign Affairs Committee, and Cleveland enthusiast. "There is with us," noted Belmont, "a yearly increasing surplus of products—agricultural and manufactured which demands new markets and new outlets." But Belmont wondered, "can they best be obtained, by participation in European conferences, and by entering on the negotiation on the general system of commercial treaties," or "can the work be better done by us independently, and by bringing to bear on the subject the revision of our own laws of taxation, currency, and finance?"[1] Clearly Belmont and most members of the Cleveland administration favored the latter approach, for it was more consistent with their general outlook, ran fewer risks of foreign entanglement, and would not contribute to the creation of trusts and monopolies at home. Once again it was a question of means and not ends, and while it is true that the foreign policy of the Cleveland years appeared less energetic, more hesitant and defensive, it did not represent a disavowal of the ultimate American goal of securing the world's markets.

Despite their concern for the domestic political impact of diplomacy, Cleveland and Bayard consciously avoided any display of anti-British bombast or jingoism. Both men were definitely more prone to interpret the popular notions of an Anglo-Saxon destiny—so eloquently expounded in those years by John Fiske and Reverend Josiah Strong—as a joint venture to be realized with the aid and cooperation, if not the lead, of Great Britain. This was especially true of Bayard, an unabashed Anglophile, who bucked the prevailing tide of anti-British nationalism and assiduously labored to prevent any friction between the two great Anglo-Saxon nations from erupting into a major conflict. Try as they may, however, Bayard and Cleveland could not simply cut off Anglophobia, and it continued to haunt them throughout their administration. Their infrequent appeals to anti-British nationalism by no means ended the persuasiveness of this approach in the political arena, nor did it purge the phenomenon from the national consciousness.

Indeed, the Democrats had employed just such campaign rhetoric in their 1884 platform. They charged that it was "Republican rule and policy" that had "managed to surrender to Great Britain, along with our commerce . . . control of the markets of the world." To restore national pride and dignity the Democrats promised to replace "the Republican party's British policy" with "an American policy."[2] Secretary of State Bayard had developed the same theme in a campaign speech to the Iroquois Club of Chicago. He decried the dwindling role of the United States in the carrying of the world's commerce when "American shipping interests no longer had any interest in what was going on in three-fourths of the surface of the globe." Then, appealing to his audience's direct self-interest, Bayard offered a standard analysis of the difficulties confronting American agriculture in a world market dominated by Great Britain. "The American farmer today could not realize for his wheat as much as it cost him to raise it because the price was regulated in Mark Lane, in London" and the existing competition "was too much for the American agriculturalist."[3] Tariff reform, Bayard and the Democrats contended, was needed to overcome this competitive disadvantage by unfettering the merchant marine from the shackles of protection and restoring it to a position of prominence.

However, any effort to disassemble the structure of protection would be a slow, painstaking process with innumerable political snares and legislative bottlenecks. Economic expansionists who desired American commercial and economic hegemony in Latin America looked for more immediate results. Initially, the Cleveland administration buoyed their hopes by sending troops to Panama in March 1885, to maintain the right of transit during revolutionary turmoil. William M. Scruggs, United States minister to Colombia and crusader against British encroachments in the Western Hemisphere, confided to Bayard that "in common, I suppose with every American who loves his country, and rejoices in its honor and glory, I feel like congratulating the Administration upon its prompt and manly course connected with the late events on the Isthmus of Panama."[4] Other friends of the administration also applauded Cleveland's forthright act. They believed that the Democrats would now assert their own foreign policy and not simply follow the lead of the Republicans. But, much to their disappointment, the Cleveland administration dragged its feet and failed to fulfill the expectations of an assertive hemispheric policy that some observers, such as Scruggs, had seen in the Panama episode.[5] Cleveland and Bayard followed a traditional and accepted pattern by dispatching marines to the isthmus. Beyond that, they had little that was imaginative to offer advocates of extended American influence in Central and South America.

Certainly the Cleveland administration did not lack for advice. A number of self-appointed advisers repeatedly urged the secretary of state and other influential members of the administration to adopt an aggressive Latin American policy. Manton Marble, the former editor of the *New York World,* who was prominent in the Democratic party and had the ear of the administration, was counseled to say "a good word for commercial treaties, upon which the destiny of the country and party now vibrates. In truth there is no principle, no party, no country that is not based on colonies and trade."[6] After several months at his post, Thomas Jordan Jarvis, minister to Brazil and former governor of North Carolina, wrote privately to Bayard about his observations concerning Latin American trade. "In the first place," Jarvis believed, "the bulk of the trade of South America, of right, belongs to the United States." He assured Bayard that "we can secure the great bulk of this trade, if we will, but it can *only* be done by the aid, and fostering care, of the government." Subsidies for steamship lines would be the first necessary step to capture this commerce, argued Jarvis, for "a great and powerful and wealthy Nation like ours, with its active, aggressive people, ought not to allow England to monopolize the trade of our neighbors, upon our own continent."[7] William Ellinger, another advocate of economic nationalism, submitted at the request of Bayard his proposals for enhancing Spanish-American trade relations. Ellinger had lived in Peru and Chile and his suggestions were almost identical to those of the South American Commission. He urged ship subsidies, international coinage, and construction of an interoceanic canal. In addition, American businessmen would have to learn the language and generally become better informed about the needs of the Latin American market.[8]

But the Cleveland administration refused to adopt such a policy for reasons that involved ideology as well as politics. Generally speaking, Cleveland and Bayard opposed direct government participation and support for overseas expansion, preferring instead a laissez-faire approach that allowed for such development as it happened at private initiative. Federal subsidies, such as those favored by GOP leaders, were denounced as nothing more than public gifts to special interests and were labelled as detrimental to the national welfare because they contributed to the already alarming concentrations of wealth and power.[9] Cleveland was not opposed to reciprocity treaties in every instance, but he refused to be bound to the Arthur-Frelinghuysen program. While he withdrew most of the treaties with Latin American countries, he retained the Mexican treaty, supported an extension of the 1875 treaty with Hawaii, and spoke in favor of reciprocity with Canada. The president defined the GOP reciprocity tactic as a transparent scheme to retain protection and to finesse any meaningful tariff reform effort. An across-the-board reduction of tariff duties, Cleveland contended, would provide the needed impetus for increased trade with Central America and South America, Europe and the Far East.

So, within a few short months after what appeared to be an auspicious beginning, the Cleveland administration dashed the hopes of the more ambitious economic expansionists by withdrawing the marines from Panama, recalling for reconsideration the Dominican treaty and the Spanish treaty for Puerto Rico and Cuba, and by failing to act upon the recommendations of the South American commissioners. The draft treaties with Colombia and El Salvador also quietly died, and no move was made to reopen negotiations with Great Britain for the British West Indies. In his December message the president, in addition to detailing his objections to the reciprocity agreements, rejected the Frelinghuysen-Zavala treaty for a protectorate in Central America and opted instead for a neutralized canal. As he explained, his administration did "not favor a policy of acquisition of new and distant territory, or the incorporation of remote interests with our own."[10] Secretary of State Bayard shared these beliefs as he confided to David A. Wells that:

> It seems clear to me that if we are to overstep our Constitutional jurisdiction—and engraft upon our Federal system—the practical realities of an Imperial system over distant and exterior dependencies—the death Knell of the Republic of our Fathers—will be sounded—and a career of territorial aggrandizement and personal and national ambitions will have commenced.[11]

The same trepidations concerning entangling alliances led Cleveland to refuse to support ratification of the Congo conference agreement.

The administration adamantly stuck to its position, even though during the next few years several Latin American countries, and Spain as well, pressed the secretary of state about the possibility of renewing negotiations for reciprocity agreements.[12] In the face of these inquiries Bayard strictly adhered to the view, as he made clear to the Salvadorean minister on one occasion, that modification or reduction of tariff duties was a legislative function and not the work of the executive department. Individual commercial agreements also were ruled out because "the disposition of the President was to lower the barriers of trade between ourselves and the Central American Countries." And when Minister Velasco submitted, at Bayard's request, a proposal for a projected commercial treaty, the secretary of state politely asserted that while he "was anxious to promote a closer condition of commercial exchange between the two nations" he believed that could only come about through the amelioration of tariff duties and not through individual commercial treaties.[13]

However, if Cleveland and Bayard hesitated to use foreign policy positively in encouraging American penetration of Central and South America, they exhibited no such reluctance in employing diplomacy in furthering domestic political goals. The president and several of his closest advisers, Secretary of the Treasury Daniel Manning, Manton Marble, and of course Bayard, were determined to maintain the integrity of the gold standard, which they believed was indispensable to fiscal stability. All of them feared that the continuation of the provisions for silver coinage of the Bland-Allison Act spelled financial suicide. To avert this contemplated disaster and, more important, to undercut the position of the silverites, the secretary of state appointed Marble as a special envoy to visit the capitals of Europe to sound out the English, French, and Germans on the possibility of a conference to establish international bimetallism.[14]

But the whole thing was a sham, a ploy designed for domestic consumption to strengthen the administration's hand in favor of gold. President Cleveland and his confidants knew full well that the Marble mission ran little risk of success; they matter-of-factly expected Great Britain to reject American overtures for international bimetallism. And since British approval of any plan for an international agreement was the sine qua non for French or German participation, the project was doomed from the start. The European refusal to back a proposed conference was of no consequence, however, as Bayard, Cleveland, and Manning, if not Marble, fully anticipated this result to justify the administration's domestic moves to buttress the gold standard.[15] This bit of diplomatic sleight-of-hand temporarily kept the silver forces off balance and on the defensive, for despite their suspicions, they remained uncertain as to the true motives of the administration.

To be sure, the silverites had received more than an inkling of the president's intentions on the currency question even before he entered the White House. In a preinauguration letter written for him by Manton Marble and addressed to a number of silver advocates—including Adoniram J. Warner, Democratic member of the House from Ohio—Cleveland announced that if necessary to avert a financial crisis he would seek the suspension of the coinage of silver.[16] True to his word, and apparently true to plan, President Cleveland, in his 1885 annual message, expressed concern that "prosperity hesitates upon our threshold because of the dangers and uncertainties surrounding this question." Accordingly, and with the European rejection of his efforts for bimetallism to support his case, he piously recommended "the suspension of the compulsory coinage of silver dollars, directed by the law passed in February, 1878."[17] Not surprisingly, this scheme backfired. The president's clever manipulation of foreign policy failed to entice numerous Democratic congressmen and senators from the South and West to follow the administration in its antisilver crusade. Unfortunately for Cleveland, this strategy not only split the Democratic party, it was unsuccessful in its objective of suspending the provisions of the Bland-Allison Act. At best the administration could claim a stalemate by asserting that it had stymied the attempts of silverites to expand the use of the white metal.

Another consequence of this venture, perhaps equally as important and damaging to Cleveland's political position as the revolt in the Democratic ranks, was the more-or-less permanent identification of his policies and actions with the interests and machinations of England. Instead of shifting the blame for the failure of the Marble mission—and indirectly, for the necessity of asking for a suspension of silver coinage—to Great Britain and the European nations, Cleveland was denounced as the "pliant tool"

of Wall and Lombard streets.[18] He and other supporters of the gold
standard were irreversibly stigmatized as being pro-British and became a favorite target of anti-British nationalism. The goldbugs
were perceived by agrarians and other silver advocates as the all-
too-willing accomplices of Great Britain in its traditional policy of
dominating and controlling the world marketplace.

The farm press and other agrarian spokesmen of the West and
South claimed the president's moves against silver sustained rather
than checked the ever-mounting competition of Indian wheat and
cotton exports. Cleveland was held responsible for the weakened
position of American agricultural exports in European grain markets. Agrarian dissatisfaction with Cleveland's monetary policy
hinged on a series of closely linked arguments. The world price
of silver relative to the value of gold was declining, and the antisilver campaign of the administration was contributing to the
cheapness of silver. Cheap silver on the international market permitted British merchants to purchase more silver in exchange for
their gold. Because the Indian rupee was a silver-backed currency,
the cheap silver bullion of the merchants, when coined into rupees,
bought a greater quantity of Indian wheat and cotton. Thus, American farmers charged that the low price of silver was subsidizing
Indian exports and displacing American farm products in the markets of England and Europe. The *Western Rural,* speaking for the
hard-pressed farmer, admonished, "let the gold standard men be-
ware that they do not deprive him wholly of this foreign market
by Indian competition."[19]

While the Indian wheat-silver connection was made repeatedly
by the congressional opposition to the president during the "silver
blizzard" of 1886, spokesmen for the administration tended to
dismiss it, as did Secretary of State Bayard, who saw the challenge
of Indian wheat as "distant and not to be feared."[20] However, one
secondary figure in the administration, Commissioner of Labor
Carroll D. Wright, devoted his first annual report to exploring the
problem of industrial depression, and acknowledged that the grain
acreage of India was fast approaching the grain acreage of the
United States. "The direct result of this Indian development," he
admitted, "has been an increase in the imports of Indian wheat
by Western Europe and a decrease in the imports of American
grain." Wright was not necessarily alarmed over the rapid emer-

gence of Indian competition. Nonetheless, he recognized the psychological implications among the producers of cotton and wheat "who feel the future has no prosperity for them." Although the commissioner of labor stopped short of espousing the explicit connection to silver that critics of Cleveland made, he conceded that the farmer's apprehension had to be removed "to aid in restoring prosperity."[21]

For the backers of silver in Congress, that was just the point: Cleveland's war against silver prolonged the economic suffering of the farmer and delayed the return of prosperity. Democrat Richard Bland of Missouri felt it was evident that the nation's "gold policy is driving the products of our silver mines to India, there to be used as money to employ Hindoos [sic] to raise wheat, corn, and cotton in direct competition with the farmers of America."[22] Hence, Cleveland's preference for gold benefited the British by providing a bounty for the agricultural exports of India. Another serious consequence, according to the analysis of Senator Thomas M. Bowen of Colorado, was that it handed England "the cudgel, or the bludgeon rather, with which to gradually drive us from the world's markets."[23] It was time for an independent "American policy" that included free coinage of silver, argued Senator Richard Coke of Texas and Congressman John W. Daniel of Virginia. For if the United States did go the full route with Cleveland and demonetize silver, it would "bend the necks of our people to the yoke of European policies."[24] Perhaps the views of western and southern members of Congress were best summed up by Representative Joseph Wheeler of Alabama when he demanded: "Let America stop legislating for our moneyed nobility, and devote its wisdom to the resuscitation of our prostrate trade and commerce, and we will be able to successfully compete with England in all the markets of the world."[25]

Economic nationalists and silverites found little to cheer in the administration's traditional and conservative approach to Latin America and what they labelled a pro-British monetary policy. The more resolute stand of Bayard and Cleveland in pushing American interests in the Pacific undoubtedly provided them with some encouragement and a measure of satisfaction. By no means, however, did the secretary of state's quiet tenacity in sustaining the nation's position in Hawaii and Samoa redeem the administration in the eyes of the more aggressive economic expansionists. Cleveland and Bayard had not initiated anything resembling a comprehensive foreign policy to supplant the vigorous and politically attractive programs of earlier Republican administrations. At best their actions, when they acted at all, were construed as a rather limpid, pale facsimile of previous commitments to extend American power and influence in the hemisphere and in the Pacific. All too frequently the administration appeared to move belatedly, and only after the path had been well traversed by such members of the Senate Foreign Relations Committee as John T. Morgan of Alabama, John Sherman of Ohio, and George Edmunds of Vermont.[26]

To some extent, and most certainly with respect to the Pearl Harbor amendment, this was true in the successful struggle for the renewal of the Hawaiian reciprocity agreement. Both Cleveland and Bayard supported an extension of the treaty, primarily in recognition of its overriding political and strategic advantages. The president had not withdrawn the Hawaiian treaty when he scrapped the Arthur-Frelinghuysen Caribbean reciprocity agreements. Bayard privately attempted to persuade William R. Morrison, Democratic member of the House from Illinois and a leading critic of Hawaiian reciprocity, to support renewal. The commercial aspects of the treaty were dismissed immediately by Bayard as "infinitely unimportant in comparison with the political interests involved." The secretary of state made no attempt to deny the "obvious selfishness" of the California sugar interests. Instead, he drew Morrison's attention to Article 4 of the 1875 treaty, which restricted the Hawaiian government from extending any lease or lien "upon any port, harbor, or other territory in their dominions, or grant any special privilege or rights of use therein to any other power, state or government." Bayard also appealed to Morrison's sense of party loyalty and concluded by virtually pleading with the Illinois Congressman "not to allow a commercial question to outweigh political considerations so important as I believe the control of these contiguous Islands on our Pacific Coast to be now, and still more so to be in the near future."[27] Morrison was immovable. He consistently maintained the treaty must be "undone," for "if we have any political rights in the Pacific they should be ours without hiring or paying for them."[28]

Bayard and Cleveland may have strongly disagreed with the

Republicans—and especially with James G. Blaine, the most recent GOP standard-bearer and nominal party head—on such issues as the tariff and ship subsidies. But on the question of the importance of Hawaii to the realization of an American Pacific empire there existed bipartisan agreement. Bayard echoed his predecessor Blaine by characterizing Hawaii as "of essential importance to us on every score" and by expressing similar fears concerning European encroachments in the Hawaiian group. In his arguments urging renewal, Bayard, who as a senator had voted for the 1875 agreement, approvingly noted that the treaty had prevented Great Britain and the other maritime powers from gaining "a foothold" in the islands.[29] Public endorsement for the renewal effort came from President Cleveland in his 1886 annual message. Cleveland believed the reciprocity treaty of 1875 had converted Hawaii into "virtually an outpost of American commerce and a stepping-stone to the growing trade of the Pacific." It would be folly to abrogate the treaty, relinquish the paramount influence the United States had acquired, and leave the way open for the nation's commercial competitors to establish a stronghold there. Accordingly, the president recommended the treaty be continued for another seven years.[30]

Traditionally, American leaders had linked the positive strategic and political gains to be acquired from a treaty with Hawaii to what was essentially a negative motivation for action—the danger that if the United States spurned this opportunity a European power would sweep in to take possession of the islands. As would be expected, the figure most often seen looming on the horizon was that of Great Britain, the national bugbear. This was the thrust of the testimony of the American minister to Hawaii, Henry A. Pierce, before the Senate Committee on Foreign Relations, in support of the original treaty. "Refuse the treaty," argued Pierce, and "necessity will drive the islanders to seek for more intimate political and commercial relations with the British colonies of [British] Columbia, New Zealand, Fee Jee [sic], and Australia, and to eventuate, in the Hawaiian Islands becoming also a colony of the British Crown." But, accept the treaty and there "cannot be a doubt that the effect will be to hold those islands with hooks of steel in the interests of the United States, and to result finally in their annexation to the United States."[31] Similar arguments, including the ever-present apprehensions over British designs, had been

aired in virtually every favorable speech during the congressional
debate over the 1875 treaty.[32]

This line of reasoning lost none of its appeal in the fight over
renewal. Actually, it picked up momentum as the result of rumors
concerning a $2 million Hawaiian loan to be floated in London.
Speculation persisted that Britain intended to make the islands, via
a reciprocity treaty with Canada, the lynchpin of its Pacific imperial network stretching from British Columbia to New Zealand and
Australia. Secretary of State Bayard eventually was assured by the
Hawaiian government that no financial transaction that granted
any European power political leverage was contemplated. However,
the Canadian threat continued, in the form of the Canadian Pacific
Railway and its announced plans to establish a steamship line to
Hawaii and the British Pacific colonies.[33] Lobbyists, among them
George Boutwell, a former secretary of the treasury working for
Boston interests supporting renewal of the treaty, relied on this
point in their propaganda efforts, as did some western interests,
including a contingent of ship builders, ship owners, and lumber
merchants of the Pacific Coast states.[34]

Ironically, and almost as if each power was acting on a mirror
image of its rival, Great Britain had perceived since the 1850s virtually every American diplomatic move as a prelude to annexation.
The British perception was perhaps a closer approximation to
reality than the corresponding American analysis of events.[35] The
English had complained bitterly about the 1875 Hawaiian
reciprocity treaty, with its installation of the conditional most-
favored-nation clause. Their main objection was that it denied Britain the opportunity of securing the identical privileges and benefits
granted to the United States. Blaine's inclusion of Hawaii in the
American system in 1881, with its extension of the Monroe Doctrine to the Pacific, was apprehensively noted. The Foreign Office
allowed the matter to ride, keeping close watch, however, on both
American moves and the state of Hawaiian opinion concerning
annexation to the United States.[36] British Commissioner James H.
Wodehouse, responding to a query from Lord Salisbury, reported
on American objectives in late 1885 by observing that "it would
seem, therefore, as if the idea of annexing these islands had never
been entirely given up by the United States government."[37] Competition and rivalry also arose over the question of cable rights for
a connection from the North American continent to Australia and
the Far East. The Foreign Office, in addition to attempting to pre-

vent the United States from gaining the upper hand, devoted its energies to keeping the way open for concessions to Canada.[38]

Britain's fears and suspicions concerning American annexationist ambitions in Hawaii bubbled to the surface again in 1887 when the Senate finally approved renewal of the reciprocity treaty. What upset the British most was an amendment in the new agreement granting the United States exclusive use of Pearl Harbor as a naval station. This addition was the handiwork of such members of the Foreign Relations Committee as George F. Edmunds; William M. Evarts; William P. Frye, the Blaine protege from Maine; future President Benjamin Harrison; and, of course, that dedicated Democratic expansionist, John T. Morgan of Alabama. Cleveland and Bayard originally opposed the Pearl Harbor amendment, but came to accept the provision by interpreting it not as a permanent territorial concession but as a lease that could be terminated if the treaty lapsed.[39] This interpretation eventually placated Great Britain as well, but only after the Foreign Office pressed the Hawaiian government for guarantees that the concession would not jeopardize its independence and neutrality. The British minister to Washington, Sir Lionel Sackville-West, also invited the United States to participate in a joint declaration with England and Germany to guarantee the "neutrality and equal accessibility of the islands and their harbors to the ships of all nations without preference."[40] Bayard rejected the proposal out of hand, citing existing American agreements providing protection for Hawaiian territory as being sufficient.

The United States pretensions in the Pacific also rankled Count Herbert Bismarck, son of the Iron Chancellor, who during the summer of 1887 warned Lord Salisbury that "the Americans would have to be restrained in every possible way." "They appeared now," the German diplomat complained, "to interpret the Monroe Doctrine as though the Pacific Ocean were to be treated as an American Lake." The American government intended "to bring under their exclusive influence not only Hawaii" but Samoa and the Tonga Islands as well to provide "stages between the future Panama Canal and Australia." Salisbury feigned indifference concerning Hawaii, but perked up when Bismarck ominously spoke of American visions of a "Republican brotherhood" linking the United States and the Australian colonies. After a brief, thoughtful pause, he conceded to the count that "we must keep a sharp eye on American fingers."[41]

Undoubtedly, Count Bismarck's blunt remarks reflected German chagrin over the hard line taken at the recently recessed Washington conference by Secretary of State Bayard. The Cleveland administration favored a formula for retaining the three-power control of Samoa that had originated at the opening of the decade. Because of its growing economic preponderance in the islands, Germany felt entitled to exclusive influence and sought sanction in its bid for hegemony from Great Britain and the United States. This German claim was based on a realpolitik division of the imperial booty of the Pacific, in which American dominance in the Hawaiian Islands was acknowledged. Britain would have the Tongas. Samoa would go to Germany. England appeared willing to accept such a scheme, but the United States had other plans that were contingent on "absolute equality of treatment in respect of commerce, navigation, jurisdiction and other matters" for the three treaty powers.[42] The Germans were probably bemused by this curious American double standard. The United States refused to grant just such equal guarantees in Hawaii, an area where it held the upper hand, but expected Germany to accede to such demands for equal treatment in Samoa, where it held the dominant position.

The Bayard formula in defense of equal opportunity quite clearly was designed to preserve America's foothold in the Samoan Islands.[43] Bayard presented several reasons for his contention that the United States deserved parity with the other powers. To begin with, the United States had been the first power to conclude a treaty with the Samoan government. Second, American interests in Samoa were as great if not greater than any other power. Finally, the islands were "less remote from the United States than from Great Britain or Germany," and "these two countries have already acquired" any outposts they might need. Perhaps the most important consideration for Bayard was the fact that Samoa lay "in a pathway of a commerce that is just being developed." With the "opening of the west coast of North America to civilization and commerce by means of the transcontinental railways" the group became even more crucial to the dream of American penetration of the Far East.[44]

Nothing was resolved at the Washington Conference of 1887,

and German-American relations remained tense for the balance of the Cleveland administration. At times the rivalry over Samoa verged on the brink of an open conflict. That it was a diplomatic tussle for high imperial stakes was succinctly pinpointed by Alvey Adee, an old hand at the State Department. The islands, while "remote and inconsiderable for Germany," were vital to the United States "for in the hands of a naval power they threaten our Pacific flank." Adee feared the recently secured advantage in Hawaii would be neutralized, for "Samoa offsets Pearl Harbor, and Bismarck so intends it."[45] The usually reserved, cool Bayard was extremely agitated and privately denounced the German government's support of "the merciless greed of the German Trading Company" in Samoa. Even more telling was his pique with Great Britain for the early support given to Germany in its push for dominance in those islands. Bayard complained to George Pendleton, the American minister to Berlin, that Britain's lack of "honorable frankness towards the United States in the Samoan affair" was "disappointing and displeasing."[46]

Eventually, Bayard's tenacity was rewarded. To avoid a conflict Chancellor Bismarck proposed that the powers convene again in Berlin in an attempt to resolve the issue. Although the negotiations took place after Benjamin Harrison had moved into the White House, the resulting tripartite agreement between Germany, Great Britain, and the United States was nonetheless a victory for the Bayard formula.[47] Above all, German ambitions had been successfully checked and American influence in Samoa was unaltered, if not enhanced. In addition to the convenient double standard concerning equal access and equal rights in the Hawaiian and Samoan island groups, the episode clearly revealed two other aspects of America's budding imperial thrust in the Pacific. To begin with, the spurt of anti-German feeling among American leaders, and to some degree the nation at large, indicated that while Great Britain normally was the target of the frustrations and anxieties of the expansionist-minded, any European power that threatened to block the American imperial path was subject to outbursts of nationalistic wrath. The other characteristic reflected the American sense of mission and destiny. It was a vision that above all was myopic and ethnocentric, and that recognized only European threats to native integrity, self-determination, and independence. Generally speaking, Americans were indifferent or perhaps oblivious to such expressions of nationalism as "Hawaii for Hawaiians" at a time when "America for Americans" was the rallying cry of many in the United States.

The momentary flare-up in German-American relations, with its trace of anti-German feeling, failed to supplant or diminish the prevailing anti-British nationalism of the period. In 1886—1887, as the movement for restrictions on alien ownership was cresting, several other issues, including silver, the tariff, the Newfoundland fisheries question, and the Bering Sea seal controversy, kept the anti-British cauldron boiling. Increasingly, the Republicans, who sniffed political victory in the winds and who sensed the vulnerability of Cleveland on the issue, capitalized on the existing hostility for Britain. Twisting the lion's tail became standard political practice as the presidential contest of 1888 drew closer, and the campaign itself was a display of Anglophobia unrivalled and unprecedented in a national election. The problem of the northeastern fisheries, long an irritant to Anglo-American diplomacy, appeared on the scene in the form of the newly negotiated Bayard-Chamberlain Treaty. The Republicans blatantly exploited the fisheries issue to defeat Cleveland in 1888. The president supplied additional ammunition to the GOP, and inadvertently contributed to the anti-British hysteria, by choosing the tariff as his battleground for the upcoming campaign. Also, an extradition treaty with Great Britain, which had been dormant for over two years, aroused Irish-Americans because it included a dynamite clause that was believed aimed at Irish nationalists and advocates of home rule. This interpretation prevailed despite a disclaimer in the treaty that no fugitive would be surrendered if his offense was "one of a political character."[48] Finally, British minister Sackville-West fueled the fires of Anglophobia when he blundered into a trap set by a Republican partisan and endorsed the Democratic ticket.

The Rosebery-Phelps extradition treaty, which a majority of both parties in the Senate rejected shortly after the election in early 1889,[49] was employed to political effect. However, it was the Bayard-Chamberlain treaty that undeniably had the greater impact and truly enlivened the campaign. This most recent dispute over

the northeastern fisheries broke out in 1885 after the expiration
of an existing settlement led to numerous seizures of American vessels by Canadian authorities. The Congress responded to the
Canadian actions in March of 1887 by adopting retaliatory
legislation that authorized the president to deny American waters
to Canadian fishermen if he found that American fishermen were
being discriminated against. Cleveland refused to use the retaliatory
club provided him by Congress. Instead, he sought to settle the
issue through the negotiation of a new treaty. It proved to be a
diplomatic move that from the start brought no end of abuse to
the administration for pursuing a pro-British policy.

The English government added to the furor by designating
Joseph Chamberlain, opponent of Irish home rule and anathema
to American Irish, as its principal negotiator. From the beginning
Chamberlain, who was extended special security protection while
in the United States, encountered considerable hostility. Shortly
after President Cleveland submitted the treaty to the Senate in February 1888, he complained to a Philadelphia audience about the
attitude and feelings of Americans: "We are treated as though we
were a foreign and rival nation." A British advocate of a special
Anglo-American relationship, Chamberlain was "astonished" by
the extent to which most Americans believed English policy to be
"a malignity" and "duplicity."[50] The Senate's rough treatment of
his diplomatic handiwork, and the pervading anti-British tone of
the election campaign, further demonstrated the depth of American
aversion to his country and its diplomacy.

In an unprecedented and openly political maneuver the Repub-
lican-controlled Senate voted to consider the fisheries treaty in open
executive session. Almost automatically the debate over an international agreement was injected with the rancor and acrimony of a
bitterly partisan national presidential canvass. The idea for open
debate originated with Harrison Holt Riddleberger, a Readjuster
from Virginia aligned with the Republicans and one of the most
rabid Anglophobes in the Senate. An implacable foe of Secretary
Bayard, who he considered little more than a British toady, Riddleberger attacked the treaty as further proof that the Cleveland administration was "a pro-English organization." During the Senate
debate he also pugnaciously announced that the United States "will
never be a national government until we have whipped England for

the third time."[51] Riddleberger earlier had emerged as the darling of the *Irish World* and a throng of Irish-Americans. He had become their favorite through his repeated attacks on the extradition treaty and his opposition to a resolution, offered in January 1885 by the then Senator Bayard, deploring the dynamiting tactics of Irish nationalists. Despite his popularity among the Irish, Riddleberger's hostility is not explained simply as a matter of trying to capture the Irish vote, which was negligible in Virginia. Perhaps his anti-British nationalism stemmed more from a Readjuster's resentment of the English creditors who held a large percentage of Virginia's debt, and who were identified as contributing to the financial woes of the state.[52]

To be sure, several other senators followed Riddleberger's Anglophobic lead in voicing their dissatisfaction with the fisheries treaty. But some, including John Sherman, chairman of the Foreign Relations Committee and an advocate of Canadian annexation, rejected the more outlandish and militant anti-British blasts in favor of what was to become the main GOP argument against ratification. The Republicans charged that Cleveland had overstepped his constitutional authority by appointing the commissioners to negotiate the treaty without first securing the approval of the Senate. This constitutional objection was repeatedly made in Senate speeches and the majority report of the Foreign Relations Committee thoroughly discussed the extent of this threat to senatorial perogatives in treaty-making. More revealing, however, was the Republican penchant for drifting from a discussion of the constitutional issue to a general denunciation of the pro-English, free trade proclivities of the Cleveland administration and which culminated in the charge that the Democrats pursued "a British economic policy." Even John Sherman, who at one point in the debate admonished his more vocal anti-British colleagues with a quote from Washington's Farewell Address warning against "habitual hatred" of any nation, found it difficult to resist the opportunity to score political points. The majority report of the Foreign Relations Committee, which he signed, contained the unsupported claim that "the President of the United States may be under influence of foreign and adverse interests."[53]

The Democrats on the committee led by Morgan of Alabama rejected the Republican contentions and documented in their minority report the number of previous cases in which presidents had made similar appointments without prior approval of the Senate.[54] In the Senate debate the Democrats also attempted to demonstrate the merits of the treaty, which they believed were considerable and most equitable to the United States. But it was to no avail, for the Republicans merely dragged out the inevitable and extracted as much political advantage as possible from the issue before they rejected the treaty. President Cleveland, however, had a surprise in store for the Republicans and once again revealed that two could play the game of manipulating foreign policy questions for domestic political profit. Almost immediately after the treaty was defeated, the president, in a bristling, nationalistic special message, asked Congress for broad retaliatory legislation that would "maintain the high standard and the becoming pride of American citizenship."[55] Of course Cleveland had outmaneuvered the Republicans and was applauded throughout the land for his courageous stand, but it was to be an ephemeral victory.

The Republicans in Congress refused to go along with Cleveland's request, and no additional retaliatory legislation was passed. Instead, the GOP, temporarily placed on the defense by the president's strong stand, continued to pound away at the tariff issue. They relied on the methods and tactics originated by the Carey group in the late 1860s and early 1870s and perfected over almost two decades of political campaigns. James Swank, president of the American Iron and Steel Association and a Carey disciple, directed the attack against the "free trade" Democrats by flooding the nation with protectionist pamphlets. The favorite theme of these polemical tracts was that "the free-traders are working for England and the English people," and that "the protectionists are working for America and the American people."[56] Actually, President Cleveland had handed the Republicans a ready-made issue for the campaign when he devoted his entire 1887 annual message to a call for revision of the tariff. James G. Blaine had immediately pounced on this opening in his famous "Paris letter," which served as the clarion call for the Republican onslaught. And in an interview with the English journalist George Smalley, Blaine reiterated the equation of the Democratic party as the pro-British party when he noted the London newspapers "all assume to declare the message is a free trade manifesto and evidently are anticipating an enlarged market for English fabrics in the United States as a consequence of the President's recommendations. Perhaps that fact stamped the character of the message more clearly than any words of mine can."[57] It was the same old, hackneyed—albeit still relatively effective—approach: tariff reform meant free trade and continued British dominance.

One Republican, George Osgoodby of California, worried over the impact of Cleveland's retaliatory message. He was unwilling to depend solely on the tariff issue to guarantee a victory for the GOP candidate, Benjamin Harrison, and so sought to neutralize the issue and win back thousands of voters who had gravitated to the Democrats. Osgoodby wrote to Sir Lionel Sackville-West, using the pseudonym Charles Murchison and posing as a naturalized American of English extraction who was perplexed as to whether he should cast a ballot for Cleveland in light of his recent hostile stand toward Great Britain. Was the president's policy "temporary only," inquired Murchison, and would he, if reelected, "suspend it for one of friendship and free trade?" Minister Sackville-West stupidly fell for the ruse and took the bait—hook, line, and sinker. He replied that while it was "impossible to predict the course which President Cleveland may pursue in the matter of retaliation should he be elected," there was "every reason to believe that, while upholding the position he has taken, he will manifest a spirit of conciliation in dealing with the question involved in his message."[58] As if that were not enough, Sackville-West, after the Republicans had gleefully published the letter, told a reporter that he realized the rejection of the fisheries treaty by the Senate and Cleveland's retaliation message were both political maneuvers. The entire episode served to hammer home the Republican charge that Cleveland and the Democrats were nothing more than the accomplices and lackeys of England. However, even with Minister Sackville-West's unintended aid, Harrison and the Republicans barely squeaked past Cleveland in the November election.

The Harrison victory signalled a return to the strident economic nationalism and vigorous support for expansion of overseas markets that had characterized earlier Republican administrations. While Cleveland and Bayard definitely had sustained the American outward thrust, their variety of overseas economic expansion provided for considerably less direct government support and was markedly more constrained vis à vis Great Britain. In one area, perhaps, the Cleveland administration, under the guidance of Secretary of the Navy William C. Whitney, did match the efforts of the Republicans—by supporting the development of a strong navy.[59] And, in the last months of his tenure Cleveland did issue a call for a Pan-American conference to convene in 1889, although the main impetus had come from congressional supporters of such a meeting. By and large, however, the first Cleveland administration was a disappointment to economic expansionists and advocates of American hegemony in the Western Hemisphere.

NOTES

1. Views of Mr. Belmont in *Participation of the United States in the Congo Conference,* House Report No. 2655, 48th Cong., 2nd Sess., 1885 (Washington: Government Printing Office, 1885), p. 16.

2. *Democratic Campaign Book, 1884* (New York: National Democratic Committee, 1884), pp. 6−7.

3. Newspaper clipping of Bayard speech to Iroquois Club of Chicago, October 13, 13, 1884, Bayard Papers, Library of Congress.

4. Ibid., William L. Scruggs to Bayard, April 24, 1885; A.M. Gibson to Thomas Lamont, April 19, 1885.

5. See, for example, William L. Scruggs, "Blundering American Diplomacy," *North American Review,* Vol. 145 (September 1887), pp. 313−18.

6. Samuel Latham Mitchell Barlow to Marble, February 26, 1885, Marble Papers, Library of Congress.

7. Thomas J. Jarvis to Bayard, September 2, 1885, Bayard Papers.

8. Ibid., William Ellinger to Bayard, August 20, 1885.

9. See letter of Secretary Bayard in *Report of the Select Committee on American Ship-Building and Ship-Owning Interests,* House Report No. 3470, 49th Cong., 1st Sess., 1886 (Washington: Government Printing Office, 1886).

10. James D. Richardson, *Messages and Papers of the Presidents VIII* (Washington: Government Printing Office, 1898), p. 327.

11. Bayard to Wells, May 1, 1885, Bayard Papers.

12. Ibid., Memoranda of interviews with Mr. Muruaga, the Spanish Minister, December 13, 1886, September 21, 1887; Memo of interview with Mr. Lainfiesta, the Guatemalan minister, November 18, 1887.

13. Ibid., Memoranda of interviews with Minister Velasco, January 14, 28, 1887.

14. Daniel Manning to Marble, April 29, 1885; Bayard to Marble, April 30, 1885, Marble Papers, Library of Congress. For a fine discussion of Cleveland's use of foreign policy for domestic ends, see John A. S. Grenville and George B. Young, *Politics, Strategy, and American Diplomacy* (New Haven: Yale University Press, 1966), pp. 44−51.

15. Marble may have been serious in his pursuit of international bimetallism. See George T. McJimsey, "The Life of Manton Marble," (Ph.D. dissertation, University of Wisconsin, 1968).

16. Robert M. McElroy, *Grover Cleveland, The Man and the Statesman* (New York: Harper & Brothers, 1923), I, pp. 107−9.

17. Richardson, *Messages and Papers,* VIII p. 346.

18. William A. Williams, *The Roots of the Modern American Empire* (New York: Random House, 1969), p. 307.

19. *Western Rural*, November 21, 1885, August 15, October 24, 1885, May 1, 1886.

20. Williams, *Roots of American Empire*, p. 307.

21. *The First Annual Report of the Commissioner of Labor, Industrial Depressions*, 1886 (Washington: Government Printing Office, 1886), pp. 247–48.

22. Remarks of April 7, 1886, *Congressional Record*, XIX, Part 3, p. 3207 (hereinafter cited as *CR*, 19:3:3207).

23. Ibid., Remarks of March 8, 1886, p. 2180.

24. Ibid., Remarks of Richard Coke, January 13, 1886, 19:1:633.

25. Ibid., Remarks of April 7, 1886, Appendix, p. 81.

26. Owen L. Burnette, Jr., "The Senate Foreign Relations Committee and the Diplomacy of Garfield, Arthur, and Cleveland," (Ph.D. dissertation, University of Virginia, 1952), pp. 383–92.

27. Bayard to Morrison, March 16, 1886, Bayard Papers.

28. Ibid., Morrison to Bayard, March 16, 1886.

29. Ibid., Bayard to Morrison, March 16, 1889.

30. Richardson, *Messages and Papers*, VIII, pp. 500–1.

31. Henry A. Pierce to Hamilton Fish, January 12, 1875, *Despatches from United States Ministers to Hawaii, 1843 – 1900*, Roll 17, Vol. 17, Records of the Department of State, National Archives, Record Group 59.

32. Chalfant Robinson, *A History of Two Reciprocity Treaties* (New Haven: Tuttle, Morehouse and Taylor Press, 1904), pp. 131–40. J. Lawrence Laughlin and H. Parker Willis, *Reciprocity* (New York: The Baker & Taylor Co., 1903), pp. 74–83.

33. Sylvester K. Stevens, *American Expansion in Hawaii* (Harrisburg: Archives Publishing Company of Pennsylvania, Inc., 1945), p. 174; and Charles C. Tansill, *The Foreign Policy of Thomas F. Bayard* (New York: Fordham University Press, 1940) pp. 378–79. The United States made an unofficial inquiry to the Foreign Office desiring to know if the Canadian government planned to subsidize a line of mail steamers between Vancouver and the Far East. The reply was negative. See Colonial Office to High Commissioner of Canada, May 26, 1886, Foreign Office 5, Vol. 1953, Public Record Office, London (hereinafter cited as F.O. 5/1953 P.R.O.).

34. George S. Boutwell, *The Reciprocity Treaty with Hawaii; Some Considerations Against Its Abrogation* (Washington: Judd and Detweiler, 1886). Petition by Ship Builders, Ship Owners, and Lumber Merchants of Pacific Coast States, Committee on Foreign Affairs, 49th Cong., records of the House of Representatives, National Archives, Record Group 233.

35. For a discussion of British reactions to American Pacific diplomacy in the 1870s, see W.D. McIntyre, "Anglo-American Rivalry in the Pacific: The British Annexation of the Fiji Islands in 1874," *Pacific Historical Review*, XXIX (November, 1960), pp. 361–80.

36. For example, see E. Hertslet memo respecting American designs on the Hawaiian Islands, January 8, 1883, F.O. 5/1844 P.R.O.

37. James H. Wodehouse to Salisbury, December 19, 1885, F.O. 115/775 P.R.O.

38. Colonial Office to Foreign Office, June 30, 1886, F.O. 5/1952 P.R.O.

39. Tansill, *Foreign Policy of Bayard,* pp. 380—98. Stevens, *American Expansion,* p. 184. Burnette argues that Bayard was being coy because he feared Hawaii would balk at the Pearl Harbor amendment and so the secretary did not support it publicly, "Foreign Relations Committee," pp. 384—85.

40. Ibid., Tansill, p. 399.

41. Memo of Count Herbert Bismarck, August 24, 1887, in E.T.S. Dugdale, *German Diplomatic Documents, 1871 — 1914,* Vol. I. (London: Methuen & Co., Ltd., 1928), p. 244.

42. Protocol of Second Samoan Conference, July 2, 1887, p. 11, Bayard Papers.

43. Ibid. See comment of Harold Marsh Sewell, the American agent sent to Samoa, to Bayard, November 7, 1887.

44. Ibid., Protocol of conference, p. 4.

45. Tansill, *Foreign Policy of Bayard,* p. 81.

46. Bayard to Pendleton, October 13, 28, 1887, Bayard Papers.

47. Tansill, *Foreign Policy of Bayard,* p. 119.

48. *Foreign Relations of the United States, 1888,* Part II (Washington: Government Printing Office, 1889), pp. 1739—43.

49. W. Stull Holt, *Treaties Defeated by the Senate* (Baltimore: The John Hopkins Press, 1933), p. 143.

50. Joseph Chamberlain, *Foreign and Colonial Speeches* (London: George Routledge & Sons, Ltd., 1897), p. 17.

51. Remarks of August 2, 1888, *CR,* 19:8:7155—7.

52. Letters of various Irish groups sent to Riddleberger, Harrison Holt Riddleberger Papers, Swem Library, College of William and Mary. On the question of foreign ownership of bonds see: William L. Royall, *Some Reminiscences* (New York: Neal Publishing Co., 1909), p. 118, and C. Vann Woodward, *Origins of the New South, 1877 — 1913* (Baton Rouge: Louisiana State University Press, 1951), p. 102.

53. *Majority Report of the Committee on Foreign Relations on the Fisheries Treaty,* Senate Misc. Doc. No. 109, 50th Cong., 1st Sess., 1888 (Washington: Government Printing Office, 1888), p. 17.

54. Ibid., Minority Report of the Committee on Foreign Relations on the Fisheries Treaty, pp. 110—34.

55. Richardson, *Messages and Papers,* VIII, p. 627.

56. E.P. Miller, *Fallacies of Free Trade* (New York: American Protective Tariff League, 1888) in collection of protection and free trade pamphlets, Wisconsin State Historical Society.

57. *New York Tribune,* December 8, 1887.

58. *Irish World,* November 3, 1888.

59. Harold and Margaret Sprout, *The Rise of American Naval Power 1776 — 1918* (Princeton: Princeton University Press, 1939), p. 189.

8

America's Commercial Crusade

What we want, then, are the markets of these neighbors of ours that lie to the south of us. We want the $400,000,000 annually which to-day go to England, France, Germany and other countries. With these markets secured new life would be given to our manufactories, the product of the Western farmer would be in demand, the reasons for and inducements to strikers, with all their attendant evils would cease.

James G. Blaine, 1886

I am thoroughly discontent with the present condition of things. We may differ as to methods, but I believe the great patriotic heart of people is stirred, and that they are bent upon recovering that share of the world's commerce which we once happily enjoyed.

Benjamin Harrison, 1891

I believe it is the duty of the national government to take such steps as will restore the American merchant marine . . . . The Nicaragua Canal should be completed. Our harbors should have adequate defence. We should have upon the sea a navy of first-class ships.

Benjamin Harrison, 1891

This [is] the era of the battle for a market.

Benjamin Harrison, 1891

The return to power of the Republican party in 1889 under the leadership of Benjamin Harrison and James G. Blaine marked the renewal of America's crusade to conquer the markets of the world. Despite Harrison's initial reluctance to appoint Blaine as secretary of state, and his uneasiness over Blaine's personal political ambitions,[1] both men agreed upon the broad strategy of economic expansion pursued by previous Republican administrations. Harrison announced during the campaign that "we do not mean to be content with our own market," and promised that his administration would "seek to promote closer and more friendly commercial relations with the Central and South American States."[2] Blaine earlier had pressed America's economic and political interests in the Western Hemisphere and the Pacific while briefly directing the nation's foreign policy under President Garfield. Confident that the United States would dominate the century about to dawn, Blaine characteristically revealed his economic nationalism when he congratulated Harrison upon his selection as the Republican presidential nominee: "Your election will seal our industrial independence as the Declaration of '76 . . . saved our political independence."[3]

Despite their oft-repeated formal expressions of confidence in their own economic power, and their tendency to dismiss those who warned of American competition as alarmists and Jeremiahs, the British were becoming increasingly uneasy over the American threat to their trade position.[4] Blaine's return to power accentuated that concern. As a leading English journal unhappily noted upon reading President Harrison's inaugural address, "the impress of Mr. Blaine's mind is upon every line. . . . Foreign nations are warned, in terms noteworthy for their haughty simplicity, to keep their hands off the American continents, and more especially off South America."[5] This blunt reassertion of the Monroe Doctrine by the new administration plainly confirmed British suspicions that "the Government of Washington assumes a protectorate of all South America."[6]

A worldwide struggle for markets raged during the last decades of the nineteenth century as Great Britain, the acknowledged leader at the start of this race for commercial primacy, faced strong challenges from Germany and the United States. Beginning in the late 1870s, and then throughout the 1880s, British leaders closely observed the American trade phenomenon and readily perceived the nature of the United States' challenge to their supremacy. Apprehension over Britain's declining trade position was especially widespread in the industrial midlands; Joseph Chamberlain of Birmingham was perhaps the most ardent spokesman for the hard-pressed British manufacturer. However, not all English observers worried over the United States trade assault. Sir Robert Giffen, Board of Trade official who acknowledged that the American economic onslaught was "great and conspicuous," denigrated the threat of foreign competition and confidently expected Britain to retain its commercial position.[7]

The optimism of such as Giffen could not conceal the obvious: Britain was losing ground to its chief competitors, the United States and Germany. In the years 1870–1871 through 1913 industrial production increased at the rate of 4.7 percent per annum for the United States and 4.1 percent for Germany, while Great Britain lagged at 2.1 percent. The American advance was even more striking in terms of total output: the United States expanded at the rate of 4.3 percent per year while Germany and Great Britain trailed at 2.9 and 2.2 percent, respectively. The story was similar in the growth of exports. Germany led in the years 1880–1913 with a 4.3 percent increase per year, the United States followed at 3.2 percent, while the rate of expansion of British exports fell to 2.2 percent per annum.[8] The German and American trade assault loomed particularly menacing because in the last third of the nineteenth century Britain suffered from recurrent economic depression, partially as a result of the decline in its share of the world's markets. As many Englishmen recognized, the battle for a market was at least three-cornered, and America was not an inconsequential participant.

The English could take some comfort, however, from the fact that Great Britain provided the principal market for American agricultural surpluses. The United States exported $123 million of breadstuffs in 1889, of which $73,800,800 million (or approximately 60 percent) was taken by Great Britain. In addition, the United Kingdom bought about two-thirds of American meat and dairy exports, and more than two-thirds of the cotton exported. These items formed three-fifths of the total exports of the United States.[9] This close connection to, and virtual dependence on, the British market had troubled and psychologically irritated American farmers for at least two decades. They denounced the price monopoly such a trade relationship bestowed upon the Liverpool and London commodity markets and supported various proposals to secure alternate markets for their exports. Understandably, enthusiasm for Blaine's announced plan of reciprocity to open Latin American markets for the nation's agricultural surpluses spread like wildfire through the western states.[10]

In an 1885 report to the Foreign Office, Sir Lionel Sackville-West, the British minister to Washington, explicitly defined the role of agricultural exports in the economic and political life of the United States. American prosperity, explained Sackville-West, depended "upon a profitable market for its surplus agricultural produce, and when, as at present, this market is wanting, the Western farmer must necessarily forego his present social status."[11] Poor harvests in Europe were no longer a sure cure for low agricultural exports, and the decreased share of the world market caused by the competition of the cheap labor of India and Russia exposed a domestic crisis which "must inevitably produce a conflict between the Western and Eastern States, which latter, under a restrictive tariff, have amassed wealth at the expense of the former by enhancing the cost of material life."[12] Sackville-West not only correctly analyzed the nature of the agrarian upheaval of the 1890s, but he also anticipated the central problem that nagged the Harrison administration and ultimately shaped American foreign policy during those years.

Sackville-West expected a movement for free trade to resolve the problem of agricultural surpluses and ameliorate agrarian discontent. He badly underestimated, as he did in connection with the Murchison letter in the 1888 campaign, the flexibility of the Republicans in meeting the challenge to their political position posed by the western farmers. Throughout the campaign, Harrison repeatedly defended the principle of the protective tariff. After the election, he and Blaine adopted a policy of reciprocity. A device traditionally viewed as a weapon in the free trade arsenal, reciprocity allowed the GOP to expand foreign markets without violating the policy of protection. It retained all the advantages of protection at home while providing the advantages of free trade abroad.

To supplement and support reciprocity, Harrison and Blaine urged a subsidized merchant marine, a new navy, closer ties with the Latin American countries through increased transportation facilities, and the creation of a monetary union. All of those measures were articles of faith in the creed of the economic expansionist. The Harrison administration consolidated the strategy begun in the depression of the 1870s under the direction of Hayes and Evarts, and sustained under Garfield and Arthur. Each successive Republican administration had refined and elaborated the ideology of economic expansion.

Another distinguishable feature of the faith was a certain fear, distrust, and jealousy directed toward Great Britain, the ruling monarch of the world marketplace. While economic expansionists varied widely in the degree and intensity of their anti-British nationalism, hostility for England visibly colored the thinking of most of them. Blaine and Harrison were students of the history of Civil War diplomacy, and to each the historical evidence irrefutably exposed English avarice, duplicity, and cunning. "Within the past year I have been reading . . . the story of our diplomatic relations with England during the Civil War," Harrison explained to an Indianapolis audience in September 1888.[13] The future president charged that the leaders of England had sympathized with the Southern cause in the hope and "expectancy of free trade with the Confederacy," and he read lengthy quotes from James Spence's *The American Union* to prove his point.[14] Spence, an Englishman, had spelled out the advantages for Great Britain in a southern victory. The destruction of the Union would open a vast market in the South and seriously weaken a powerful rival that threatened British supremacy in foreign markets.[15] Great Britain invariably had "attempted to coin commercial advantage out of the distress of other nations." But the Union victory had thwarted England's "commercial greed," Harrison believed, and now the "New South," with its burgeoning cotton textile trade, also was engaged in the industrial rivalry with Great Britain.[16]

Blaine interpreted the British role in an identical manner. The American people had "recognized that England's hand had been against us, concealed somewhat, and used indirectly, but still heavily against us."[17] The English upper classes, and especially the Tory party, had desired the destruction of the Union. In Blaine's mind the English government had been Janus-faced, for its actions belied its formal expressions of amity and cordiality. Particular venom was reserved for Lord Robert Cecil, the Marquis of Salisbury, with whom Blaine had many a memorable diplomatic bout. Salisbury very nearly lost his sanity brooding over the outcome of the American struggle and Blaine noted that "[t]his extraordinary madness may at least be said to have a method": to destroy the Union and eliminate a powerful rival.[18] Blaine never forgot or forgave Salisbury for his active and overt support of the Confederacy.

Reflecting their anti-British nationalism and fully alive to the appeal of such a stance, the Republicans, with Harrison and Blaine in the forefront, twisted the lion's tail throughout the entire 1888 campaign. Posters pictured Cleveland under the British flag while Harrison benignly appeared under the American flag. Republican campaign slogans included "Cleveland runs well in England," and the ever-popular "America for Americans—No Free Trade."[19] At a parade in his honor in Indianapolis at the close of the campaign, Harrison was immensely pleased by the center of attraction, a bull covered with a white cloth carrying the slogan "John Bull Rides the Democratic Party and We Ride John Bull."[20] Cleveland's 1887 tariff message, which had established the major campaign issue, was denounced by Republicans as proof of his truckling to British interests. The GOP was aided considerably by Sackville-West's blunder in publicly favoring Cleveland, which served to nail down the image of the Democrats as the pro-British party. As Blaine wrote Harrison: "Lord Sackville's letter is I think having a wonderful effect upon the Irish here and proves more at the dash of a sentence than we could by argument during the whole campaign."[21] Even with Sackville-West's unthinking help, however, the Republicans won only narrowly, and Cleveland polled a plurality of the popular vote.

The first order of business for the new administration in its desire to improve commercial relations with the countries of Central and South America had been predetermined by the actions of Cleveland. Prior to the election and in response to growing congressional pressure, he had issued a call for a conference of Latin American nations to meet in Washington during 1889.[22] By a quirk of fate,

Blaine again headed the State Department when the long debated—and delayed—Pan-American Conference finally convened. The proposed agenda was inclusive: the subjects were a customs union, inter-American rail and steamship lines, arbitration treaties, trademark and copyright laws, and common silver coins.

The conference itself accomplished very little, even though it did arouse the suspicions of European nations and the representatives of several Latin American states who feared the object was "to secure the political and commercial ascendancy of the United States on this continent."[23] Some British observers attacked it as another example of the Monroe Doctrine being interpreted to mean "America for the United States," and as a poorly disguised attempt to "dictate from Washington the external and even the internal policy of the most important South American States."[24] In a broad sense, the fears of the Latin Americans were justified. For implicit in this drive to establish American commercial hegemony was the creation of economic and political influence and control that would lead to the type of intervention familiar in the twentieth century.

The most important result of the Pan-American Conference for the Harrison administration was the suggestion to use individual reciprocity treaties as a substitute for the impractical customs union. Blaine moved rapidly to realize his dream of capturing the trade of the hemisphere from the British. But the reciprocity campaign had a domestic goal as well. The rumblings from the prairies were threatening the Republican party's supremacy in the key northwest states. The opening of foreign markets via reciprocity, reasoned Harrison and Blaine, would calm the agrarian tempest and overcome the powerful and seductive appeal of the Populists and free silver. A Connecticut judge candidly explained the strategy to fellow Republicans: "Upon Mr. Blaine's platform we can hold our majorities in the great Western States where corn and cattle are raised."[25] More important, reciprocity would open new outlets and thereby dampen the social unrest caused by the recurrent depressions of the late nineteenth century. Blaine explained this relationship:

> What we want, then, are the markets of these neighbors of ours that lie
> to the south of us . . . . With these markets secured new life would be given
> to our manufactories, the product of the Western farmer would be in de-

mand, the reasons for and inducements to strikers with all their attendant evils would cease.[26]

This was the raison d'être of the ideology of economic expansion. Foreign policy, in addition to allowing for control of foreign markets per se, served to alleviate and ameliorate domestic ills; it preserved the existing social order and, not incidentally, furthered the direct political ends of the Republicans.

The McKinley tariff bill was considered in Congress while the International American Conference was in session and the delegates closely followed the debate. Blaine believed the proposals to remove the duties on sugar and coffee, while imposing them on hides and raising those on wool, would preclude the negotiation of successful reciprocity agreements. The secretary was not opposed to free sugar, but he argued that the United States "ought to have, in exchange for free sugar from certain countries, a free market for breadstuffs and provisions."[27] Sugar and coffee would be used as the "crowbars" to pry open the markets of the Central and South American countries, and reciprocity would provide the quid pro quo for access to the American market. He vigorously entered the fray and began an educational campaign to convince the doubters, especially among Republicans, of the viability of reciprocity. The first move was to dissuade Congress from taking hides from the free list; that was "a slap in the face to the South Americans with whom we are trying to enlarge our trade." He pleaded with McKinley to stem the tide, for "movements as this for protection will protect the Republican party into a speedy retirement."[28]

In the conference report submitted to President Harrison, Blaine recommended reciprocity treaties, stressing that the United States would gain the most from the agreements. If wool, hides, and sugar were used as the basis for successful bargaining, the resulting treaties would enlarge the nation's trade with Latin America by diverting the flow of their commerce from Europe to the United States. Opposition to Blaine's scheme arose immediately within the Republican party and, naturally, among the Democrats. Some Republicans felt his plan was contrary to the GOP promise for a "free breakfast table." Among Democratic spokesmen and newspapers, meanwhile, reciprocity was misinterpreted in order to gleefully proclaim that one of the high priests of protection had finally seen the light and had begun to advocate what amounted to free trade policy.[29]

Others, including many Republicans, doubted whether the proposed treaties would actually provide new outlets for American agricultural surpluses. They argued that if the trade was controlled by Great Britain and other European nations, the exports had to be manufactured goods rather than agricultural products. In addition, the South American countries produced many of the same raw materials as the United States, and that implied tougher competition rather than larger markets. Some critics argued that the most-favored-nation clause inserted in many treaties would negate the value of reciprocity. Finally, McKinley and his colleagues were more concerned with protection per se, and were not at that time "looking for enlarged commercial relations with South America or any other countries."[30]

Blaine promptly answered his GOP critics who feared abandonment of the "free breakfast table" promise. Then, in the pages of the *New York Tribune* and the *Chicago Tribune,* the Democrats, and some skeptical Republicans, were instructed that reciprocity was in no way an abandonment of protection: it was "not in conflict with a protective tariff, but supplementary thereto" because "the enactment of reciprocity is the safeguard of protection."[31] In reply to the query of how the United States could sell farm products in South America when the same things were produced there, Blaine pointed out that, while some cereals were grown in the southern countries of South America, "the sugar countries of South and Central America and the West India Islands contain 40,000,000 people who import the largest part of their breadstuffs."[32] Finally, to answer opponents who doubted that it would displace European exports of manufactured goods, Blaine quickly added that reciprocity was not "only a Western interest" for "it will prove beneficial and profitable both to the farm and the shop."[33]

The mechanics of reciprocity were explained by the *Chicago Tribune.* If the duties on breadstuffs and pork were dropped via reciprocity, agricultural exports would increase, which would open the way for increased manufactured exports. It would have the ancillary result of fostering increased American shipping facilities.

At present, Great Britain controlled the carrying trade, which was detrimental to American exports. But if a vessel "found awaiting it at New York a consignment of breadstuffs for Bahia it would take manufactured goods as part of its cargo . . . . Pork and flour will open the way for cotton goods and certain classes of machinery."[34] The lack of shipping had hindered American exports of cotton cloths from making more headway against British textiles in Latin American markets. Happily, reciprocity would benefit the American farmer, open the way for the American manufacturer, and foster the growth of the American merchant marine.

Though the McKinley Tariff Act as finally passed incorporated a reciprocity article, it signified only a partial victory for Blaine. He had doggedly persisted in the Senate after the House had passed the bill without a reciprocity provision. President Harrison aided Blaine in his campaign, and it gained more support from three crucial sources. William McKinley, author of the bill, guided the revised Senate version through the House. Agrarians, particularly flour milling and meat packing groups, jumped on the reciprocity bandwagon, and a significant number of manufacturers' and industrial journals, convinced by Blaine's arguments of the importance of reciprocity, also supported the amendment.[35] Sugar, coffee, hides, and several tropical products were placed on the free list. Reciprocity was reconciled with free sugar by inserting a retaliatory provision that stipulated duties would be restored if the United States was not granted "reciprocal advantages." This retaliatory aspect differed sharply from previous reciprocity agreements, particularly those negotiated during Arthur's administration.

The economic nationalism evident in the McKinley Tariff stunned the British. The staid *Times* of London charged it was an "act of economic war," entirely unprovoked, and denounced it as "a gigantic electioneering job" designed to appeal to Irish-Americans. The *Times* petulantly remarked that the law was particularly galling to British exporters since American agricultural products had unfettered access to the English market.[36] One American in Europe, Titian J. Coffey, disagreed with their analysis of the tariff as simply a political maneuver. He informed the editors (and readers) that protection was the accepted policy of the Republican party, was not an "unfriendly act," and was justified to establish American hegemony in Latin America since Great Britain had appropriated all of unabsorbed Africa and had "not offered your American offspring a share of the 'swag'."[37]

If some American spokesmen defended the bill in terms of overseas commercial expansion, the initial fear of the English was that the new tariff would "strike a heavy blow at British industry."[38] Members of Parliament from the industrial Midlands voiced their concern throughout the summer of 1890 and pressed the Foreign Office to make representations to Washington expressing opposition to the proposed duties. Several cities and towns, including Sheffield, sent resolutions and memorials imploring Lord Salisbury to take action against this declaration of "commercial war." But the Salisbury government politely rejected all such proposals as impractical and an intrusion on the internal affairs of the United States.[39] Official rebuffs aside, the immediate effect of the McKinley Tariff was to resurrect the sagging fortunes of the protectionist movement within the United Kingdom. Shortly after the new duties went into force, Sheffield firms reduced wages by five percent, cutlery firms exporting to America suffered immensely, and the tin plate industry of Wales was all but decimated. More alarming was the notice that "four well-known English textile firms . . . moved a whole or a portion of their plant across the Atlantic." Petitioning for relief from the disastrous impact of the McKinley Act, the Birmingham Chamber of Commerce offered another alternative by suggesting that a monetary conference be held in London and that in return for European and British support for silver the United States ease its tariff policy.[40]

Prime Minister Salisbury pinpointed the British dilemma in a speech at Hastings in May 1891, and in so doing moved toward a policy of protection. Great Britain, he asserted, had stripped itself of any weapons since it would "levy no duties," a policy that may "be noble, but it is not business."[41] Salisbury, foreseeing the future commercial triumph of the United States, informed his nation that "the power we have most reason to complain of is the United States, and what we want the United States to furnish us with mostly are articles of food essential to the feeding of the people, and raw materials necessary to our manufactures, and we cannot exclude one or the other without serious injury to ourselves."[42] While some members of his party moved to support of an imperial preference system, Salisbury campaigned in the 1892 election on a retaliatory and protectionist platform, although fully aware that Britain had little recourse against the United States.[43]

Prior to the passage of the McKinley Tariff, Blaine and the English Liberal leader, William E. Gladstone, publicly exchanged views on the question of protection versus free trade. Gladstone reiterated his earlier prediction that the United States would replace Great Britain in commercial supremacy, but only after adopting free trade "would she outstrip us in the race."[44] The Englishman willingly accepted his own analysis and judgment, for he anticipated only beneficial results for England through expanded commerce and increased wealth. There was little "doubt as to the position of power the United States will assume"; the question of how the Americans would use this power in the future caused Gladstone some anxiety, for he feared the subtle influences of wealth and fame might subvert the American love of freedom.[45]

Blaine disagreed with Gladstone's assumption that the United States must adopt free trade to succeed. The secretary of state argued that the different stages of economic development that prevailed between the two nations necessitated different policies. While free trade might suit Great Britain, protection was best for the United States. He fell back upon the historical analysis of the Careyites by asserting that Britain had maintained protection as long as it was advantageous, moving to a policy of relative free trade only when it became expedient and profitable. If the United States abandoned protection in 1890, it ran the risk of having its trade recolonized by England, and it would become a dependency to "a greater degree than is Canada or Australia to-day." Britain's true design was revealed in Gladstone's comment that the United States "produced more cloth and iron at high prices, instead of more cereals and more cotton at low prices."[46] Thus, Blaine angrily commented: "the mechanic arts and the manufacturing processes should be left to Great Britain and the production of raw materials should be left to America. It is the old colonial idea of the last century."[47] The real basis for English hostility to protection was its detrimental impact on the trade and industry of the United Kingdom, its role in lessening American dependence on Britain, and its threat to the profits of British merchants.

The challenge inherent in the reciprocity article of the McKinley Tariff also excited and vexed British leaders. Not only were the members of the Salisbury government troubled by the possible threat to their trade with the nations of Latin America, they feared as well for the future prosperity of Britain's Caribbean colonies. Early in 1891 the Colonial Office suggested the possibility that some sort of reciprocal arrangement between Canada and the British West Indies be explored by an interdepartmental committee. This tentative step toward an imperial preference scheme was rejected by the Board of Trade on the grounds that Canada would not offer a sufficient market for the West Indies and because such a projected system of differential duties violated free trade principles. Salisbury, displeased with the orthodoxy of the Board of Trade, complained of their effort "to fasten the most rigorous doctrines of the Manchester school not only upon us but upon our colonies." Labelling the situation a "grave matter," he groped for some alternative policy. In the end, however, London abandoned the plan for Canadian—West Indian reciprocity and sanctioned negotiations which led to agreements with the United States for Jamaica, Trinidad, Barbados, Guiana, and the Leeward and Windward islands.[48]

In the discussions between the two governments preceding the conclusion of the treaties, the British opened by asserting that none of the duties levied by the West India colonies were "reciprocally unequal and unreasonable.". Secretary of State Blaine took issue with this claim by exposing a tariff structure that discriminated against American farm products and bore little resemblance to free trade. Taking Jamaica as an example, Blaine pointed out that "the highest rate of duty attaches to agricultural and food products, while . . . the lowest rate of duty is invariably affixed to goods of a high grade of manufacture." In practice this meant that the highest rates were paid on goods from the United States and the lowest on those from Great Britain. That was not all. While the United States offered an "open door" for almost all the products of the West Indies, nearly half of Jamaica's exports to Great Britain were subject to "duties of an enormous character." This, at least to the American secretary of state's satisfaction, explained why "the United States affords a market for 54 per cent of the total exports of Jamaica, and Great Britain for only 34 per cent. But in its import trade the figures are almost exactly reversed, as the consumption of British goods on the Island amounts to 56 per cent of the entire imports, and those of the United States to only 34 per cent."[49]

It was precisely such impediments to American exports that Blaine and other economic expansionists hoped to eliminate via reciprocity. Under the provisions of Article 3 of the McKinley Bill, the United States concluded agreements with all countries in Latin America except Colombia, Haiti, and Venezuela. In addition, the retaliatory aspect forced Germany, Denmark, Austria, and France to repeal their prohibitions on American meat, another gain for the GOP among American farmers.[50] As Cecil Spring-Rice, then secretary to the British legation, wrote to his brother Ferguson: "We must reconcile ourselves to it and look for new markets. A serious aspect of it is the reciprocity clause, which drives us out of the West Indies and South America."[51] Sir Lyon Playfair, hatchetman for the Liberal party in its campaign against the Salisbury government, labelled the reciprocity article a "safety valve" that would prevent protection from "blowing up" American society by securing markets in Latin America and Asia.[52] All of the agonizing by the British amused and pleased Americans. The *Farmers' Voice* happily reported that Britain was "becoming seriously uneasy" over the effectiveness of reciprocity in Latin America.[53]

But the domestic benefits of reciprocity did not appear soon enough to save the GOP. The congressional elections of November 1890, which occurred little over a month after the tariff went into effect, returned the Democrats to control of the House. One Iowa Republican believed Blaine's criticism of the original McKinley Bill did "great harm" to the party's cause. Ultimately he expected reciprocity to win out, although the "distrust" sown among the farmers by the Democrats could prove "dangerous."[54] William McKinley angrily commented that:

> the Democratic victory had its uses. It established beyond dispute or controversy the existence of a partnership between Democratic free trade leaders in the United States and the statesmen and ruling classes of Great Britain . . . they are both for the same unpatriotic cause . . . [a] crusade against our industries.[55]

President Harrison responded to the loss by staging an extended cross-country tour to mend party fences and to keep the farmers

in the fold. The president pointed out to H. B. Kelley, chairman
of the Western States Commercial Congress, that agricultural production had created the "necessity of larger markets," and explained that he looked to reciprocity agreements to furnish "new
and large markets for meats, breadstuffs, and an important line
of manufactured products."[56] Later in the tour he called for a subsidized merchant marine, a strong navy, and a completed Nicaragua
canal. Only then could the United States displace its European rivals in the markets of Latin America. Harrison repeated this theme
in May 1891, at Portland, Oregon, where he declared that government aid was a necessity and "a duty." In Texas the president confided that "I have before me constantly the need of the American
farmer of a larger market for his products."[57]

William E. Chandler, Republican senator from New Hampshire
and secretary of the navy during the Arthur administration, commented to Harrison in June 1891 that England was "our mother"
and should be friendly, but was "our greatest commercial rival."
He advised the president that it was time for Americans as a nation
to "show our teeth."[58] Harrison had complained on the West Coast
that the United States had "been content to see the markets of
these American republics lying south of us mastered and controlled
by European nations." But no more, and the president heeded
Chandler's advice when in August he told Vermont citizens that
it was "the era of the battle for a market."[59] The United States
would not push its "trade forward at the point of the bayonet,"
but Harrison subtly warned the British that:

> Larger foreign markets for the products of our farms and of our factories,
> and a large share in the carrying trade of the world, peaceful relations with
> all mankind, with naval and coast defences that will silently make an effec-
> tive argument on the side of peace, are the policies that I would pursue.[60]

The administration basically adhered to this formula for the
peaceful conquest of hemispheric markets. On at least one occasion, however, Harrison was quite willing for the United States to
bare its teeth. A crisis with Chile erupted in 1891–1892 over a
fracas in Valparaiso between the crew of the *Baltimore* and a Chilean mob, in which two American sailors were killed and a number
injured. Chile dragged its feet by refusing to offer an apology or

reparations; the president threatened force and brought the nation to the brink of war to avenge what he deemed an unpardonable insult to the United States uniform. So enraged was Harrison that he very nearly toppled the painstaking efforts of his administration to build a Pan-American movement designed to enhance the United States' position in the hemisphere.

Chilean animosity for the United States stretched back a number of years and to a considerable extent focused on the activities and official statements of James G. Blaine. Blaine had earned their enmity during his stint as secretary of state under Garfield. His diplomatic support of Peru in the War of the Pacific and his allegation that Chile's military adventure had been inspired by England were among his sins. In addition, Chileans were stung during the 1880s by Blaine's denunciation of the growing British control of the nitrate industry. They may have shared his concern over the increasingly dominant role English capital played in their economy, but they resented his meddling in their affairs and the implication that the United States was the acknowledged caretaker for all the nations of Latin America.

When Blaine returned to the State Department in 1889 he discovered, to his pleasant surprise, that the government of Jose Manuel Balmaceda was intent upon curtailing British influence in Chile. To take advantage of this fresh opportunity to undercut British predominance on the Pacific coast of South America, he appointed Patrick Egan as American minister to Santiago. An implacable foe of Great Britain and a dedicated exponent of the Blaine variety of economic expansion, Egan was an Irish patriot who had come to the United States in 1883. He settled in Nebraska, became extremely successful in the milling business, and worked with the GOP to wean other Irish-Americans from the Democratic fold. He understood and sympathized with the goals of Balmaceda's drive to preserve "Chile for Chileans." His expertise in the milling industry provided an entree among Chilean nationalists interested in economic development. Egan and President Balmaceda discussed the possibility of bringing American capital in to break the British stranglehold of the nitrate enterprises. The American minister also proposed the creation of an American steamship service to challenge "Britannia's rule of the South Pacific waves." While both these plans came to naught,

Egan did help secure a cable concession for an American firm which eventually broke the English monopoly in this field.[61]

Any hope Egan and the administration had for extending American commercial interests faded in early 1891 when Chile was plunged into civil war as a consequence of Balmaceda's attempt to seize legislative powers. Although nominally neutral, the United States, particularly Minister Egan, tended to favor Balmaceda, and the actions of the Harrison administration embittered the eventually successful insurgents. Their ship, the *Itata,* which was loaded with arms purchased in the United States, was pursued and apprehended by the American Navy off the Chilean port of Iquique. The rebels vehemently protested this action, and later—but too late to help in their struggle against Balmaceda—were vindicated by a United States court which decreed that American vessels were unjustified in stopping the *Itata.* The situation deteriorated further with the defeat of Balmaceda and the creation of a new government. Not only did the State Department briefly delay recognition of the new regime, but Egan, ignoring the protests of the new government, granted asylum to a number of Balmaceda supporters.[62]

American leaders, especially President Harrison, had little enthusiasm for the new government of the triumphant congressional forces. The overthrow of Balmaceda was a bitter setback to American ambitions in South America. All the more galling was the awareness among members of the administration that European backing, and that of several British nitrate kings in particular, had contributed significantly to the rebel victory.[63] Undoubtedly, this partially accounts for the president's militant reaction to the *Baltimore* incident. Harrison's "war message" of January 25, 1892, and his apparent readiness to apply force, bullied the new Chilean government into an apology and acceptance of American demands. This bellicose outburst of American assertiveness may have bolstered the national ego, but throughout Latin America it wiped away much of what little goodwill had been engendered by the Pan-American Conference. Europeans also noted the aggressive and belligerent character of American foreign policy that was taking shape at the end of the nineteenth century. One British spokesman, Cecil Spring-Rice, worriedly observed that "the moral for us is: what will the U.S. be like when their fleet is more powerful, if the administration acts in a similar manner?"[64]

Spring-Rice's fears may have been somewhat premature, but they were not totally unwarranted. In the United States' campaign to displace the British in the hemisphere, perhaps the greatest achievement of the Harrison administration was that it accelerated the construction of a major, modern navy.[65] A strong navy was seen as the concomitant to commercial expansion, and a necessary requisite for the establishment of American influence in the Western Hemisphere. The teachings of Alfred Thayer Mahan dictated, in addition to the construction of a large navy, American strategic expansion into the Caribbean and Anglo-American solidarity at sea. Eventually all phases of the Mahan formula were acted upon, but in the years before the Spanish-American War his call for Anglo-American naval cooperation ran counter to the prevailing feeling among Americans. Great Britain was seen as frustrating the United States economically, politically, and strategically.

Many Americans believed the United States was encircled by English military and naval power, in addition to being engulfed by the United Kingdom's financial and economic might. They pointed to the 11 naval bases and 33 coaling stations the British maintained in the seas around the United States. During the congressional debate on the naval bill of 1890, for example, senators such as Matthew Calbraith Butler of South Carolina, and representatives such as Henry Cabot Lodge of Massachusetts, repeatedly called the nation's attention to England's tremendous naval strength off the country's shores. Secretary of the Navy Benjamin F. Tracy expressed similar concern over the preponderance of British naval strength in American waters.[66]

Small-navy adherents quickly ridiculed such cries of alarm and discounted the existence of any real danger to American security. They believed any threat of British aggressiveness was nullified by the importance of English capital investment in the United States, the difficulty of defending Canada, and the traditional fear of Russia entering such a conflict on the side of America. However, the debate revealed that more than security was at issue. For advocates of a powerful navy it was a question of power and prestige, and the recognition of American hegemony in the Western Hemisphere.

Part of the anxiety and fear about encirclement was directed toward Canada, which was identified by numerous Americans as an extension of England; but to most Canada symbolized British commercial competition more than military might.[67] The hostility that appeared as security consciousness cloaked a fear of Canada as competitor in the race for markets. This danger was especially evident in the construction and completion of the Canadian transcontinental railroads. American concern over the threat of the Canadian roads reached its peak during the years of the Harrison administration, and was focused by an investigation initiated under the leadership of Shelby M. Cullom. James J. Hill, a Canadian turned American, testified before the committee that the Canadian Pacific was simply another British tactic to secure the Asian trade. The empire-builder agreed with Chairman Cullom's suggestion that the United States ought to annex Canada to eliminate this challenge. "I was born in Canada," Hill concluded, "and I think the Canadians make very good Americans."[68]

Joseph Nimmo, Jr., erstwhile supporter of American railroads, was one of the critics who labelled the Dominion government "as much of a transportation company as a government."[69] Nimmo noted that Sir John MacDonald "has not concealed the fact that the object is to sweep the commerce of the ocean under the British flag."[70] While the tone of the Senate *Report* was hostile, the actual recommendations were mild, and officially nothing was done to counter the alleged Canadian threat. Nimmo later complained to Charles Perkins, president of the Chicago, Burlington, and Quincy, that "Mr. Blaine has been the chief obstacle to a just consideration of Canadian Pacific aggression;—not perhaps from a spirit of opposition, but for the reason that he has given his whole attention to South America."[71]

Despite dissatisfaction among such men as Nimmo, the administration's emphasis on Latin America, and especially the policy of reciprocity, was the most effective phase of its strategy of overseas economic expansion. The *London Trade Journal* attested to its success when it complained that "the United States steps into the Cuban and Porto Rico [*sic*] market, while British goods are shut out. It is a decided victory for the commercial policy introduced by Mr. Blaine."[72] Clearly, their experience with the McKinley Tariff educated the British as to the nature of the economic expansionism implicit in the reciprocity tactic. In 1897, while evaluating another GOP effort to resurrect reciprocity, Prime Minister Salisbury noted that "under the last Republican tariff Act, the reciprocity clause was very much a deception. The United States secured in various nations special privileges which in practice could benefit the United States alone." True, in return the United States gave free entry for a limited number of articles, but "as all countries producing these entered into reciprocity arrangements with the United States the result was that the various Foreign Countries gave the United States positive privileges and in return got nothing more than liberty to compete in the United States market on equal terms with all their trade rivals."[73] Of course that was exactly what Blaine, Harrison, and other American leaders desired: privileged entry for American products in overseas markets without any sacrifice in the home market.

President Harrison crowed over the effectiveness of the reciprocity treaties, and especially stressed the harm wrought to British trade. In his letter accepting the 1892 Republican presidential nomination he noted that "the British board of trade has presented to the government a memorial asking for the appointment of a commission to the best means of counteracting what is called the 'commercial crusade of the United States.' "[74] To further prove the worth of the treaties, Harrison revealed that the associated chambers of commerce of Great Britain had reported that British exports to "the Latin-American countries during the last year had decreased £ 23,700,000," which "was not due to temporary causes, but directly to the reciprocity policy of the United States."[75]

The impact of the reciprocity policy upon the national rival may have elated Harrison, but the domestic benefits derived from the treaties were not enough to avert the Republican debacle of 1892. Cleveland and the Democrats not only recaptured the White House, they also gained control of both houses of Congress for their most decisive victory since the 1850s. As is the case in any election, a number of factors influenced the outcome and contributed to the demise of the GOP. First, neither Harrison nor Blaine was able to campaign as he had in 1888. The president was preoccupied with the welfare of an ailing wife and Blaine, beset by personal tragedies and ill health, had left the administration in June 1892. Second, and perhaps most important, the newly formed People's party had a strong appeal among Republicans west of the Mississippi. Agrarians were attracted to the comprehensive reform program of the Populists which included demands for free silver, a subtreasury plan, government ownership of railroads, prohibition of alien ownership of land, and a graduated income tax. On the strength of their platform the Populists garnered electoral votes in six middle western and western states. And it was the inability of the Republicans to keep the farmers of the West in the fold that more than anything else accounts for the GOP defeat.

Blaine and Harrison consciously and boldly, if unsuccessfully, employed foreign policy as a tool to keep the Republicans in power. Their efforts were exceptional in carrying the American challenge to the British, and in many ways it was the key Republican administration in the last decades of the nineteenth century. More than any previous GOP administration, it formally and explicitly fostered economic expansion and an aggressive foreign policy with a determination and vision that were absent in the earlier efforts of Hayes and Evarts, Arthur and Frelinghuysen. They set the pattern for the future course of American foreign policy and, equally important, their actions turned Great Britain toward the more active pursuit of a rapprochement with the United States.

NOTES

1. Whitelaw Reid to W. W. Phelps, May 3, 1890, Reid Papers, Library of Congress. Reid explained that Harrison originally had not wanted to include Blaine in the cabinet, and "only complied when we had all crowded him on this point."

2. Speech to delegation from Henry County, Indiana, July 31, 1888, in Charles Hedges, *Speeches of Benjamin Harrison* (New York: John W. Lovell Co., 1892), p. 68.

3. Blaine to Harrison, June 26, 1888 in Albert Volwiler, ed., *The Correspondence Between Benjamin Harrison and James G. Blaine, 1882 — 1893* (Philadelphia: American Philosophical Society, 1940).

4. Desmond C.M. Platt, *Finance, Trade, and Politics in British Foreign Policy 1815 — 1914* (Oxford: Clarendon Press, 1968), pp. 362—68. Bernard Semmel, *Imperialism and Social Reform* (Garden City: Doubleday & Co., 1968), pp. 76—88.

5. See the editorial remarks in *The Spectator*, March 9, 1889, p. 327. Blaine's return to the State Department also caused apprehension in Spain and Chile; see William S. Robertson, "The Pan-American Policy of James G. Blaine," (Master's thesis, University of Wisconsin, 1900), p. 125.

6. Ibid., *Spectator*, March 9, 1889.

7. See R. Giffen's report to British Board of Trade entitled "Recent Progress of Foreign Trade" in United States Consular Report No. 98 (October 1888) (Washington: Government Printing Office, 1888), p. 147.

8. Derek H. Aldcroft, ed., *The Development of British Industry and Foreign Competition* (Toronto: University of Toronto Press, 1968), p. 13.

9. David S. Muzzey, *James G. Blaine, A Political Idol of Other Days* (New York: Dodd, Mead & Co., 1934), p. 446.

10. Gail Hamilton, *Biography of James G. Blaine* (Norwich, Conn.: Henry Bill Publishing Co., 1895), p. 688.

11. "Report on Imports and Exports in the United States," Commercial No. 8 (1886) Parliamentary Papers, Vol. 67, Part II, p. 151.

12. Ibid.

13. Hedges, *Speeches,* p. 140.

14. Ibid.

15. Ibid.

16. Ibid., speech of March 20, 1888, pp. 16–20.

17. James G. Blaine, *Twenty Years of Congress* (Norwich, Conn.: The Henry Bill Publishing Co., 1884), p. 482.

18. Ibid.

19. Harry J. Sievers, *Benjamin Harrison Hoosier Statesman, 1865 – 1888* (New York: University Publishers, Inc., 1959), p. 408.

20. Ibid., p. 406.

21. Blaine to Harrison, October 25, 1888 in Volwiler, *Correspondence Between Harrison and Blaine.*

22. For a discussion of the support for a Pan-American conference in the 1880s see Walter LaFeber, *The New Empire, An Interpretation of American Expansion, 1860 – 1898* (Ithaca: Cornell University Press, 1963), pp. 112–13.

23. Matias Romero, "The Pan-American Conference" *North American Review,* 1890, Vol. 151, p. 356. The United States' movement for a customs union was blocked by Argentina, since it saw this move would damage its meat and wheat exports to Europe by limiting European manufactured exports into Latin America.

24. *London Times,* July 15, 1890. See also Board of Trade memo of June 18, 1889, Foreign Office 5, Vol. 2069, Public Record Office, London (hereinafter cited as F.O. 5/2069 P.R.O.).

25. *New York Tribune,* September 17, 1890.

26. Speech of Blaine's contained in Blaine to Reid, May 16, 1886, Reid Papers, Library of Congress.

27. *Chicago Tribune,* June 17, 1890.

28. Alice Felt Tyler, *The Foreign Policy of James G. Blaine* (Minneapolis: The University of Minnesota Press, 1927), p. 185.

29. *New York Tribune,* August 31, 1890; *Chicago Tribune,* July 3, 1890.

30. *Chicago Tribune,* June 20, 1890.

31. *New York Tribune,* August 30, 31, September 17, 1890, *Chicago Tribune,* July 3, 1890.

32. Ibid., *New York Times,* September 17, 1890.

33. Ibid.

34. *Chicago Tribune,* August 9, 1890.

35. LaFeber, *New Empire,* pp. 116–18. For McKinley's views and his acceptance of reciprocity strategy see *Rural New Yorker,* October 31, 1891.

36. *London Times,* October 3, 1891.

37. Ibid., October 7, 1890.

38. Ibid., October 9, 1890.

39. See, for example, the question in House of Commons by Mr. Howard Vincent, June 9, 1890; resolutions of public meeting in Sheffield, July 15, 25, 1890; Town of Worcester resolution against McKinley Tariff, September 13, 1890, F.O. 5/2101 P.R.O.

40. *London Times,* April 26, 1892. Memorial of Birmingham Chamber of Commerce, May 25, 1892, F.O. 5/2165 P.R.O. There also were several cabinet papers devoted to the question of trade with the colonies and imperial preference. See, for example, Development of trade with the colonies, December 8, 1890, Cab. 37/28/64; C. M. Kennedy memo on position of British colonies in relation to commercial treaties and the most-favored-nation clause, January 1, 1891, Cab. 37/29/1; Commercial union between the United Kingdom and the colonies, board of trade report, February 9, 1891, Cab. 37/29/7 P.R.O. See also Benjamin H. Brown, *The Tariff Reform Movement in Great Britain, 1881 − 1895* (New York: Columbia University Press, 1943), pp. 74−81.

41. James A. Tawney, *Reciprocity is the complement of a protective tariff. Its achievements already mark the triumph of American trade in foreign markets,* Speech in the House of Representatives, Thursday, January 25, 1894 (Washington: 1894).

42. Ibid.

43. Earl of Dunraven. "Commercial Union Within the Empire," *Nineteenth Century,* March 1891, Vol. 29, pp. 507−22; Brown, *Tariff Reform Movement,* p. 81.

44. See "Free Trade or Protection," *North American Review,* January, 1890, Vol. 150, pp. 1−54.

45. Ibid., p. 26.

46. Ibid., p. 45.

47. Ibid., p. 46.

48. Board of Trade to the Colonial Office, June 1, 1891: Colonial Office to Foreign Office, June 12, 1891, F.O. 5/2129 P.R.O. See also J. Lawrence Laughlin and H. Parker Willis, *Reciprocity* (New York: The Baker & Taylor Co., 1903), pp. 210−12.

49. Blaine to Sir Julian Pauncefote, October 31, 1891, in Report on the Negotiations with the Government of the United States in the Matter of the McKinley Act. For an admission of the discriminatory nature of West Indian duties see Neville Lubbock to Lord Knutsford, December 8, 1891, F.O. 5/2165 P.R.O.

50. LaFeber, *New Empire,* p. 120. John L. Gignilliat, "Pigs, Politics, and Protection: The European Boycott of American Pork, 1879−1891," *Agricultural History,* XXXV (January, 1961), pp. 3−12. See also James L. Erlenborn, "The American Meat and Livestock Industry and American Foreign Policy, 1880−1896," (Master's thesis, University of Wisconsin, 1966).

51. Cecil Spring-Rice to Ferguson, November 6, 1891 in Stephen Gwynn, ed., *The Letters and Friendships of Sir Cecil Spring-Rice* (Boston: Houghton Mifflin Co., 1929), p. 116. For other examples of British concern over the effectiveness of reciprocity see Alexander Gollen to Roseberry, March 31, 1893, Commercial

No. 1213, Foreign Office, Annual Series Parliamentary Papers, 1893; *New York Tribune*, October 15, 1892 for a collection of British newspaper comments. See also Tawney, *Reciprocity*, for a British West Indian newspaper appraisal.

52. *London Times*, November 14, 1890.

53. *Farmers' Voice*, June 27, 1891.

54. Issac P. Brewer to William B. Allison, November 17, 1890, Allison Papers, Iowa Historical Society, Des Moines.

55. *London Times*, February 14, 1891.

56. Hedges, *Speeches*, p. 287.

57. Ibid., pp. 332, 409.

58. William E. Chandler to Harrison, June 18, 1891, Harrison Papers, Library of Congress.

59. Hedges, *Speeches*, pp. 522, 540.

60. Ibid.

61. Osgood Hardy, "Was Patrick Egan a Blundering Minister," *Hispanic American Historical Review*, Vol. 8 (1928), pp. 65—81. Frederick Pike, *Chile and the United States, 1880 — 1962* (South Bend: University of Notre Dame Press, 1963), pp. 69—70.

62. William R. Sherman, *The Diplomatic and Commercial Relations of the United States and Chile, 1820 — 1914* (Boston: The Gorham Press, 1926), pp. 143—68. Pike, *Chile and the United States*, pp. 71—72.

63. Harrison to Blaine, September 26, 1891 in Volwiler, *Correspondence Between Harrison and Blaine*. Osgood Hardy, "British Nitrates and the Balmaceda Revolution," *Pacific Historical Review*, Vol. XVII (May 1948), pp. 165—80.

64. Cecil Spring-Rice to Ferguson, April 1892, in Gwynn, *Letters and Friendships of Spring-Rice*, p. 118.

65. Harrison and Blaine also tasted some success in their drive to reestablish the American merchant marine with the passage of the Ocean Mail Act of 1891. But the bill failed to stem the decline of the merchant fleet when only 11 of 53 of the authorized bids were awarded to steamship firms during the Harrison years. See John G.B. Hutchins, *The American Maritime Industries and Public Policy, 1789 — 1914*, (Cambridge: Harvard University Press, 1951).

66. Forrest Davis, *The Atlantic System: The Story of Anglo-American Control of the Seas* (New York: Reynal and Hitchcock, 1941). Henry C. Lodge, "Our Blundering Foreign Policy," *The Forum*, 19 (1890), pp. 8—17.

67. See testimony in *Relations with Canada*, Senate Report 1530, 51st Cong., 1st. Sess., 1890 (Washington: Government Printing Office, 1890).

68. See Hill's testimony in *Transportation Interests of the United States and Canada*, Senate Report No. 847, 51st Cong., 1st Sess., 1890 (Washington: Government Printing Office, 1890), p. 179.

69. Nimmo to Charles Perkins, March 24, 1890, Perkins Papers, Chicago, Burlington, and Quincy Archives, Newberry Library, Chicago.

70. Ibid.

71. Ibid., June 24, 1892.

72. *Bradstreets,* July 23, 1892.

73. Foreign Office memo to the Colonial Office, April 14, 1897, F.O. 5/2344 P.R.O.

74. *Proceedings of the Tenth Republican National Convention, 1892* (Minneapolis: Harrison and Smith, Printers, 1892), p. 167.

75. Ibid.

9

The Battle for Silver

Our farmers and cotton growers, for lack of silver coinage, are co-laborers in aiding England to obtain cheap wheat and cotton.

Southern Mercury, 1894

The gold monometallic policy of Great Britain now in force among all great civilized nations, is, I believe, the great enemy of good business throughout the world at this moment. Therefore, it seems to me, if there is any way in which we can strike England's trade or her moneyed interest, it is our clear policy to do it in the interest of silver.

Henry Cabot Lodge, 1894

The people of the United States are opposed to remaining a financial colony of Great Britain, and any reference to London is regarded as a badge of our humiliation . . . . Our object is to abolish financial slavery.

Senator William Stewart, 1896

America must rule herself.

People's Party Paper, 1895

Gold monometallism is a British policy . . . . It is not only un-American, but anti-American.

Democratic Platform, 1896

I am sorry to say that I am afraid that a large number, and probably a majority, of Americans would look forward without horror to a war with this country . . . . At bottom, I believe it is due to the extreme sensitiveness and vanity of the Americans as a nation. They are jealous of this country, and suspect us always of an assumption of superiority, of which we are not conscious ourselves, but they are convinced nevertheless that we look down upon them, and they would not be sorry to prove that they are bigger and stronger and better than we are.

Joseph Chamberlain, 1895

While Americans are all united on the Monroe Doctrine, nevertheless, the recent manifestation of hostile feeling towards Great Britain did not grow out of any real apprehension of danger to our interests by the dispute over the boundary in Venezuela. That was only the occasion. The real cause of the feeling in this country is the deep-seated belief that England by her financial maneuvering beginning with the demonetization of silver in 1873, has gained an advantage, not only over the States, but other countries, which will yet lead to trouble.

A. J. Warner, 1896

During the last two decades of the nineteenth century the free silver issue came to represent all of America's grievances against England. The remonetization of silver promised to liberate the American farmer from the grip of the English market, to open alternate markets in South America and Asia for his agricultural surplus, and to end the nation's humiliating reliance on foreign capital with its attendant evils of alien ownership and bond issues. Millions of Americans came to believe free coinage of silver at the ratio of 16 to 1 offered a panacea for the country's social and economic ills. And silverites frequently cast their crusade in the idiom of a second declaration of independence, demanding a return to the Spirit of '76. The question, as one silverite senator declared, was "whether we propose to surrender our own independence and manhood and follow the dictates of England" or whether the American people, "striking out in the spirit of 1776, dare to take our own course for ourselves."[1] The choice was clear for many agrarians. They advocated free silver in the belief that it would solve the problems of market expansion while simultaneously ridding the nation of British economic influence.

Essentially what the free silver advocates sought was a return to the bimetallic gold and silver standard that prevailed under the Coinage Act of 1837. That legislation provided for the coinage of gold and silver in unlimited amounts. In addition to favoring a bimetallic system, the silverites accepted a quantity theory of money based on the premise that the amount of money in circulation dictated the general level of prices as well as the level of economic activity and growth. In this analysis, the general deflationary trend and the low price levels that plagued the nation in the last quarter of the nineteenth century were directly attributable to the short supply of money in circulation, and were the unfortunate result of the demonetization of silver in 1873. The silverite obsession with the curative powers of money hardly constituted a radical departure from American tradition. It was based on the long held notion that access to money and credit was necessary to keep the way open for material success and social mobility.[2] In that sense, the silver crusade reflected the same incipient capitalist mentality that had sparked and sustained the campaign against alien ownership of land.

The free silver argument appealed to western and southern farmers because, first of all, they recognized that remonetization would inflate the country's currency, put more money in circulation, keep interest rates low, and broadly serve to relieve their economic plight. Despite long-standing arguments to the contrary, this analysis was not particularly irrational. As two noted economists recently have pointed out, the remonetization of silver "would certainly have reduced the monetary demand for gold and increased the monetary demand for silver and in both respects would have contributed to a higher gold price of silver." That, in turn, would have arrested the deflationary spiral, and in all likelihood would have alleviated some of the financial woes of the American farmer.[3]

Second, spokesmen for the West and South repeatedly advanced the silver analysis when they defined their regions as being colonial in relation to the English metropolis and its extension in the American Northeast.[4] They argued that money when in short supply tended to concentrate in the financial centers, and little remained to foster economic growth in the outlying regions. One such representative, Herman E. Taubeneck, national chairman of the People's party, detected "a deep and wide gulf between the interests

of the East and those of the South and West" and the only way
for these sections to secure "commercial independence from the
East is first to become financially independent."[5] And that could
only be accomplished through free silver, for the adherence of metropolitan business and political leaders to the gold standard riveted
the United States to the British financial system. To the silverites
it was clear that Great Britain, the world's creditor, only stood to
gain from any continued rise in the price of gold and corresponding
decline in the price of silver.

The steady decline of the world price of silver relative to gold
in the years following demonetization, which was paralleled by a
corresponding drop in agricultural prices, appeared to support the
contentions of Taubeneck and other silverites. The ratio of silver
to gold at the beginning of the 1870s was roughly 16 to 1, or, in
other words, 16 ounces of silver equaled the value of one ounce
of gold. By 1880 silver fell to 19 to 1, in 1894 it was 32 to 1,
and by the end of the century it stood at about 35 to 1.[6] The collapse of farm prices was nearly as dramatic. For example, a bushel
of wheat sold at $1.19 in 1881; by 1894 the price had plummeted
to an average of 49.1 cents per bushel. In 1881 corn sold at 63
cents per bushel; by 1891 it had dropped to 28 cents per bushel.[7]
Of course, the primary benefactor of the decline in the price of
silver, according to agrarian leaders, was Great Britain, the world's
chief importer of foodstuffs.

It was widely accepted among American farmers that unlimited
silver coinage would check the collapse in agricultural prices and
improve their competitive position in several ways. To begin with,
free coinage would increase the world's money supply and sup-
posedly enhance the world price of their wheat, cotton, corn, and
meat exports. Second, it would undermine the price monopoly of
the London and Liverpool commodity markets. Finally, silver
remonetization would terminate the farmer's dependence on English markets by opening alternate markets in the Western Hemisphere and Asia. To restore a bimetallic system in the United States
would allow the silver standard nations of Latin America and the
Far East to buy American farm products and manufactured goods
without losing in the exchange, as they would if they traded through
a gold standard nation such as Great Britain. The adoption of silver
was seen as the key to capturing new outlets for it would help
undercut existing British credit, banking, and transportation advantages in those areas. The silver fight, Colorado's Senator Henry

M. Teller asserted, "is for the control of the great industries of this country" and for the world's "great avenues of commerce and trade."[8]

Throughout the currency debates of the late nineteenth century supporters of the gold standard persistently opposed and tirelessly attacked the free silver analysis. Although they may have shared the silverite concern for economic development and market expansion, the goldbugs feared that unlimited coinage of silver would destroy the stability of the fiscal structure, result in silver monometallism, and seriously disrupt the economic health of the nation. The commercial and financial success of Great Britain confirmed the superiority of the gold standard. Some economic expansionists, including James G. Blaine, argued that it was necessary for the United States to remain within the gold system in order to overwhelm England in the markets of the world. Just such logic had prompted John Sherman and other gold advocates to push for the demonetization of silver and commit, according to silverites, the "Crime of '73." Both the goldbugs and the silverites insisted that their approach and their monetary system offered the more viable fulcrum for continued internal economic development and projected overseas commercial expansion.

During the 1880s the rapidly emerging competition of Indian wheat and cotton exports, especially in the British market, alarmed American farmers and quickly aroused national concern over the money standard. American producers became increasingly receptive to the charge that English "nabobs," with the cooperation of the English government, were actively backing the development of Indian wheat and cotton exports to destroy American agriculture. In the eyes of silverites, this was accomplished through Britain's hostility for silver and its refusal to support any move for international bimetallism. The 1886 comment of Sir Robert N. Fowler, English banker and member of Parliament, that "the effect of the depreciation of silver must be the ruin of the wheat and cotton industries of America, and the development of India as the chief wheat and cotton exporter of the world" was repeatedly cited as proof of the British plot by silverites in their speeches, pamphlets, and campaign tracts.[9]

More disturbing to the agrarians than the British scheme to "ruin" their export trade was the tacit support given the British efforts by the American government. The main advantage enjoyed by the exports of India stemmed from the demonetization of silver in the United States, which depressed the world price of silver. And the failure of the United States government to remonetize silver only sustained the low price of silver bullion. This allowed English merchants to buy more silver with the same amount of gold, and when they had the bullion coined into rupees it purchased a greater quantity of wheat and cotton in Indian markets. To American farmers, at any rate, the cheapness of silver subsidized Indian exports and served to displace American products in English and European markets.

The India wheat-silver argument appeared with monotonous regularity in the agrarian journals during the late 1880s and early 1890s.[10] A typical explanation of the relationship came from the *Western Rural* when it charged that the United States, by discriminating against silver "to the extent of depreciating its value forty per-cent," allowed England to purchase the breadstuffs of India and "thus swindle our own wheat and corn growers out of forty per-cent of the value of their product."[11] But, as agrarian spokesmen and their journals repeatedly made clear, not only would adoption of silver destroy Great Britain's special position vis à vis India, it also would give the United States a definite competitive edge in securing the markets of silver-using countries in Latin America and Asia.

This facet of the silverite dogma was shared by a contingent of Eastern conservatives who advocated international bimetallism for the commercial and trade advantages it would bestow upon the United States. The primary appeal of bimetallism among this group was that it offered a means to expand overseas markets. They organized the Boston Bimetallic Club in 1893 and among their number were such important figures as Henry Cabot Lodge, Thomas Reed, George F. Hoar, Brooks Adams, William C. Whitney, and E. Benjamin Andrews. This group took an intermediate position between that of the free silverites and the goldbugs. They favored the restoration of bimetallism and an expanded use of silver through an international agreement. Their basic disagreement with the silverites was that they did not accept the notion that the United States could unilaterally reestablish silver.

Surprisingly, throughout the last two decades of the nineteenth century there existed rather widespread support among American leaders for international bimetallism. From the administration of President Hayes to that of President McKinley, all major leaders supported, at least publicly, efforts to achieve that objective. They backed various proposals for international conferences and special commissions, sent confidential agents abroad to sound out the Europeans on the possibility of an international bimetallic agreement, and dispatched American representatives to world monetary conferences in 1867, 1878, 1881, and 1892.[12] All such efforts to secure an international accord were unsuccessful. As a result, by the late 1880s agrarians and silverites had dismissed that course of action as a typical political evasion of the issue. Certainly the activities of Grover Cleveland during his first administration supported the view that any plan for an international agreement was simply a political tactic designed to quell the agitation for free silver. Above all, silverites realized that Britain's determined opposition doomed any movement for an international bimetallic pact. And John Hay, in a private letter to Whitelaw Reid, cynically acknowledged the political opportunism of international bimetallism. When commenting on the threat of free silver, he predicted in 1895 that the Republicans "shall hold the great bulk of our strength on the platform of international bimetallism, which of course is impracticable, and means nothing more than the present state of things."[13]

Despite the suspicions and doubts of the free silver forces, not all bimetallists who pursued an international agreement did so in hopes of defusing the remonetization campaign. A number of American leaders genuinely endorsed a bimetallic pact in the belief that it would avert domestic financial chaos, stabilize the international monetary system, and increase America's share of world commerce. As the ex-senator from Wisconsin, Timothy O. Howe, a delegate to the 1881 conference in Paris, explained to the assembly, the American concern was not primarily for "our so-called precious metals," but because the United States "wish[ed] to find a busy and lusty world to help consume the really precious fruits of our agriculture."[14] Another American representative to the conference, former Secretary of State William M. Evarts, bluntly announced to the other delegates that "we want to sell our raw materials to Europe." And at the same time Evarts fully expected the United States to contest Europe for industrial supremacy in "the markets of the world."[15]

The disagreements over the most effective method to implement silver in behalf of overseas economic expansion split American bimetallists in the 1890s. The more militant silverites, who ultimately united around the banner of William Jennings Bryan in 1896, demanded immediate free and unlimited coinage of silver at the ratio of 16 to 1. The nationalistic silverites dismissed the objection that their policy inevitably would force the United States to silver monometallism and a total debasement of its currency. They were economic nationalists of the first order who believed that the overwhelming economic power of the United States would dictate that the other nations of the world fall in line and follow the American lead in support of silver. William Windom, Harrison's secretary of the treasury, offered the principal objections to such a solution in his report for 1889. He observed that "rich and powerful as the United States is, we are not strong enough, nor rich enough, to absorb the silver of the world," even though the unilateral adoption of silver might be "the heroic remedy."[16] Their differences aside, both international and national bimetallists agreed that Great Britain blocked the path to any international agreement.

The India wheat-silver argument offered by American farmers and silverites presented a rather one-sided picture of a complicated international trade pattern. They tended to overlook the damaging impact the fall in the gold price of silver had on certain segments of the British Empire and among specific economic interests in Britain.[17] The disadvantages were detailed frequently by English bimetallists, who urged their government to support an international agreement. First, the general decline in farm prices was decimating British agriculture and carrying the landed interest to ruin. Second, British manufacturers, while profiting to some degree from the price drop of such raw materials as cotton, were losing ground in the markets of the silver-using countries of the Far East. Their goods, produced on the gold standard, were more costly to Chinese and Japanese purchasers who had to absorb the exchange difference when they paid in silver. Third, the financial solvency of the Indian government was threatened because it had to remit its international deficits in gold. Finally, Britain's position as world creditor was endangered by the continuing deflationary trend which made it increasingly difficult for debtor nations to meet their obligations.[18]

While some British leaders favored more extensive use of silver in the international monetary system, the official policy of the English government was to refuse to give any firm commitment to international bimetallism. British supporters of gold feared that participation in an international accord would result in the diminution in the purchasing power of gold. Debtor nations on a silver standard might then repay their obligations on the basis of inflated prices. As a consequence, Britain's standing as the leading financial nation of the world would be jeopardized. One London banker, Bertram Currie, accurately focused on the main concern of British goldbugs: "I do not say that England would lose her natural advantages if she parted with the gold standard, but if she did she would be in very great danger of losing her supremacy."[19]

Some American advocates of international bimetallism understood that the appreciation in the price of gold relative to silver inflicted hardships within the British Empire as well as in the United States, and they hoped that ultimately enough pressure would be brought to bear to force a change in British policy favorable to international bimetallism. Patience, however, was not a noticeable virtue among free silverites, and they disdainfully rejected the notion that all the United States needed to do was to wait for Great Britain to act on its true interest. Any policy that promised monetary relief primarily through the actions of England convinced farmers and silverites of America's subservient financial status and intensified their already strong anti-British nationalism.

Historians of the American silver movement contend that the free silverites actually played England's game by allowing Europe to stand by while the United States carried the ball in support of silver.[20] The farmers, according to this view, proved to be their own worst enemies. Their continued agitation resulted in measures such as the Bland-Allison Act and the Sherman Silver Purchase Act, and committed the American government to a policy of buying silver, which in effect placed the United States in the position of upholding the world price of silver. To be sure, silverites and agrarians did enhance their own dilemma by accepting the self-defeating legislation of political compromise. But they clearly recognized the

inadequacies of the Bland-Allison Act, and they remained cool to
the Sherman Silver Purchase Act, which received the bulk of its
support from American silver producers and owners of silver in
New York and London. In the end such half measures reluctantly
were accepted as better than none.[21] Any other course would have
been a policy of passivity and one that again gave the initiative
and the upper hand to the English. That was intolerable, for to
sit idly by and wait for the largesse of England was only a
reaffirmation of American dependence. More important, the economic crisis of the 1890s precluded a policy of watchful waiting;
it demanded immediate action and efforts for relief.

The cry for remonetization at 16 to 1 and the rhetoric of free
silver dominated the political arena in the 1890s. The debates leading to the passage of the Sherman Silver Purchase Act were
marked by charges of conspiracy. Congressional supporters of the
white metal repeatedly framed their logic in terms of the Crime
of '73. The financial classes of the United States and Great Britain
were accused of attempting to keep the producing classes in a state
of financial servitude. One farmers' newspaper complained that
"since 1873 England had made war on the wheat industry by depressing the value of silver, and has found obedient servants among
the bankers and speculators of Wall Street; and . . . willing tools
in Congress."[22] Passage of the act failed to placate the free silver
advocates nor did it abet their campaign spirit. Farm organizations,
especially the Alliances and Granges, mounted an extensive petition
barrage of the Congress.[23] But it was the formation of the People's
party in 1892, with a plank calling for unlimited coinage of silver
at 16 to 1, that mobilized farmer and labor unrest and drew thousands to the free silver banner.

The monetary issue not only internally split both major political
parties, it also thinned their ranks as more and more farmers rallied
to the People's party. However, many veteran Populists (such as
Tom Watson of Georgia, Senator William V. Allen of Nebraska
and William A. Peffer of Kansas) worried that the sole reliance
on the curative powers of silver would subvert the other major
reforms outlined in the Omaha platform.[24] Nonetheless, the Panic
of 1893 and the ensuing crisis of the 1890s reinforced the convic-
tions of the faithful and steadily swelled the ranks of the silver
army. The actions of the newly inaugurated Cleveland administra-

tion further enhanced the credibility of the silverites. The president's various attempts to preserve the gold standard smacked of a gigantic deal among the "bloated plutocrats" of Wall and Lombard streets. Cleveland's grim determination to repeal the Sherman Act aroused his enemies and created an irreparable split among his own party. One editor complained that "Mr. Grover Cleveland is not a representative of Democratic principles, nor of true Democrats," for "his policies on Silver and the Tariff are true English policies."[25] Cleveland confronted the heresy of silver even within his official family. Vice-President Adlai Stevenson of Illinois was a free silver advocate who drew supporters to him in what amounted to a parallel cabinet. Secretary of the Navy William C. Whitney also converted to the white metal, having been convinced it offered a means of expanding trade to the Orient.

The successive bond issues promoted by Cleveland and Secretary of the Treasury John Carlisle during the period 1893—1896 infuriated the agrarians of the West and South. Such was especially the case with the secretly negotiated bond issue of February 1895 handled by the Morgan-Belmont-Rothschild syndicate. That particular deal revealed the extent to which the administration was beholden to the Wall Street interests and their British-Jewish partners. To the silverites, the whole sordid transaction confirmed their belief that the country's financial system was manipulated in the interest of the East and England, while the colonial areas, the West and South, suffered unrelieved.

Ironically, the arch-villian J. Pierpont Morgan secretly visited England in 1893 at the request of Grover Cleveland to negotiate a bimetallist agreement, but the English government flatly rejected the proposal. Had the silverites known of the effort, perhaps they would have been less critical of Cleveland and the House of Morgan. It is more likely, however, that the incident would have been interpreted as a further illustration of America's financial dependence upon England. The bond issues increased the national debt for a crisis that never came. Most of the borrowed funds went for current expenditures of the government, but it provided no relief for the depression-ridden people. Throughout the anguish of Cleveland's administration, the silver men gleefully predicted the day of reckoning and the demise of the gold standard.

Amidst the hue and cry for remonetization, American bimetallists who remained hopeful of an international accord tried to arrange another monetary conference in 1894. The abortive movement was spearheaded by Henry Cabot Lodge, who candidly admitted the problems surrounding such a scheme were "enormous."[26] Lodge attempted to employ the tactics of economic nationalism to force Great Britain to support international bimetallism. He introduced an openly hostile amendment to the tariff bill that would have doubled the existing duty on items from Great Britain and the Empire and added 35 percent *ad valorem* to goods on the free list until Great Britain accepted an international bimetallic agreement. The Massachusetts Republican justified this acknowledged act of "commercial warfare" by claiming that England was "the one obstacle across the path of bimetallism," and asserting that such drastic action was the only way to bring Great Britain to an agreement.[27] To illustrate the workability of the scheme, Lodge drew upon the historical example of the colonists' response to the Stamp Act. He believed that his amendment would once again provide the means to bring the London merchants to heel. Thomas Reed of Maine also attempted to browbeat Great Britain. He warned that if England did not accept bimetallism, the United States and other nations friendly to silver would form a tariff union with reciprocity being the reward for free coinage of silver.[28]

The Senate eventually tabled Lodge's proposal, but not before 33 senators expressed their support for the amendment in a letter addressed to Moreton Frewen, an active British bimetallist with a number of important contacts in the United States. The bipartisan letter argued that Great Britain was responsible for the failure of past monetary conferences. And to overcome British intransigence on the currency question, the senators threatened coercion by making it clear they favored discriminatory American duties that would "strike at England's colonial interests." Presumably Frewen was to employ the document in his English campaign for bimetallism.[29] Lodge confided to his English friend, in a tone of self-satisfaction, that it was "evident that in England my amendment is better understood and the reasons for it better appreciated than among the mugwumps of the eastern coast."[30] The Populists, however, were suspicious. Senator Allen concluded that Lodge's amendment was "a piece of Yankee ingenuity," and warned that all the talk of international bimetallism "is a subterfuge by which the Republican party hopes to deceive the people in 1896."[31]

Frewen also intended to capitalize on his friendships with various prominent American senators by securing their support for an increase of the duty on diamonds, an increase that promised him considerable personal gain.[32] He hoped to raise the existing 10 percent duty to 30 percent. That would be prohibitive and thus seriously injure South Africa's diamond exports because the United States took one-third of all Cape diamonds. The threat of an increase could be used as an economic lever to force Cecil Rhodes to "get the Rothschilds to support the calling of a Monetary Conference in London." If Rhodes obtained the London banking firm's approval, then "diamonds will be fairly treated." In the interim, Frewen expected to "make a little fortune" from "the fall in shares" since "I alone shall know how the cat may be made to jump."[33] The fantastic scheme never materialized. Senate supporters of the diamond increase failed to have it included in the Wilson tariff bill of 1894.[34] The manipulative features of the plan were based on assumptions shared by silverites and which invariably appeared in Populist campaign rhetoric. Only when the interests of the British capitalists were directly threatened would they acquiesce to bimetallism and the restoration of silver in the world's currency. The various attempts to bring England to the conference table through threats of economic harassment failed. Lodge and other senators, even with the diligent efforts of Frewen, pushed Great Britain no closer to accepting international bimetallism.

Anyone familiar with the character and background of Henry Cabot Lodge might be puzzled by the avowedly anti-British nature of his foreign policy, both in this incident and throughout the 1890s. On the one hand, Lodge represented the epitome of the Anglo-Saxon tradition in the United States. Personally friendly with many leading Englishmen of his generation, he was a Boston patrician steeped in English history and literature with unabashed pride in his ancestry and the New England of his birth. Self-appointed protector of the purity of the Anglo-Saxon race, he labored for immigration restriction and was an intellectual leader of late nineteenth century nativism. On the other hand, he was a fierce defender of American interests in the Western Hemisphere who feared and resented British activities in Central and South

America. In addition, English resistance to his hopes for international bimetallism compounded and reinforced his suspicions, excited his patriotic fervor, and laid bare the anti-British side of his Americanism. In this respect Lodge reflected the outlook of a number of American leaders in the last decades of the nineteenth century, who saw the rivalry with England as a contest for commercial and economic supremacy. They protested British policies that encroached upon American hemispheric interests and overseas ambitions without abandoning their reverence for the nation's English heritage and Anglo-Saxon culture.[35]

Lodge not only berated Great Britain, but he also had long been a thorn in the side of Cleveland and the Democrats, and his attacks were mainly concentrated on what he labelled their pro-British conduct of foreign policy. He and his Republican cohort from Massachusetts, George F. Hoar, delighted in slinging barbs at Cleveland's secretary of state, Walter Q. Gresham, a political apostate who deserted the GOP to support Cleveland in 1892. They were particularly angered by the handling of the Hawaiian situation and the refusal of Cleveland to accept the Harrison treaty of annexation. In 1895 Lodge worriedly confided to fellow senator Cushman K. Davis that he hated "to think of the dangers we are in with such an administration at the helm. They may yield to England in Venezuela and Nicaragua to such a point that we can never recover the lost ground."[36] Later that year, these fears were publicly expressed by Lodge in a magazine article dealing with the English threat in Venezuela and what it portended for American interests in the Orinoco River system. "The supremacy of the Monroe doctrine," he concluded, "should be established and at once—peaceably if we can, forcibly if we must."[37] Actually, the vigorous stand of Cleveland and Gresham's successor, Richard Olney, would more than satisfy Lodge and other critics.

Although he was the frequent target of Republicans demanding a more vigorous and "American" foreign policy, Gresham was in truth a sophisticated economic expansionist who during the 1893–1894 domestic crisis came to see overseas markets as a means of eliminating the depression and preserving the system. He wrote his friend Judge Charles E. Dyer early in 1894 recommending that "our manufactures of all kinds should have free raw materials—that is to say, all such imported materials as they need in their business should come in free." Gresham believed "this would lower the cost of the manufactured article and enable our people to compete in foreign markets with Great Britain." In addition to tariff reform for free raw materials, Secretary Gresham advocated international bimetallism and expected the repeal of the Sherman Silver Purchase Act would prompt England and other nations to "join us in a movement for a larger use of silver."[38]

The Nicaraguan question provided another example of the bipartisan commitment to extending American political and commercial influence in Latin America that prevailed in the last decades of the nineteenth century. So adroitly did Gresham handle the issue that not only was the United States' influence in Nicaragua enhanced, but a virtual American protectorate ultimately supplanted British dominance in the Mosquito reservation area. The secretary of state balanced concern for a projected canal route and the protection of American commercial interests with the efforts of Nicaraguan President Zelaya to gain control over the reservation territory. In the process Gresham successfully finessed the British and neutralized their special protective status over the Mosquito Indians.[39]

However, the Cleveland administration attained little immediate benefit from Gresham's astute diplomacy. In April 1895 the British landed troops and occupied Corinto in a dispute with Zelaya over an apology and indemnity for the arrest of a British diplomat. Democrats and Republicans throughout the nation, as well as the press, blasted England for its role "of bully against a minute and defenseless people." Several state legislatures passed resolutions deploring this latest example of British aggression. The jingoistic display of anti-British nationalism generated by the Corinto incident soon spread to a hostile and bitter denunciation of the administration for its cautious response to the English intervention. Cleveland was castigated for his spineless and "un-American" policy. The comment of the Philadelphia *Press* was typical of the criticism: "what is the most amazing and embittering is that this act of British aggression is consumated with the assent and sanction of the American Administration." The eventual withdrawal of the British did not halt the anti-Cleveland barrage and amidst this wave of Anglophobic abuse the administration formulated its Venezuelan policy.[40]

Before his death in May 1895, Gresham was preparing a note on the boundary controversy between Great Britain and Venezuela. The dispute was of long duration, and Venezuela had vainly attempted to submit the question to arbitration before 1887, when in desperation it severed diplomatic relations with Great Britain. As early as 1881, James G. Blaine, then serving as secretary of state in the Garfield administration, had warned the English that as long as he was at the head of the State Department they would not gain another foot of territory in the Western Hemisphere.[41] President Cleveland, believing the Monroe Doctrine to be involved, decided to press the issue. He announced in December 1894 that the United States would renew its efforts to bring about "a restoration of diplomatic relations" and "to induce a reference to arbitration."[42] Gresham proceeded in the spring of 1895 to act on Cleveland's rhetoric by urging Venezuela to restore diplomatic relations with England so that the United States might use its influence for arbitration.

Simultaneously, members of Congress began a push for arbitration. Leonidas F. Livingston of Georgia entered a resolution calling for arbitration of the dispute. The Orinoco River was defined as "the key to more than one-quarter of the South American continent," and if England secured control a grave danger would arise because this would "revolutionize the commerce and political institutions of at least three of the South American Republics."[43] Livingston had been induced to enter the resolution by William L. Scruggs, a nominal member of his district and an able propagandist and lobbyist in the employ of the Venezuelan government. Scruggs began his campaign for American support of Venezuela in October 1894 with the publication of a pamphlet entitled *British Aggression in Venezuela, or the Monroe Doctrine on Trial*. It contained a brief outline of the history of the dispute and cogently presented the Venezuelan case. Scruggs sent copies to the leading newspapers and magazines in the United States and England, members of Congress, to governors and leading members of the state legislatures, and to various clubs and libraries in the nation's major cities.[44] The pamphlet aroused Americans against the British threat and, along with Scruggs' diligent lobbying efforts, convinced Livingston, Cleveland, Lodge, and others that some action was necessary.[45]

Scruggs may have awakened the United States to the danger and intensified American leaders' concern, but the administration earlier recognized that British encroachments in Latin America directly threatened American interests. British success would give London control of the Orinoco River, close the Caribbean, dominate the interior trade and, in effect, undermine the Monroe Doctrine. Richard Olney, Gresham's blunt and stubborn successor in the State Department, prepared, at Cleveland's direction, a strong note that was forwarded to Great Britain on July 20, 1895. It was approved by members of the cabinet, and the president commented that the note "entirely satisfied him," particularly since it "caught the national spirit perfectly."[46] Olney aimed to reassert and preserve the Monroe Doctrine by declaring that "today the United States is practically sovereign on this continent, and its fiat is law upon the subjects to which it confides its interposition." He pointedly concluded that American interests were directly involved because the "political control at stake . . . is of no mean importance, but concerns a domain of great extent . . . and if it also directly involves the command of the mouth of the Orinoco, is of immense consequences in connection with the whole river navigation of the interior of South America."[47]

Lord Salisbury and England disagreed. In an unintentionally delayed reply the British prime minister disdainfully rejected the applicability of the Monroe Doctrine and reasserted the correctness of Britain's claims. Cleveland responded with a special message to Congress in which he called for the United States to take upon itself the responsibility of inquiring and determining the true boundary line. He asked the Congress for adequate appropriations for a commission to make such an investigation. When the commission had established the boundary, the United States would determinedly resist any English efforts to transgress the decision. President Cleveland concluded by revealing that he was "fully alive" to the consequences of this course of action.[48]

Cleveland's salvo touched off an Anglo-American crisis and overnight the man who John Hay believed did "not seem to have a friend in the world" became a popular hero, with most of the nation applauding his newly discovered backbone.[49] W. W. Cox wrote Secretary of Agriculture J. Sterling Morton that the message "was like an electric spark kindling the fires of patriotism."[50] Illinois Senator Shelby M. Cullom, normally a critic of Cleveland, set the tone when he spoke in behalf of enforcement of the Monroe Doctrine. "Our policy," Cullom announced, "is the American policy, our doctrine is the protection of American interests, and our motto is 'America for Americans.' " The *Union Signal* of Milwaukee screamed that it "Means a Fight," and the Portland *Oregonian* welcomed the prospect for "we are at the mercy of England as far as our finances go, and this is our only out."[51] The reaction within the business community was mixed, and substantially reflected the metropolis-colonial dichotomy. Financiers in New York and Boston, and to some extent in Chicago, were appalled by Cleveland's belligerent tone. Merchants and industrialists of the Midwest, South, and West, especially those interested in overseas market expansion, backed the president. *Bradstreet's* reported that 22 of 23 boards of trade, chambers of commerce and commercial exchanges supported Cleveland, while such prominent leaders as William C. Whitney, Chauncey Depew, Oscar Straus, Charles E. Adams, and Andrew Carnegie hailed the message.[52]

There also was a lack of unanimity among reformers, Populists, and silverites. The renowned spokesman for America's social conscience, Henry Demarest Lloyd, looked upon a war with Great Britain as a battle against "those which in the past have stood against Liberty and Progress" and he would "extend the Monroe doctrine to the defense of every Republic as far as Andorra and San Marino." Such a conflict would be a welcome purgative and purifier, for "if anything could save America from her apparently impending Midas-like doom it would be such a Mission."[53] But one southern Populist editor snapped that Cleveland's "jingo message is all rot" and he only "seeks by a show of Americanism, to recover some of the ground lost by his party by his culpable course, but it will fail." Tom Watson's *People's Party Paper* concurred, and declared that "the war scare is to be utilized for the purpose of riveting the goldbug shackles."[54]

They were not far from the mark, for Cleveland was motivated—at least to a significant extent—by political considerations. He recognized the Venezuela question was "a winner," and an issue by which he might retain control of the Democratic party. Such an analysis does not discount the president's genuine nationalistic concern for America's interests, nor his commitment to overseas economic expansion. But his anti-British stand momentarily disoriented the Republicans and temporarily cheered the disenchanted among his own ranks. Cleveland's post-master-general, William L. Wilson, acknowledged the political importance by noting in his diary: "The Venezuela matter has dwarfed or relegated to the background all other and lesser foreign questions on which the Republicans were getting ready to attack the administration for its 'weak and un-American' foreign policy, and to that extent has done us good politically."[55] The action was consistent with Cleveland's earlier use of foreign policy for domestic political ends. In the summer of 1888, for example, he had asked congressional support for stronger measures against Great Britain in the dispute over fishing rights in Canadian waters. That was a maneuver to squelch the Republican charge that he was pro-British. Likewise, his withdrawal of the Hawaiian treaty in 1893 was at least partially designed to cast the GOP in a bad light. As W. T. Stead of the London *Review of Reviews* commented to Lloyd on the Venezuela finesse, "it must be admitted that President Cleveland has left us no room for difference of opinion."[56]

The seething anti-British nationalism exposed by the Venezuelan crisis surprised and shocked the English. Even such members of the Atlantic community as James Bryce, Moreton Frewen, and Joseph Chamberlain, who frequently visited the United States and had numerous American friends, were caught off guard by the emotionalism of the public outcry. They undoubtedly understood from their contact with the Americanism of Lodge or Theodore Roosevelt what Chamberlain described as "the extreme sensitiveness and vanity of the Americans as a nation." But while most British leaders remained perplexed and sought some explanation from their American contacts, Chamberlain readily, and rather perceptively, analyzed the nature of the outburst. He believed that probably the majority of Americans "would look forward without horror to war" with England because they "are jealous of this country." Americans "suspect us always of an assumption of superiority of which we are not conscious ourselves" and "they would not be sorry to prove that they are bigger and stronger and better than we are."[57]

Several American leaders, in replying to inquiries from their English friends about the nature of the anti-British reaction, displayed their share of national sensitiveness and jealousy. They also detailed a number of specific factors that helped detonate the explosion. The first thing made clear to the English correspondents was that the widespread anti-British feeling was not generated exclusively by apprehension for American interests in the Western Hemisphere. The president of the American Bimetallic League, Adoniram J. Warner, wrote Frewen that Americans were "all united on the Monroe Doctrine." But the difficulty in Venezuela "was only the *occasion*" and the "real cause of the feeling" against Britain arose from "the deep-seated belief that England by her financial maneuvering beginning with the demonetization of silver in 1873, has gained an advantage" which "will lead to trouble." Warner believed that the American people resented England's position "as the great creditor nation of the world" which allowed Britain "to dominate other countries more by the power this gives her than by her own navy." The United States was determined to break free of English financial dominance "even if it takes another war."[58]

Frewen also heard from several other prominent Americans who supported Warner's analysis. Henry C. Lodge initially complained to his friend that "the whole of this trouble has grown out of Lord Salisbury's . . . refusal to arbitrate coupled with an assault on the Monroe Doctrine, which the American people do not like . . . . We do not meddle with Africa or Europe or anything," Lodge argued, "but in the Americas we must be let alone. . . ." At the bottom of the "outburst against England here" was "England's attitude on the money question and the way in which she has snubbed all our efforts to do anything for silver." "Do you not see," Lodge admonished his bimetallist ally, "that gold, which you have been fighting for years, is really at the bottom of all this business?"[59]

Frewen forwarded Lodge's angry letter to Arthur J. Balfour, the first lord of the treasury in Salisbury's cabinet. An active bimetallist who had served on the Royal Commission on Gold and Silver in the 1880s, Balfour continued to seek a means to create an international agreement on bimetallism. His famous Mansion House statement of 1893 strongly urged Great Britain to adopt the double standard to guarantee international monetary stability and to aid "in oiling the wheels of commerce."[60] In his reply to Frewen concerning the Lodge letter, Balfour agreed that the gold issue was responsible. But, he asked, making an analysis similar to that of the American national bimetallists, "why do not the USA, if they think as they do (quite rightly in my opinion) that Bimetallism is for their advantage, force Bimetallism on the world whether England likes or or not?" Balfour believed the United States would succeed because Germany and the Latin union would accede "*with* England or *without* her." The British bimetallist was confident that, once such a combination had been established, "England would do a very great deal to help" and "large portions of the British Empire would join it."[61] That, of course, was exactly what American silverites had argued for years.

Lodge also wrote directly to Balfour concerning the Anglo-American crisis. Much ill will had been engendered by the British action in the Corinto affair, Lodge informed the Englishman, but basically the American outburst over the Venezuela crisis was symptomatic of deep-seated and long-standing grievances against Great Britain. He reiterated the argument that Cleveland's message was only the occasion to vent this pent-up hostility and resentment. "When," Lodge explained, "the President suddenly took a stand which the country thought right in Venezuela, the materials were ready and the explosion followed." The whole episode hinged on the defense of the Monroe Doctrine "which is our balance of power and rests on the great law of self-preservation." There was to be no mistake or misunderstanding on this basic premise. American hegemony in the Western Hemisphere had to be clearly and explicitly acknowledged.[62]

The ultimate capitulation of the Salisbury government in the Venezuela affair resulted in good part from the pressure of other diplomatic problems, especially in South Africa and the Middle East. The German kaiser's telegram to President Kruger of the Transvaal Free State congratulating him on the capture of the Jameson raiders was the event that helped precipitate a change of opinion within the British cabinet. In a meeting on January 11, 1896, the cabinet informed Prime Minister Salisbury it no longer supported his strong stand against the United States and urged him to abandon the policy of refusing arbitration of the dispute. Salisbury did not surrender without a fight, and at one point angrily threatened that if England "were to yield unconditionally to American threats another Prime Minister would have to be found."[63] In the end, however, Salisbury begrudgingly acquiesced.

Two cabinet members, Arthur Balfour and Colonial Secretary Joseph Chamberlain, were instrumental in bringing about the shift within the British government. Both men were fully cognizant of America's present and future economic potential and favored an Anglo-American detente. They impressed Salisbury with the growing importance of the United States as a power to befriend—rather than antagonize—in the face of a hostile world. And while Balfour deemed bimetallism a viable course for Britain to follow in order to retain its commercial position, Chamberlain was moving toward trade and tariff preference within the Empire as a way to meet the growing competition of Germany and the United States. Chamberlain, in particular, scurried about for solutions to the Venezuelan mess. In the midst of the crisis he suggested to Lord Salisbury that England offer the United States an alliance against Turkey in the Near East. Doubtful of the feasibility of such a plan from the start, the Prime Minister rejected it because the difficulties were so "formidable." He questioned whether the United States "could really help us," for it was unlikely the Americans would be willing to commit troops to such an operation. Perhaps what on the surface appears to be an outlandish scheme actually underscores Chamberlain's rather perceptive insight into the American national psyche. He probably was prepared to include the United States in the games played by the imperial powers in the hope that this appeal to their imperial ambitions and Anglo-Saxon race pride might mollify their resentment and jealousy of Great Britain.[64]

Negotiations over the exact nature of the Venezuelan agreement continued throughout the spring and summer of 1896. A treaty was finally approved in November that called for a tribunal consisting of two Americans, two British citizens, and a Russian versed in international law. In the final settlement England received most of the disputed territory, although Venezuela remained in control of the Orinoco River. The details of the settlement provided somewhat of an anticlimax. The main issue of British acceptance of American hegemony in the Western Hemisphere had already been decided. Throughout the negotiations the United States barely consulted the Venezuelans. They were mere pawns in the power struggle who were granted representation on the tribunal only after making a vehement protest. American disdain for Venezuelan interests left a reservoir of ill feeling that manifested itself in the pro-Spanish position of that nation during the Spanish-American war.

While the Venezuela issue may have had a cathartic effect, Cleveland's triumph was shortlived. The president's bold foreign policy stroke was not supplemented by a program for economic expansion and thus failed to overshadow the monetary issue in the 1896 Democratic convention. The Democrats dumped Cleveland and the gold standard in favor of William Jennings Bryan and free silver. In his campaign the Nebraskan focused almost exclusively on the benefits of unlimited silver coinage at 16 to 1. Remonetization would bring the nation relief from the depression by arresting the deflationary trend and broadly serving to expand overseas markets. Bryan declared "it was the issue of 1776 over again," for unlimited silver coinage would not only end the exploitation of the farmers by the metropolitan East, it also would allow the United States to bring England's reign as king of the world marketplace to a close. The Democrats, castigated by Republican protectionists for over twenty years as the party of England and John Bull, hoped to turn the tables on the GOP with their charge that "gold monometallism is a British policy, and its adoption has brought nations into financial servitude to London. It is not only un-American but anti-American."[65] When the People's party convention also nominated Bryan, the forces of the colonial South and West were merged under the free silver banner.

However, some Populist leaders—including Tom Watson—rather reluctantly backed Bryan. They doubted that free silver could unilaterally unfetter the domestic marketplace without the assistance of their broad program of domestic reforms aimed at transportation abuses, alien ownership of land, and monopolistic concentrations of wealth. In addition, Bryan neglected to buttress his promise of remonetization with other proposals for overseas commercial expansion. William McKinley quickly sensed the weakness of Bryan's sole reliance on free silver. He and the GOP shrewdly capitalized on the narrowness of the Democratic approach by erecting a more comprehensive economic nationalist platform that was coupled with a safe commitment to silver through an international bimetallic agreement. On the monetary issue the Republicans had a flexibility that permitted them to stress their adherence to gold in the East, while in the crucial pivot states of the old

Northwest they emphasized their pledge to seek international bi-metallism as the most effective way of remonetizing silver.[66]

The key features of the Republican economic composite were protection and reciprocity. A protective tariff was "the bulwark of American industrial independence" for "it builds up domestic industry and trade and secures our own markets for ourselves." To augment protection and "secure enlarged markets for the products of our farms, forests, and factories," the GOP urged a return to the Blaine formula of reciprocity which "builds up foreign trade and finds an outlet for our surplus."[67] McKinley and the Republicans constantly assured the voters that their integrated approach to overseas commercial expansion would restore prosperity and bring relief to a depression-ridden nation. They argued that their program would provide sufficient economic rewards throughout the land to overcome the colonial-metropolitan tension and eliminate the need for internal market reforms.

McKinley's convincing victory over Bryan testified to the wisdom and effectiveness of the Republican formula. By putting all their eggs in the free silver basket, the Democrats had very little to fall back on when just before the election a sudden upturn in agricultural prices occurred without a corresponding hike in the price of silver. This appeared to disprove the cause-effect relationship of their analysis, which said that the decline in the price of silver since demonetization accounted for the steady drop of farm prices over the past two decades. The Republicans successfully blunted the simplistic appeal of free silver among the agrarians of the Midwest with the balanced economic nationalism of protection and reciprocity and the promise of international bimetallism. At the same time, the Republican stand retained the allegiance of eastern industrial workers and tied metropolitan industrial and business leaders to the McKinley ticket.

The campaign of 1896, frequently billed as the epic "battle of the standards," went beyond the question of determining the most advantageous domestic currency system. It represented the culmination of more than twenty years of debate over the issue of how best to foster overseas commercial expansion and provide for more equitable internal economic development. Both parties relied heavily on the appeal of economic nationalism and pursued virtually the same objectives. They offered alternatives designed to establish domestic financial and industrial independence and eradicate British economic influence. But in 1896 neither the Democrats nor the Republicans were able to monopolize the prevailing anti-British nationalism of the electorate. The attempt of the Democrats, through their free silver commitment, to transfer the stigma of the pro-British label to the GOP faltered. Republican flexibility on the money issue neutralized the goldbug charge and thwarted this attack on their Americanism. In the end, the Republican program, which highlighted protection and reciprocity, was the choice of Americans as the more viable alternative to insure industrial independence and to challenge Great Britain throughout the hemisphere and the Pacific.

NOTES

1. Remarks of James K. Jones, January 28, 1898, *Congressional Record*, XXXI, Part 2, 1135 (hereinafter cited as *CR*, 31:2:1135).

2. Walter T.K. Nugent, *Money and American Society, 1865 – 1880* (New York: The Free Press, 1968). Robert B. Sharkey, Review of *Money and American Society, 1865 – 1880*, by Walter T.K. Nugent, *American Historical Review*, LXXIV (February 1969), pp. 1093—94.

3. Milton Friedman and Anna Schwartz, *A Monetary History of the United States* (Princeton: Princeton University Press, 1964), p. 134, Roy Harrod, *The Dollar* (New York: W. W. Norton and Co., 1963), pp. 1—34.

4. For an extensive discussion of the colonial status of the West and South see William A. Williams, *The Roots of the Modern American Empire* (New York: Random House, 1969).

5. *People's Party Paper*, January 5, 1894.

6. Harrod, *Dollar*, p. 17. John Garraty, *The American Nation* (New York: Harper & Row, 1966), p. 614.

7. Stanley Jones, *The Presidential Election of 1896* (Madison: University of Wisconsin Press, 1964), p. 8.

8. Remarks of January 7, 1898, *CR*, 31:1:426.

9. *Western Rural*, May 1, 1886. C. P. Wright and J. S. Davis, "India as a Producer and Exporter of Wheat," *Wheat Studies*, 3:8 (July 1927), pp. 317—412. Petition of Southwest Silver Convention, December, 1892 to Senate Committee on Finance, 52nd Cong., records of the United States Senate, National Archives, Record Group 46. Thomas C. Power, *Silver, The Friend of the Farmer and the Miner* (Washington: n.p., 1893). Herman E. Taubeneck, *The Condition of the American Farmer* (Chicago: The Schulte Publishing Co., 1896), p. 51.

10. See, for example, the pages of the *Western Rural, Pacific Rural Press, Rural New Yorker, Prairie Farmer*, and the Alliance organs *National Economist* and *Southern Mercury*.

11. *Western Rural,* October 15, 1892.

12. Henry B. Russell, *International Monetary Conferences* (New York: Harper & Brothers, 1898). Jeannette P. Nichols, "Silver Diplomacy," *Political Science Quarterly,* XLVIII (December 1933), pp. 583–84.

13. Hay to Reid, May 2, 1895, Whitelaw Reid Papers, Library of Congress.

14. Russell, *International Monetary Conferences.* p. 293.

15. William M. Evarts, *The Monetary Conference. What America Asks From Other Nations* (New York: Douglas Taylor, Printer, 1881).

16. *Annual Report of the Secretary of the Treasury,* 1889 (Washington: Government Printing Office, 1889), pp. lxxi, lxxii.

17. See Ralph Robey, *The Monetary Problem, Gold and Silver* (Final Report of the Royal Commission on Gold and Silver, 1888), (New York: Columbia University Press, 1936).

18. *Report of the Royal Commission on the Depression of Trade and Industry* (London: Eyre and Spottiswoode, 1886). *The Proceedings of the Bimetallic Conference held at Manchester, 4th and 5th April 1888* (Manchester: The Bimetallic League, 1888).

19. Testimony of Bertram Currie, *Reports from Commissioners, Inspectors, and Others* (1888) House of Commons, Vol. 22, pp. 43, 49.

20. Russell, *International Monetary Conferences,* and Nichols, "Silver Diplomacy."

21. J. Laurence Laughlin, *The History of Bimetallism in the United States* (New York: D. Appleton & Co., 1892), p. 264.

22. *Pacific Rural Press,* November 14, 1891.

23. See petitions to Senate Committee on Finance, 51st Cong., records of the United States Senate, NA, RG 46.

24. John D. Hicks, *The Populist Revolt* (Minneapolis: The University of Minnesota Press, 1931). C. Vann Woodward, *Tom Watson, Agrarian Rebel* (New York: The MacMillan Company, 1938).

25. *National Bulletin,* October 22, 1892, copy in Lemeul H. Weller Papers, Wisconsin State Historical Society.

26. Henry C. Lodge to Moreton Frewen, November 16, 1894, Frewen Papers, Library of Congress.

27. Remarks of May 9, 1894, *CR,* 26:5:4528,

28. *Fortnightly Review* (June 1894), LXI, pp. 837–38. See also Thomas B. Reed to Frewen, May 15, 1894, Frewen Papers.

29. See letter of April 23, 1894, Frewen Papers.

30. Ibid., Lodge to Frewen, June 4, 1894.

31. Hicks, *Populist Revolt,* p. 320.

32. Frewen was a nineteenth century entrepreneur in the pattern of Cecil Rhodes. He ranched in Wyoming during the 1870s and lost heavily. His marriage to Clare Jerome, sister of Jenny Jerome Churchill, eased his monetary problems, but he always remained on the verge of bankruptcy. Frewen served as economic advisor to the Nizam of Hyberdad and engaged in numerous business ventures in North and South America, Africa, and Australia. See Shane Leslie, *Studies in Sublime Failure* (London: Ernest Benn, Ltd., 1932).

33. Frewen to his wife, April 10, 1894, Frewen Papers.

34. Among the supporters were Edward Wolcott, William Stewart, John T. Morgan, Anthony Higgins, Joseph Daniel, James K. Jones, and of course, Lodge. William C. Whitney of Cleveland's cabinet also backed the plan. See Whitney to Frewen, July 31, 1894, and Wolcott to Frewen, June 5, 1894, Frewen Papers.

35. John Higham, *Strangers in the Land, Patterns of American Nativism 1860 — 1925* (New York: Atheneum, 1967), p. 96. Howard K. Beale, *Theodore Roosevelt and the Rise of America to World Power* (New York: Collier Books, 1965), pp. 85–99.

36. Lodge to Davis, April 9, 1895, Cushman K. Davis Papers, Minnesota Historical Society.

37. Henry C. Lodge, "England, Venezuela, and the Monroe Doctrine," *North American Review*, Vol. 160 (June 1895), p. 658.

38. Gresham to Dyer, May 2, 1894. Gresham to General F.M. Force, August 30, 1893, Gresham Papers, Library of Congress.

39. For a succinct analysis of the Cleveland administration's Nicaragua policy see Walter LaFeber, *The New Empire* (Ithaca: Cornell University Press, 1963), pp. 218–28.

40. *Review of Reviews*, XI (June 1895), p. 621. Nelson M. Blake, "Background of Cleveland's Venezuelan Policy," *American Historical Review*, XLVII (January 1942), pp. 263–66.

41. Remarks of Sir Edward Thornton to Lord Granville, June 14, 1881, in Paul Knaplund and Carolyn M. Clewes, *Private Letters From the British Embassy in Washington to the Foreign Secretary Lord Granville, 1880 — 1885*, Annual Report of the American Historical Association, Vol. I, 1941 (Washington: Government Printing Office, 1942), p. 137.

42. James D. Richardson, *Messages and Papers of the Presidents*, IX (Washington: Government Printing Office, 1902), p. 526.

43. Remarks of February 6, 1895, *CR*, 27:2:1832.

44. William L. Scruggs, *The Colombian and Venezuelan Republics* (Boston: Little, Brown & Co., 1900), p. 296.

45. John A. S. Grenville and George B. Young, *Politics, Strategy, and American Diplomacy* (New Haven: Yale University Press, 1966), pp. 125–57.

46. George F. Parker, *Recollections of Grover Cleveland* (New York: The Century Company, 1909), pp. 197–98.

47. *Foreign Relations of the United States, 1895*, II (Washington: Government Printing Office, 1896), pp. 1483–88.

48. Richardson, *Messages and Papers*, IX, p. 655.

49. Hay to Whitelaw Reid, May 2, 1895, Reid Papers.

50. W.W. Cox to Morton, December 19, 1895, J. Sterling Morton Papers, Nebraska State Historical Society.

51. Remarks of December 10, 1895, *CR*, 28:1:111. James A. Barnes, *John G. Carlisle, Financial Statesman* (New York: Dodd, Mead and Company, 1931), p. 410.

52. Walter LaFeber, "The American Business Community and Cleveland's Venezuelan Message," *Business History Review*, 34:4 (Winter 1960), pp. 393–402.

53. Lloyd to John C. Pirie, December 30, 1895, Lloyd Papers, Wisconsin State Historical Society.

54. *Southern Mercury,* December 26, 1895. *People's Party Paper,* December 27, 1895.

55. Wilson diary entry of January 3, 1896 in Festus P. Summers, ed., *The Cabinet Diary of William L. Wilson, 1896 − 1897* (Chapel Hill: The University of North Carolina Press, 1957). See also Blake, "Cleveland's Venezuelan Policy."

56. W.T. Stead to H.D. Lloyd, December 24, 1895. Henry D. Lloyd Papers.

57. Chamberlain to Selborne, December 20, 1895, Chamberlain Papers, University of Birmingham, England.

58. A. J. Warner to Frewen, January 28, 1896, Frewen Papers.

59. Ibid., Lodge to Frewen, January 9, 17, 1896.

60. *Address by the Right Honorable Arthur James Balfour* (London: n.p., 1893), p. 19. Correspondence of Henry H. Gibbs to Balfour, 1896−97, Balfour Papers, British Museum.

61. Balfour to Frewen, February 3, 1896, Frewen Papers.

62. Lodge to Balfour, February 1, 1896, Lodge Papers, Massachusetts Historical Society. Lodge also made this point to Frewen when discussing possible American intervention to Cuba in support of the insurgents and the question of annexation. "There is nothing in the Monroe Doctrine," Lodge maintained, "preventing ourselves or any other American state from acquiring additional territory if we so choose. The Monroe Doctrine applies solely to the prevention of the extension of European territory in this hemisphere." Lodge to Frewen, March 11, 1896, Frewen Papers.

63. Memo of cabinet meeting, January 11, 1896, Chamberlain Papers.

64. Ibid., Salisbury to Chamberlain, December 30, 1895, January 6, 1896.

65. William J. Bryan, *The First Battle* (Chicago: W. B. Conkey Company, 1896), pp. 199−206. Kirk H. Porter and Donald B. Johnson, *National Party Platforms, 1840 − 1956* (Urbana: The University of Illinois Press, 1956), p. 98.

66. For an excellent contemporary analysis of the situation in the Midwest and West see the letter of James Clarkson to Samuel Fessenden, October 15, 1896, Clarkson Papers, Library of Congress. See also Lawrence J. Scheidler, "Silver and Politics, 1893−1896," (Ph. D. dissertation, Indiana University, 1936).

67. Porter and Johnson, *Party Platforms,* p. 107.

10

Conclusion

Why is it that the seat of commerce and finance now in control of and dominating the United States and the whole world is located on the little island of England? Why does not the United States control both the finance and commerce and proclaim herself mistress of the seas?

James S. Hogg, 1894

We have come to the time when we must make up our minds whether we are to be dominant in the Western Hemisphere and keep it free from foreign invasion or whether we are to stand aside and let it all be seized as Africa has been.

Henry Cabot Lodge, 1896

Throughout the last quarter of the nineteenth century the United States challenged Great Britain for commercial and economic supremacy in the Western Hemisphere and the Pacific. A progression of American leaders, from Henry C. Carey to James G. Blaine and Henry Cabot Lodge, directed their energies to supplanting England as the ruling monarch of the marketplace and to establishing true economic and financial independence for the United States. Governor James S. Hogg of Texas spoke for much of the nation in the mid-1890s as he rhetorically asked, "Why is it that the seat of commerce and finance now in control and dominating the United States and the whole world is located in the little island of England?" Many Americans undoubtedly also understood his impatience when he demanded to know why the United States does not "control both the finance and commerce and proclaim herself mistress of the seas?"[1] The belief that Britain's economic and financial power thwarted the fulfillment of the nation's destiny was shared by dirt farmers, sharecroppers, agrarian editors, and labor leaders as well as businessmen, industrialists, and politicians. This perception, and the hostility and frustration it evoked, gave rise to the anti-British nationalism that pervaded the American consciousness in the late nineteenth century.

Actually, American visions of commercial preeminence coincided with the necessity of coping with the difficulties created by the recurrent economic depression and business stagnation that marked the period. Beginning in the depression of the 1870s and continuing to the turn of the century, American leaders accepted and acted upon the doctrine that overseas economic expansion would insure domestic peace and prosperity, social stability, and perhaps most important, preserve the existing system.[2] Foreign markets for America's surplus argicultural and manufactured goods were defined by these leaders as the best remedy for the destructive economic and social effects of depression; they tied the nation's domestic health, and its very viability, directly to foreign policy. And in this battle for the marketplace such leaders as William M. Evarts, Hugh McCullough, Frederick Frelinghuysen, Terence V. Powderly, and President Benjamin Harrison, to name but a few, consciously and repeatedly defined the contest as one with England for world economic supremacy.

A world-wide struggle for markets began during the 1870s as Great Britain, the acknowledged leader at the start of this race for commercial primacy, faced strong challenges from Germany and the United States. However, it was the United States and not Germany (as is so often maintained) that presented the greater initial, and for that matter sustained, challenge to Britain's economic hegemony. In those years America assumed world industrial leadership and asserted control of its home market. Whereas earlier in the century the United States had been Britain's largest foreign customer, in 1898 Americans purchased only one-sixteenth of English exports. And while the United States became less important as an outlet for British goods it continued to furnish about one-fifth of Britain's imports, mostly foodstuffs and raw materials.[3]

British leaders such as William E. Gladstone, Joseph Chamberlain, and Lord Salisbury closely observed the American industrial and trade phenomenon and readily perceived the nature of the United States' challenge to their supremacy. Even before England's European isolation and the threat of Germany were fully visible on the horizon, Gladstone led the Liberals in openly courting the United States. "The future of the world belongs to us," he predicted in 1884 when discussing the necessity of an Anglo-American friendship, "to us who are of the same blood and language, if we are true to ourselves, and to our opportunities, not of conquest or aggression, but of commercial development and beneficent influence." Chamberlain, initially less sanguine about Britain's future, scurried about for a policy that might preserve the English lead while Salisbury only grudgingly acknowledged America's new position. By and large, however, the British patiently endured the excesses of the adolescent power and shared the assessment of Gladstone, and ultimately Chamberlain as well, that Britain's destiny lay in closer ties with its North American offspring.[4]

But the majority of Americans during the latter half of the nineteenth century reacted unfavorably to any movement for a closer relationship with the national rival. The United States may have gained ground in the economic competition by breaking the traditional client-patron trade pattern that existed with England and by establishing a favorable trade balance after the years of 1876–1877. Nonetheless, a balance of payments deficit remained that in the American view gave Britain the upper hand in the commercial race. It was abundantly clear that despite impressive American advances, Britain's influence and power were quite intact. It possessed a global empire. It was the world's banker. Its merchant fleet controlled the ocean trade lanes. And to protect these far-flung interests, Her Majesty's Navy ruled the waves. Above all, as part of these activities Britain enjoyed a preeminent position in the Western Hemisphere that provided the main obstacle to an expanded American trade to Central and South America.

In the ensuing political and economic confrontations with Great Britain in Latin America, many American leaders—including the most notorious twisters of the lion's tail such as Blaine or Lodge—frequently revealed a certain ambivalence toward the former mother country. This mixed emotional and psychological response resembled a love-hate, or more accurately a hate-love relationship. It was characterized on the one hand by immense distrust, hostility, and resentment which stemmed from an intense jealousy of Britain's dominance of the international arena. On the other hand, there existed a grudging admiration born of envy and a commitment to an Anglo-Saxon destiny that inspired occasional attempts to emulate the obvious and phenomenal imperial success of Great Britain. This ambivalent attitude toward England— hostility and resentment tempered by admiration—was a central characteristic in the outlook of American leaders during the years between the Civil War and the end of the century.

England, however, was perceived as more than just a menace to American overseas commercial expansion. At the domestic level anti-British nationalism mushroomed as the result of the popular awareness of the dominant role played by Britain in American economic and political life. Beginning with Henry C. Carey and his cadre of economic nationalists, large portions of the population identified England as the primary opponent of American industrial, economic, and financial independence. The expressions of hostility and resentment were particularly apparent among farmers of the trans-Mississippi West and the South. Not only was the presence of British capital strongly felt in these regions, but a sense of dependence upon England as a vital market for agricultural exports prevailed as well. The farmers of the West and South, painfully aware that the price for their wheat and cotton was set in the Liverpool and London commodity markets, explicitly defined their status as that of domestic colonials and usually compared their plight to that of other colonial societies such as British-controlled India and Ireland. In expressing their grievances, the agrarians continually denounced their inferior position at the colonial end of an imperial axis that extended from the metropolitan centers of Britain and the Northeast to the West and South. Consequently, it appears that in the last quarter of the nineteenth century a direct correlation existed between the level of economic development of a region and the intensity of anti-British sentiment.

Certainly a festering source of antagonism among Americans,

especially those engaged in developing the West, was the prevalence of British capital in various enterprises such as cattle ranches, railroads, grain elevators, stockyards, mines, and land companies. To be sure, the role of British investment in the total development of the American economy was not crucial. Yet, it was quite important to the development of these capital scarce regions. Total British investment in the United States amounted to approximately $2 billion in 1890 and approached somewhat more than $2.5 billion at the turn of the century.[5] While these speculative activities were focused predominately in the West, large outlays also existed in the old Northwest and the South. Anti-British nationalism flourished in these sections, most noticeably in the region between the Mississippi River and the Rocky Mountains. Even here, however, Anglophobia was touched with a trace of ambivalence as westerners, displaying a trait apparently common to members of capital scarce areas, desired and sought the benefits of foreign capital but resented the influence and control it gave the outsider.

Concern over the extensive landholdings of foreigners was not restricted to the actual pioneers in the regions where the British corporations prevailed. Americans in general were fearful that the frontier as a positive social force shaping American life and institutions soon would disappear. Veterans groups, labor organizations, and major and minor political parties were aroused at the prospect of a vanishing frontier. Newspapers, journals, and periodicals throughout the nation worriedly expressed their misgivings about the emergence of this evil and published lists of alien holdings and recent acquisitions to document the extent and nature of this alleged threat to the republic. And in the 1880s a national campaign for legislation to curb alien ownership swept the country. The issue played a prominent part in the 1884 presidential campaign as both major parties inserted a call for restrictions in their platforms. A typical nationalist response came from the New Hampshire legislature in a joint resolution that patriotically declared that "American soil is for Americans, and should be exclusively owned and controlled by American citizens."[6] The sustained public outcry brought the passage of federal legislation in 1887 that curbed alien holdings in the territories and by 1900 all but fifteen of the forty-five states had statutes that made some distinction between domestic and alien owners.[7]

The phenomenon of Anglophobia undoubtedly reached its high-water mark with the Populist movement and the free silver crusade of the 1890s. The Populists viewed their political struggle as basically a revolt against a progressively more oppressive financial and economic imperialism centered in the East and directly linked to, and dominated by, Great Britain. And while popular enmity for the national rival had been on the rise for over two decades, it was the free silver campaign that mobilized this discontent by providing a single issue that not only incorporated all of America's grievances against England but promised to end the United States' financial servitude to Great Britain. Free silverites contended that remonetization would release the American farmer from his dependence on the English market and open alternate markets in Latin America and Asia for his agricultural surplus. In addition, they argued that unlimited coinage at 16 to 1 would terminate the United States' rather humiliating reliance on foreign capital and thereby overcome the attendant evils of alien ownership and bond issues—both of which benefited British investors and speculators at the expense of the American people. What the free silver campaign did for the farmer and his allies was to unite their concern for solutions to the problems of market expansion and British influence on the course of American economic development. As such, it gave specific form to their burgeoning economic nationalism and intensified their anti-British nationalism.

In the climactic presidential campaign of 1896 both major parties stressed economic nationalist remedies and presented alternatives designed to establish domestic financial and industrial independence and eliminate British economic influence. The Democrats, allied with the Populists, advocated silver remonetization to end the nation's economic woes and release it from British thralldom. In response, the Republicans offered an integrated economic composite based on protection and reciprocity with a commitment to international bimetallism. And while both the Democrats and the Republicans proclaimed that their program was the more patriotic "American" course to follow, neither group was successful in pinning the pro-British tag on the other, nor was one party able to exclusively capitalize on the prevailing anti-British nationalism of the electorate. In the end, the Republicans convinced the voters that their alternative would insure industrial independence and carry the challenge to the British in the Western Hemisphere and the Pacific.

The central features of the silver crusade and the debates surrounding the 1896 campaign essentially verify the general conclusion that Anglophobia can best be understood as a corollary to the dynamic economic nationalism that emerged in the United States during the last decades of the nineteenth century. This admittedly negative emotional response went hand-in-hand with the nation's expanding power and its awakening national consciousness. In those years the United States obviously felt hemmed in and frustrated by Great Britain. Consequently, England was constantly identified and understood as thwarting American aspirations for commercial and economic preeminence in the Western Hemisphere in particular, and the world in general. That led to frequent emotional outbursts and vehement denunciations against the former mother country. And while Americans claimed that Britain presented the principal obstacle to the fulfillment of their destiny, England's actions, such as its role in the War of the Pacific, its intransigence in refusing alteration of the Clayton-Bulwer Treaty, its show of force in the Corinto affair, and its consistent territorial encroachments in the Venezuelan boundary dispute, gave form and substance to this view of John Bull as devil.

The defeat of the free silver movement signaled the eventual disappearance of Anglophobia as a dominant and pervasive feature of the American national consciousness. One of the last outright displays of anti-British nationalism came in the debate over ratification of the Olney-Pauncefote arbitration treaty and its rejection in the Senate by three votes.[8] The return of prosperity and the events surrounding America's burst of imperialism at the end of the century dissipated the force of Anglophobia and effectively drove anti-British sentiments to the background. The acquisition of an overseas empire and the recognition of America's power by Great Britain and the nations of Europe eradicated the feelings of inferiority and overcame the jealousy of England's imperial success. The United States was now acknowledged as a partner among equals on the international scene.

This acceptance was dramatically illustrated by Britain's acquiescence on a number of key issues that prompted the "great rapprochement" at the dawn of the twentieth century. Isolated on the continent and fearful of the growing industrial and military might of Germany, England eagerly sought to cement the bonds of Anglo-American friendship. Britain's sympathy for the United States in the war against Spain, its concessions on the interoceanic canal question, its tacit acknowledgment of American hegemony in the Caribbean, and its approval and support for the Open Door principle based on a mutuality of interest in the Far East, all paved the way for the removal of American hostility and ill feeling.[9] No longer was Britain accused at every turn of trying to block the fulfillment of this nation's destiny. Perhaps more than anything else, British recognition of the United States as a world power, not as a junior partner, and the satisfaction Americans felt with their recent imperial success, help to explain the gradual submergence of Anglophobia.

The remarkable turnabout in public opinion allowed for an informal Anglo-American alliance that only a few short years earlier would have been unthinkable. However, anti-British sentiment never entirely disappeared. Several sources of friction remained and the first two decades of the twentieth century saw sporadic Anglophobic outbursts, such as those that tinged the debates over entry into World War I and ratification of the Versailles Treaty. British capital continued to flow into the United States and in Latin America the economic rivalry between the two nations grew increasingly fierce. It was only with the conclusion of the First World War that active Anglophobia declined. Not only were British investments in the United States virtually liquidated by the 1920s, but more important, America assumed the role of the world's creditor and possessed a clear economic supremacy in the Western Hemisphere. Even then, anti-British feelings had not vanished, and they reappeared in the 1930s as an element in what has been labelled isolationism in the Midwest and West, but what perhaps more accurately can be understood as a mixture of the traditional distrust of England, and Europe in general, united with a sincere desire for nonintervention. Ironically, Great Britain's support of the United States after World War II has made the reversal complete and turned many Americans into Anglophiles.

NOTES

1. Speech advocating an isthmian canal, Philadelphia, July 2, 1894 in Robert C. Cotner, ed., *Addresses and State Papers of James Stephen Hogg* (Austin: University of Texas Press, 1951), p. 374.

2. For a discussion of the McKinley administration's commitment to economic expansion see Thomas J. McCormick, *China Market: America's Quest for Informal Empire, 1893 – 1901.* (Chicago: Quadrangle Books, 1967). William A. Williams, *The Roots of the Modern American Empire* (New York: Random House, 1969).

3. Bradford Perkins, *The Great Rapprochement, England and the United States, 1895 – 1914* (New York: Atheneum, 1968), pp. 8–9.

4. William E. Gladstone, "Kin Beyond the Sea," *North American Review,* September-October 1878. George W. Smalley, *London Letters and Some Others* (London: Macmillan Company, 1890), II, p. 349. A. P. Thornton, *The Imperial Idea and Its Enemies* (London: St. Martin's Press, Inc., 1959), p. 77. For some British expressions of concern at the turn of the century see F. A. McKenzie, *The American Invaders* (London: Grant Richards, 1902), and Sir Christopher Furness, *The American Invasion* (London: Simpkin, Marshall, Hamilton, Kent & Co. Ltd. 1902).

5. A. K. Cairncross, *Home and Foreign Investment, 1870 – 1913* (Cambridge: Cambridge University Press, 1953), pp. 183–85. Bruce M. Russett, *Community and Contention, Britain and America in the Twentieth Century* (Cambridge: The MIT Press, 1963), p. 229.

6. Joint resolution of the New Hampshire legislature, November 11, 1885, Senate Committee on Public Lands, 49th Cong., records of the United States Senate, National Archives, Record Group 46.

7. *London Times,* October 3, 1901, p. 5.

8. For a discussion of the Senate's rejection of the treaty see Howard K. Beale, *Theodore Roosevelt and the Rise of America to World Power* (Baltimore: The Johns Hopkins Press, 1956).

9. Perkins, *The Great Rapprochement.* Charles S. Campbell, Jr., *Anglo-American Understanding,* 1898–1903 (Baltimore: The Johns Hopkins Press, 1957). Lionel Gelber, *The Rise of Anglo-American Friendship* (Hamden, Connecticut: Archon Books, 1966).

SELECTED BIBLIOGRAPHY

Archival and Manuscript Sources

Arthur J. Balfour Papers. British Museum. London, England.
Wharton Barker Papers. Library of Congress. Washington, D. C.
Thomas F. Bayard Papers. Library of Congress. Washington, D. C.
Albert Beveridge Papers. Library of Congress. Washington, D. C.
James G. Blaine Papers. Library of Congress. Washington, D. C.
Joseph Chamberlain Papers. University of Birmingham. Birmingham, England.
James S. Clarkson Papers. Library of Congress. Washington, D. C.
Grover Cleveland Papers. Library of Congress. Washington, D. C.
Cushman K. Davis Papers. Minnesota Historical Society. St Paul, Minnesota.
Charles Dilke Papers. British Museum. London, England.
Grenville Dodge Papers. Iowa State Historical Society. Des Moines, Iowa.
William M. Evarts Papers. Library of Congress. Washington, D. C.
Moreton Frewen Papers. Library of Congress. Washington, D. C.
Robert Arthur Talbot Gascoyne-Cecil Papers. (Third Marquis of Salisbury). Christ Church College. Oxford, England.
William E. Gladstone Papers. British Museum. London, England.
Great Britain, Records of the Foreign Office. Public Records Office. London, England.
Walter Q. Gresham Papers. Library of Congress. Washington, D. C.
Benjamin Harrison Papers. Library of Congress. Washington, D. C.
Charles L. Kurtz Papers. Ohio Historical Society. Columbus, Ohio.
Henry D. Lloyd Papers. Wisconsin State Historical Society. Madison, Wisconsin.
Henry Cabot Lodge Papers. Massachusetts Historical Society. Boston, Massachusetts.

Manton Marble Papers. Library of Congress. Washington, D. C.
William McKinley Papers. Library of Congress. Washington, D. C.
J. Sterling Morton Papers. Nebraska Historical Society. Omaha, Nebraska.
National Archives of the United States. Legislative Records. Washington, D. C.
National Archives of the United States. General Records of the Department of
    State. Washington, D. C.
Richard C. Olney Papers. Library of Congress. Washington, D. C.
Whitelaw Reid Papers. Library of Congress. Washington, D. C.
Harrison Holt Riddleberger Papers. College of William and Mary. Williamsburg,
    Virginia.
William F. Vilas Papers. Wisconsin State Historical Society. Madison, Wisconsin.
Lemeul H. Weller Papers. Wisconsin State Historical Society. Madison, Wisconsin.

Public Documents

A. Congressional:
Congressional Record.
House of Representatives. House Executive Document No. 267. 48th Cong., 2nd
    Sess., 1885.
_____. House Report No. 2308. 48th Cong., 2nd Sess., 1885.
_____. House Report No. 3455. 49th Cong., 1st Sess., 1886.
_____. *Report from the Central and South American Commission-
ers.* House Executive Document No. 226. 48th Cong., 2nd Sess., 1885.
_____. *Report of a Commission Appointed for the Revision of the
Revenue System of the United States.* House Executive Document No. 34.
39th Cong., 1st Sess., 1866.
_____. *Report of the Committee on Foreign Affairs on the Rela-
tions of the United States with Mexico.* House Report No. 701. 45th Cong.,
2nd Sess., 1878.
_____. *Reports of the Silver Commission of 1876.* House Miscella-
neous Document No. 396. 49th Cong., 1st Sess., 1887.
_____. *Report on the Commercial Relations of the United States
with Foreign Countries for the year 1877.* House Executive Document No. 102.
45th Cong., 2nd Sess., 1878.
Senate. *Promotion of Commerce and Increase in Foreign Trade, etc.* Document
No. 60. 55th Cong., 3rd Sess., 1899.
_____. *Report of the International American Conference Relative
to an Intercontinental Railway Line.* Senate Executive Document No. 125. 51st
Cong., 1st Sess., 1890.
_____. *Report of the Select Committee on Relations with Canada.*
Document No. 1530. 51st Cong., 1st Sess., 1890.
_____. *Report of the Select Committee on Transportation Routes
to the Seaboard.* Report No. 307. 43rd Cong., 1st Sess., 1874.
_____. *Report on Unauthorized Fencing of Public Lands.* Senate
Executive Document No. 127. 48th Cong., 1st Sess., 1883–1884.
B. Other:
Bureau of the Census. *Tenth Census of the United States: 1880. Report of the Produc-
tions of Agriculture,* Vol. 3.

———————————. *Eleventh Census of the United States: 1890. Statistics of Agriculture, Irrigation, Fisheries*, Vol. 5.

Department of Agriculture. Bureau of Statistics. *Exports of Farm Products From the United States, 1851 — 1908*. Statistical Bulletin 75. Washington, 1890.

Department of Commerce. Bureau of Statistics. *Historical Statistics of the United States, Colonial Times to 1957*. Washington, 1960.

Department of State. *Consular Reports*. 1880–1896.

———————————. *Papers Relating to the Foreign Relations of the United States*. 1876–1896.

Department of the Treasury. *Annual Report of the Secretary of the Treasury*. 1878–1894.

Great Britain. *Parliamentary Papers. Diplomatic and Consular Reports*. 1877–1879.

Journals and Newspapers

American Economist; Bradstreet's; Breeder's Gazette; The Economist (London); *Farm, Field, and Fireside; Manufacturers' Record; National Economist; National Stockman; Northwestern Miller; Pacific Rural Press; People's Party Paper; Prairie Farmer; Public Opinion; Rural New Yorker; Saturday Review* (London); The *Spectator* (London); *Southern Mercury; London Times; Chicago Tribune; New York Tribune; New York Times;* and *Western Rural.*

Pamphlets and Proceedings

Balfour, Arthur J. *Address by the Right Honorable Arthur James Balfour*. London: 1893.

Bland, T. A. *People's Party Shot and Shell*. Chicago: Charles H. Kerr & Co., 1892.

Carey, Henry C. *Appreciation of the Price of Gold. Evidence Before the United States Monetary Commission*. Philadelphia: Collins, Printer, 1876.

———————————. *Monetary Independence*. Philadelphia: 1875.

———————————. *The British Treaties of 1871 and 1874*. Philadelphia: Collins, Printer, 1874.

———————————. *The Way to Outdo England Without Fighting Her*. Philadelphia: Henry Carey Baird, Industrial Publisher, 1865.

Elder, William. *How the Western States Can Become the Imperial Power in the Union*. Philadelphia: Ringwalt and Brown, 1865.

———————————. *The American Farmer's Markets at Home and Abroad*. Philadelphia: Ringwalt and Brown, 1870.

Evarts, William M. *The Monetary Conference. What America Asks From Other Nations*. New York: Douglas Taylor, Printer, 1881.

Michels, Ivan C. *The True Cause for the Decline in Prices for Wheat and A Remedy*. Washington: Ivan C. Michels, Publisher, 1887.

Proceedings of the National Convention of Ship-Owning and Other Commercial Bodies for the Encouragement of the Ocean Commerce of the United States. New York: Burr Printing House, 1880.

Record of the Proceedings of the Regular Sessions of the General Assembly, Knights of Labor of America, 1880–1890.

Report of the Joint Committee of the Commercial Bodies of New Orleans to the United States, Mexican, Central American Commission. New Orleans: A. W. Hyatt, 1884.

Roach, John. *The Successful Maritime Policy. An Investigation into the Causes of the Decline of Our Shipping Interest.* New York: The Metropolitan Industrial League, n.d.

Swank, James M. *British Efforts to Prevent the Development of American Industries.* Philadelphia: The American Iron and Steel Association, 1892.

————————. *The Industrial Policies of Great Britain and the United States.* Philadelphia: The American Iron and Steel Association, 1876.

Tawney, James A. *Reciprocity Is the Complement of a Protective Tariff.* Washington: 1894.

Thompson, Robert Ellis. *The Commercial Future.* Philadelphia: Edward Stern and Company, 1878.

Worrall, Thomas D. *Direct Trade between Great Britain and the Mississippi Valley.* Manchester: North of England Co-op Printing Society, 1875.

Unpublished Sources

Burnette, Owen Lawrence, Jr. "The Senate Foreign Relations Committee and the Diplomacy of Garfield, Arthur, and Cleveland." Ph.D. dissertation, University of Virginia, 1952.

Erlenborn, James L. "The American Meat and Livestock Industry and American Foreign Policy, 1880–1896." Master's Thesis, University of Wisconsin, 1966.

Hearden, Patrick Joseph. "Cotton Mills of the New South and American Foreign Policy." Master's Thesis. University of Wisconsin, 1966.

Leach, Duane M. "The Tariff and the Western Farmer: 1860–1890." Ph.D. dissertation, University of Oklahoma, 1965.

McJimsey, George T. "The Life of Manton Marble." Ph.D. dissertation, University of Wisconsin, 1968.

O'Grady, Joseph Patrick. "Irish-Americans and Anglo-American Relations, 1880–1888." Ph.D. dissertation, University of Pennsylvania, 1965.

Reuter, William C. "Anglophobia in American Politics." Ph.D. dissertation, University of California, Berkeley, 1966.

Robertson, William Spence. "The Pan-American Policy of James G. Blaine." Master's Thesis, University of Wisconsin, 1900.

Scheidler, Lawrence John. "Silver and Politics 1893–1896." Ph.D. dissertation, Indiana University, 1936.

Schonberger, Howard B. "Transportation to the Seaboard: A Study in the "Communication Revolution" and American Foreign Policy, 1860–1900." Ph.D. dissertation, University of Wisconsin, 1968.

Terrill, Tom E. "The Tariff and Foreign Policy, 1880–1892." Ph.D. dissertation, University of Wisconsin, 1966.

Tucker, James F. "British Agriculture Under Protection and Free Trade, 1815–1895." Ph.D. dissertation, University of Pennsylvania, 1957.

Wilgus, Alva Curtis. "James G. Blaine and the Pan American Movement." Master's Thesis, University of Wisconsin, 1921.
Winchester, Richard C. "James G. Blaine and the Ideology of American Expansion." Ph.D. dissertation, University of Rochester, 1966.

Articles

Airlie, Lord. "The United States as a Field for Agricultural Settlers," *Nineteenth Century,* 9 (February 1881), 292—300.
Albion, Robert G. "British Shipping and Latin America, 1806—1914," *Journal of Economic History,* 11 (1951), 361—77.
Andrew, A. Piatt. "The Influence of the Crops Upon Business in America," *Quarterly Journal of Economics,* 20 (May 1906), 323—52.
Bastert, Russell H. "A New Approach to the Origins of Blaine's Pan American Policy," *Hispanic American Historical Review,* 39 (August 1959), 375—412.
——————————. "Diplomatic Reversal: Frelinghuysen's Opposition to Blaine's Pan-American Policy in 1882," *Mississippi Valley Historical Review,* 42 (March 1956), 653—71.
Blaine, James G. "Foreign Policy of the Garfield Administration," *Chicago Weekly Magazine,* (September 16, 1882).
Blake, Nelson. "Background of Cleveland's Venezuelan Policy," *American Historical Review,* 47 (January, 1942), 259—77.
Brayer, Herbert O. "The Influence of British Capital on the Western Range Cattle Industry," *The Westerners Brand Book,* 4 (May 1948), 1—19.
——————————. "The 76 Ranch on the Powder River," *The Westerners Brand Book,* 7 (December, 1950), 73—75, 77—80.
——————————. "When Dukes Went West," *The Westerners Brand Book,* (Denver Posse), (1948), 54—76.
Bryan, William Jennings. "Foreign Influence in American Politics," *The Arena,* 19 (April 1898), 433—38.
Campbell, Charles S. "The Dismissal of Lord Sackville," *Mississippi Valley Historical Review,* 44 (March 1958), 635—48.
Clements, Roger V. "British Investment and American Legislative Restrictions in the Trans-Mississippi West, 1880—1900," *Mississippi Valley Historical Review,* 42 (September 1955), 207—28.
——————————. "British-Controlled Enterprise in the West Between 1870 and 1900, and Some Agrarian Reactions," *Agricultural History,* 27—28 (1953—1954), 132—41.
——————————. "The Farmer's Attitude Toward British Investment in American Industry," *Journal of Economic History,* 15 (March 1955), 151—59.
Conant, Charles A. "The Economic Basis of Imperialism," *North American Review,* 167 (1898), 236—40.
Currie, A. W. "British Attitudes Toward Investment in North American Railroads," *Business History Review,* 34 (Summer 1960), 194—215.
Del Mar, Alexander. "Henry C. Carey's Round Table," *Gunton's Magazine,* 13 (August 1897).

Desmond, A. J. "America's Land Question," *North American Review*, 142 (February 1886), 153–58.

Gallagher, John and Robinson, Ronald. "The Imperialism of Free Trade," *Economic History Review*, 6 (August 1953), 1–15.

Gates, Paul W. "Frontier Landlords and Pioneer Tenants," *Journal of the Illinois State Historical Society*, 38 (June 1945), 143–206.

Gignilliat, John L. "Pigs, Politics, and Protection: The European Boycott of American Pork, 1879–1891." *Agricultural History*, 35 (January 1961), 3–12.

Gladstone, William E. "Free Trade or Protection," *North American Review*, 150 (January 1890), 1–26.

——————————. "Kin Beyond the Sea," *North American Review*, 127 (September–October 1878), 179–212.

Graham, Richard. "The Investment Boom in British-Texan Cattle Companies, 1880–1885," *Business History Review*, 34 (Winter 1960), 421–45.

Greenwood, Fred. "The Anglo-American Future," *The Nineteenth Century*, 44 (July 1898), 10.

Grohman, W. Baillie. "Cattle Ranches in the Far West," *Fortnightly Review*, 34 (1880), 438–57.

Hardy, Osgood. "Was Patrick Egan a Blundering Minister," *Hispanic American Historical Review*, 8 (1928), 65–81.

——————————. "British Nitrates and the Balmaceda Revolution," *Pacific Historical Review*, 17 (May 1948), 165–80.

Hernon, Joseph M. Jr. "British Sympathies in the American Civil War: A Reconsideration," *Journal of Southern History*, 33 (August 1967) 356–67.

Jones, Wilbur Devereux. "The British Conservatives and the American Civil War," *American Historical Review*, 58 (April 1953), 527–43.

Kasson, John A. "The Monroe Declaration," *North American Review*, 133 (September 1881), 247–49.

Keenleyside, Hugh L. "American Economic Penetration of Canada," *Canadian Historical Review*, 8 (March 1927), 31–40.

Kiernan, V. G. "Foreign Interests in the War of the Pacific," *Hispanic American Historical Review*, 35 (February 1955), 14–36.

LaFeber, Walter, "The American Business Community and Cleveland's Venezuela Message," *Business History Review*, 34 (Winter 1960), 393–402.

Lodge, Henry C. "England, Venezuela and the Monroe Doctrine," *North American Review*, 160 (June 1895), 651–58.

——————————. "Our Blundering Foreign Policy," *The Forum*, 19 (1895), 8–17.

Mills, Roger Q. "The Gladstone-Blaine Controversy," *North American Review*, 150 (February 1890), 145–76.

Mulhall, Michael G. "Thirty Years of American Trade," *North American Review*, 165 (1897), 572–81.

Mundella, A. J. "The Conditions on Which the Commercial and Manufacturing Supremacy of Great Britain Depend," *Journal of Statistical Society*, 41 (February 1878), 87–134.

Munson, A. E. "British Industrial Growth during the Great Depression (1873–1896): Some Comments," *Economic History Review*, 15 (April 1963), 529–33.

Nixon, Herman C. "The Populist Movement in Iowa," *Iowa Journal of History and Politics*, 24 (January 1926), 3−107.

O'Leary, Paul M. "The Scene of the Crime of 1873 Revisited: A Note," *Journal of Political Economy*, (August 1960), 392.

Radke, August C. "Senator Morgan and the Nicaraguan Canal," *Alabama Review*, 12 (January 1959), 5−34.

Rippy, J. Fred. "British Investments in Texas Lands and Livestock," *Southwestern Historical Quarterly*, 58 (January 1955), 331−41.

Snyder, Louis L. "The American-German Pork Dispute, 1879−1891." *Journal of Modern History*, 16 (March 1945), 16−28.

Socolofsky, Homer E. "The Scully Land System in Marion County," *Kansas Historical Quarterly*, 18 (November 1950), 337−75.

Spence, Clark C. "When the Pound Sterling Went West: British Investment and the American Minerial Frontier," *Journal of Economic History*, 16 (December 1956), 482−91.

Terrill, Tom E. "David A. Wells, The Democracy, and Tariff Reduction, 1877−1894," *Journal of American History*, 56,3 (December 1969), 540−55.

Tischendorf, Alfred. "North Carolina and the British Investor, 1880−1910," *North Carolina Historical Review*, 32 (October 1955), 512−18.

Van Alstyne, Richard W. "The Significance of the Mississippi Valley in American Diplomatic History, 1686−1890," *Mississippi Valley Historical Review*, 36 (September 1949), 215−38.

Volwiler, Albert T. "Tariff Strategy and Propaganda, 1887−1888." *American Historical Review*, 36 (1930), 76−96.

Weinstein, Allen. "Was There a 'Crime of 1873'?: The Case of the Demonetized Dollar," *Journal of American History*, 54 (September 1967), 307−26.

Williams, William Appleman. "The Vicious Circle of American Imperialism," *New Politics*, 4 (Fall 1965), 49−55.

Wiman, Erastus. "British Capital and American Industries," *North American Review*, 150 (February 1890), 220−34.

Winther, Oscar O. "The English and the Far West," The *Westerners Brand Book*, 11 (1954), 57−59, 64.

Books

Adams, Brooks. *The New Empire*. New York: MacMillan Company, 1902.

Adams, George Burton. *Why Americans Dislike England*. Philadelphia: Henry Altenmus, 1896.

Aldcroft, Derek H., ed. *The Development of British Industry and Foreign Competition*. Toronto: University of Toronto Press, 1968.

Allen, Harry Cranbrook. *Great Britain and the United States. A History of Anglo-American Relations, 1783 − 1952*. New York: St. Martin's Press Inc., 1955.

Allen, John H. *The Tariff and Its Evils*. New York: G. P. Putnam Company, 1888.

Armstrong, William M. *E. L. Godkin and American Foreign Policy, 1865 − 1900*. New York: Bookman Associates, 1957.

Bancroft, Frederic, ed. *Speeches, Correspondence and Political Papers of Carl Schurz*. New York: G. P. Putnam Company, 1913.

Barnes, James A. *John G. Carlisle, Financial Statesman*. New York: Dodd, Mead and Company, 1931.

Barrows, Chester L. *William M. Evarts, Lawyer, Diplomat, Statesman.* Chapel Hill: University of North Carolina Press, 1941.

Beale, Harriet S. Blaine, ed. *Letters of Mrs. James G. Blaine,* New York: Duffield and Company, 1908.

Beale, Howard K. *Theodore Roosevelt and the Rise of America to World Power.* New York: Collier Books, 1965.

Belmont, Perry. *An American Democrat.* New York: Columbia University Press, 1940.

Blaine, James G. *Political Discussions, Legislative, Diplomatic and Popular, 1856 − 1886.* Norwich, Conn.: Henry Bill Publishing Company, 1887.

_____. *Twenty Years of Congress: Lincoln to Garfield.* Norwich, Conn.: Henry Bill Publishing Company, 1884.

Bourne, Kenneth. *Britain and the Balance of Power in North America, 1815 − 1908.* Berkeley: University of California Press, 1967.

Bourne, Stephen. *Trade, Population and Food, A Series of Papers on Economic Statistics.* London: George Bell & Sons, 1880.

Boyd, Charles W. *Mr. Chamberlain's Speeches.* London: Constable and Co., Ltd., 1914.

Brebner, John Bartlet. *North Atlantic Triangle: The Interplay of Canada, the United States and Great Britain.* New Haven: Yale University Press, 1945.

Bryan, William Jennings. *The First Battle.* Chicago: W. B. Conkey Company, 1896.

Cairncross, A. K. *Home and Foreign Investment 1870 − 1913.* Cambridge: The University Press, 1953.

Callahan, James M. *American Foreign Policy in Mexican Relations.* New York: MacMillan Company, 1932.

Campbell, Charles S. Jr. *Anglo-American Understanding, 1898 − 1903.* Baltimore: Johns Hopkins Press, 1957.

Carey, Henry C. *Principles of Social Science.* Philadelphia: J. B. Lippincott & Company, 1858.

_____. *The Harmony of Interests.* Philadelphia: Henry Carey Baird, Publisher, 1865.

Cecil, Lady Gwendolen. *Life of Robert Marquis of Salisbury.* London: Hodder and Stoughton, 1922.

Chamberlain, Joseph. *Foreign and Colonial Speeches.* London: George Routledge and Sons, Ltd., 1897.

Chambers, J. D. *The Workshop of the World.* London: Oxford University Press, 1961.

Chapman, Sydney J. *The History of Trade Between the United Kingdom and the United States.* London: Swan, Sonnenschein and Company, Ltd., 1899.

Clark, Gordon. *Shylock: as Banker, Bondholder, Corruptionist, Conspirator.* Washington: By the Author, 1894.

Clay, John. *My Life on the Range.* New York: Antiquarian Press Ltd., 1961.

Cotner, Robert C., ed. *Addresses and State Papers of James Stephen Hogg.* Austin: University of Texas Press, 1951.

Cowing, Cedric. *Populists, Plungers and Progressives.* Princeton: Princeton University Press, 1965.

Crawford, Theron C. *James G. Blaine, A Study of His Life and Career.* Philadelphia: Edgewood Publishing Company, 1893.

Curtis, William E. *From the Andes to the Ocean.* Chicago: Herbert S. Stone and Company, 1900.

—————————. *Trade and Transportation Between the United States and Spanish America.* Washington: Government Printing Office, 1889.

Davies, Wallace Evan. *Patriotism on Parade.* Cambridge: Harvard University Press, 1955.

Democratic Campaign Book. New York: National Democratic Committee, 1884.

DeSantis, Vincent P. *Republicans Face the Southern Question, The New Departure Years, 1877 – 1897.* Baltimore: Johns Hopkins Press, 1959.

Destler, Chester McArthur. *Henry Demarest Lloyd and the Empire of Reform.* Philadelphia: University of Pennsylvania Press, 1963.

Dugdale, Blanche E. C. *Arthur James Balfour, 1848 – 1906.* New York: G. P. Putnam and Sons, 1937.

Dunham, Harold H. *Government Handout: A Study in the Administration of the Public Lands, 1875 – 1891.* Ann Arbor, Mich.: Edwards Bros., Inc., 1941.

Dunning, William A. *The British Empire and the United States.* New York: Charles Scribner's Sons, 1916.

Dyer, Brainerd. *The Public Career of William M. Evarts.* Berkeley: University of California Press, 1933.

Evarts, Sherman, ed. *Arguments and Speeches of William Maxwell Evarts.* New York: MacMillan Company, 1919.

Ferleger, Herbert Ronald. *David A. Wells and the American Revenue System.* New York: By the Author, 1942.

Foster, John W. *Diplomatic Memoirs.* New York: Houghton, Mifflin Company, 1909.

Frewen, Moreton. *Melton Mowbray and Other Memories.* London: Herbert Jenkins, 1924.

Friedman, Milton and Schwartz, Anna J. *A Monetary History of the United States, 1867 – 1960.* Princeton: Princeton University Press, 1963.

Furness, Sir Christopher. *The American Invasion.* London: Simpkin, Marshall, Hamilton, Kent & Company, Ltd., 1902.

Garvin, James L. *The Life of Joseph Chamberlain.* London: MacMillan and Company, Ltd., 1933.

Gates, Paul W. *Fifty Million Acres: Conflicts Over Kansas Land Policy, 1854 – 1900.* Ithaca: Cornell University Press, 1954.

—————————. *The Illinois Central Railroad and Its Colonizations Work.* Cambridge: Harvard University Press, 1934.

Gelber, Lionel. *The Rise of Anglo-American Friendship.* Hamden, Connecticut: Archon Books, 1966.

George, Henry. *Progress and Poverty.* New York: Robert Schalkenbach Foundation, 1948.

Glad, Paul W. *The Trumpet Soundeth.* Lincoln: University of Nebraska, 1960.

Gollin, Alfred. *Balfour's Burden: Arthur Balfour and Imperial Preference.* London: Anthony Bland, Ltd., 1965.

Green, Arnold W. *Henry Charles Carey, Nineteenth Century Sociologist.* Philadelphia: University of Pennsylvania Press, 1951.

Grenville, John A. S. *Lord Salisbury and Foreign Policy.* London: The Athlone Press, 1964.

———————————— and Young, George B. *Politics, Strategy and American Diplomacy.* New Haven: Yale University Press, 1966.

Gresham, Matilda. *Life of Walter Quintin Gresham, 1832 — 1895.* Chicago: Rand McNally and Company, 1919.

Gwynn, Stephen, ed. *The Letters and Friendships of Sir Cecil Spring-Rice.* Boston: Houghton Mifflin Co., 1929.

Hamilton, Gail (Mary Abigail Dodge). *Biography of James G. Blaine.* Norwich, Conn: Henry Bill Publishing Company, 1895.

Harrod, Roy. *The Dollar.* New York: W. W. Norton and Company, Inc., 1963.

Hedges, Charles, ed. *Speeches of Benjamin Harrison.* New York: John W. Lovell Company, 1892.

Helper, Hinton R. *The Three Americas Railway.* St. Louis: W. S. Bryon, 1881.

Hibbard, Benjamin H. *A History of the Public Land Policies.* New York: Peter Smith, 1939.

Hicks, John D. *The Populist Revolt.* Lincoln: University of Nebraska Press, 1961.

Hirshon, Stanley P. *Farewell to the Bloody Shirt.* Bloomington: Indiana University Press, 1962.

Hoar, George F. *Autobiography of Seventy Years.* New York: Charles Scribner's Sons, 1903.

Hoffman, Ross J. S. *Great Britain and the German Trade Rivalry, 1875 — 1914.* Philadelphia: University of Pennsylvania Press, 1933.

Hofstader, Richard. *The Age of Reform.* New York: Alfred A. Knopf, Inc., 1955.

————————————. *The Paranoid Style in American Politics and Other Politics and Other Essays.* New York: Alfred A. Knopf, Inc., 1966.

Hollingsworth, J. Rogers. *The Whirligig of Politics, The Democracy of Cleveland and Bryan.* Chicago: University of Chicago Press, 1963.

Hutchins, John G. *The American Maritime Industries and Public Policy, 1789 — 1914.* Cambridge: Harvard University Press, 1941.

Ingalls, John James. *The Writings of John James Ingalls.* Kansas City, Missouri: Hudson-Kimberly Publishing Company, 1902.

Jackson, A. P. and Cole, E. C. *Oklahoma: Politically and Topographically Described.* Kansas City, Missouri: Ramsey, Millett, and Hudson, 1885.

Jackson, William Turrentine. *When Grass Was King: Contributions to the Western Range Cattle Industry Study.* Boulder: University of Colorado Press, 1956.

————————————. *The Enterprising Scot: Investors in the American West After 1873.* Chicago: Aldine Publishing Company, 1968.

Jenks, Leland H. *The Migration of British Capital to 1875.* New York: Alfred A. Knopf, 1938.

Jones, Stanley. *The Presidential Election of 1896.* Madison: University of Wisconsin Press, 1964.

Joyner, Fred B. *David Ames Wells, Champion of Free Trade.* Cedar Rapids, Iowa: The Torch Press, 1939.

Kaplan, A. D. H. *Henry Charles Carey, A Study in American Economic Thought.* Baltimore: Johns Hopkins Press, 1931.

Keasbey, Lindley M. *The Nicaragua Canal and the Monroe Doctrine.* New York: G. P. Putnam's Sons, 1896.

Knaplund, Paul. *Gladstone's Foreign Policy.* New York: Harper Brothers, 1935.
——————————— ed. *Letters From the Berlin Embassy, 1871 — 1874, 1880 — 1885.* Annual Report of the American Historical Association, 1942, Vol. II. Washington: Government Printing Office, 1944.

——————————— and Clewes, Carolyn M. eds. *Private Letters From the British Embassy in Washington to the Foreign Secretary Lord Granville, 1880 — 1885.* Annual Report of the American Historical Association, Vol. I, 1941. Washington: Government Printing Office, 1942.

LaFeber, Walter. *The New Empire: An Interpretation of American Expansion, 1860 — 1898.* Ithaca: Cornell University Press, 1963.

Laughlin, J. Lawrence. *The History of Bimetallism in the United States.* New York: D. Appleton and Company, 1901.

———————————. and Willis, H. Parker. *Reciprocity.* New York: The Baker and Taylor Company, 1903.

Leslie, Shane. *Studies in Sublime Failure.* London: Ernest Benn, Ltd., 1932.

Lodge, Henry C. ed. *Selections From the Correspondence of Theodore Roosevelt and Henry C. Lodge, 1884 — 1918.* New York: Charles Scribner's Sons, 1925.

Mahan, Alfred T. *The Influence of Sea Power Upon History, 1660 — 1783.* Boston: Little, Brown, 1917.

Malin, James C. *A Concern About Humanity: Notes on Reform, 1872 — 1912 at the National and Kansas Levels of Thought.* Lawrence, Kansas: By the Author, 1964.

———————————. *Confounded Rot About Napoleon: Reflections Upon Science and Technology, Nationalism, World Depression of the Eighteen-Nineties, and Afterwards.* Lawrence, Kansas: The Author, 1961.

Manchester, Alan K. *British Preeminence in Brazil, Its Rise and Decline.* Chapel Hill: University of North Carolina Press, 1933.

May, Ernest R. *Imperial Democracy.* New York: Harcourt, Brace & World, 1961.
———————————. *American Imperialism: A speculative essay.* New York: Atheneum, 1968.

McElory, Robert M. *Grover Cleveland, The Man and the Statesman.* New York: Harper & Bros., 1923.

McGann, Thomas F. *Argentina, the United States, and the Inter-American System 1880 — 1914.* Cambridge: Harvard University Press, 1957.

McKenzie, F. A. *The American Invaders.* London: Grant Richards, 1902.

Miller, Clarence Lee. *The States of the Old Northwest and the Tariff, 1865 — 1888.* Emporia, Kansas: Emporia Gazette Press, 1929.

Millington, Herbert. *American Diplomacy and the War of the Pacific.* New York: Columbia University Press, 1948.

Mitchell, B. R. *Abstract of British Historical Statistics.* Cambridge: University Press, 1962.

Morgan, W. Scott. *History of the Wheel and Alliance and the Impending Revolution.* Fort Scott, Kansas: J. H. Rice and Sons, 1889.

Muzzey, David S. *James G. Blaine: A Political Idol of Other Days.* New York: Dodd, Mead and Company, 1934.

Neale, R. G. *Great Britain and United States Expansion 1898 – 1900.* East Lansing: Michigan State University Press, 1966.

Nevins, Allan. *Grover Cleveland: A Study in Courage.* New York: Dodd, Mead and Company, 1947.

─────────────. *Henry White, Thirty Years of American Diplomacy.* New York: Harper & Bros., 1930.

Nordyke, Lewis, *Cattle Empire: The Fabulous Story of the 3,000,000 Acre XIT.* New York: William Morrow and Company, 1949.

Nugent, Walter T. K. *Money and American Society, 1865 – 1880.* New York: The Free Press, 1968.

Official Proceedings of National Democratic Convention 1884. New York: Douglas Taylor's Democratic Printing House, 1884.

Official Proceedings of the Republican National Conventions. 1884 – 1888. Minneapolis: Charles W. Johnson, Publisher, 1903.

Osgood, Ernest S. *The Day of the Cattleman.* Minneapolis: University of Minnesota Press, 1929.

Parker, George F. *Recollections of Grover Cleveland.* New York: The Century Company, 1909.

Pelzer, Louis. *The Cattleman's Frontier.* Glendale, California: Arthur H. Clarke Company, 1936.

Perkins, Bradford. *The Great Rapprochement: England and the United States, 1895 – 1914.* New York: Atheneum, 1968.

Pike, Frederick. *Chile and the United States 1880 – 1962.* South Bend: University of Notre Dame Press, 1963.

Platt, Desmond C. M. *Finance, Trade and Politics in British Foreign Policy 1815 – 1914.* Oxford: Clarendon Press, 1968.

Pletcher, David M. *The Awkward Years: American Foreign Relations Under Garfield and Arthur.* Columbia: University of Missouri Press, 1962.

Porter, Kirk H., and Johnson, Donald B. ed. *National Party Platforms, 1840 – 1964.* Urbana: University of Illinois Press, 1966.

Powderly, Terence V. *Thirty Years of Labor 1859 to 1889.* Columbus, Ohio: Excelsior Publishing House, 1889.

Ramm, Agatha. ed. *The Political Correspondence of Mr. Gladstone and Lord Granville, 1876 – 1886.* Oxford: Clarendon Press, 1962.

Report of the Royal Commission on the Depression of Trade and Industry. London: Eyre and Spottiswoode, 1886.

Republican Campaign Text Book for 1884. New York: Republican National Committee, 1884.

Richardson, James D. ed. *Messages and Papers of the Presidents, 1789 – 1897.* Washington: Government Printing Office, 1898.

Ridge, Martin. *Ignatius Donnelly. The Portrait of a Politician.* Chicago: University of Chicago Press, 1962.

Robey, Ralph. *The Monetary Problem. Gold and Silver.* (Final Report of the Royal

Commission on Gold and Silver, 1888). New York: Columbia University Press, 1936.

Robinson, Chalfant. *A History of Two Reciprocity Treaties.* New Haven: Tuttle, Morehouse and Taylor Press, 1904.

Russell, Henry B. *International Monetary Conferences.* New York: Harper and Brothers, 1898.

Russett, Bruce M. *Community and Contention.* Cambridge: The M.I.T. Press, 1963.

Saul, S. B. *Studies in British Overseas Trade.* Liverpool: Liverpool University Press, 1960.

Sayers, R. S. *A History of Economic Change in England, 1880 − 1939.* New York: Oxford University Press, 1967.

Schonberger, Howard B. *Transportation to the Seaboard, A Study in the "Communications Revolution" and American Foreign Policy, 1860 − 1900.* Westport, Conn.: Greenwood Publishing Corporation, 1971.

Scruggs, William L. *The Columbian and Venezuelan Republics.* Boston: Little, Brown and Company, 1900.

Semmel, Bernard. *Imperialism and Social Reform.* Garden City, N. Y.: Doubleday & Company, 1968.

Sheffy, Lester F. *The Life and Times of Timothy Dwight Hobart.* Canyon, Texas: The Panhandle-Plains Historical Society, 1950.

Sheldon, Addison E. *Land Systems and Land Policies in Nebraska.* Publications of the Nebraska State Historical Society. Lincoln: Nebraska State Historical Society, 1938.

Sherman, Thomas H. *Twenty Years with James G. Blaine.* New York: The Grafton Press, 1928.

Sherman, William R. *The Diplomatic and Commercial Relations of the United States and Chile, 1820 − 1914.* Boston: Gorham Press, 1926.

Sievers, Harry J. *Benjamin Harrison, Hoosier Statesman, 1865 − 1888.* New York: University Publishers, Inc., 1959.

Smith, Theodore C. *The Life and Letters of James A. Garfield.* New Haven: Yale University Press, 1925.

Spence, Clark C. *British Investments and the American Mining Frontier, 1860 − 1901.* Ithaca: Cornell University Press, 1958.

Sprout, Harold and Margaret. *The Rise of American Naval Power 1776 − 1918.* Princeton: Princeton University Press, 1939.

Stanwood, Edward. *James Gillespie Blaine.* New York: Houghton, Mifflin Company, 1905.

Stead, William T. *The Americanization of the World.* New York: Horace Markley, 1901.

Steevens, G. W. *The Land of the Dollar.* New York: Dodd, Mead & Company, 1898.

Stevens, Sylvester K. *American Expansion in Hawaii.* Harrisburg: Archives Publishing Company of Pennsylvania, Inc. 1945.

Strauss, William L. *Joseph Chamberlain and the Theory of Imperialism.* Washington: American Council on Public Affairs, 1942.

Summers, Festus P. ed. *The Cabinet Diary of William L. Wilson, 1896 − 1897.* Chapel Hill: University of North Carolina Press, 1957.

Swann, Leonard Alexander, Jr. *John Roach: Maritime Entrepreneur.* Annapolis: United States Naval Institute, 1965.

Tansill, Charles Callan. *The Foreign Policy of Thomas F. Bayard.* New York: Fordham University Press, 1940.

Tate, Merze. *The United States and the Hawaiian Kingdom: A Political History.* New Haven: Yale University Press, 1965.

Thomas, H. C. *The Return of the Democratic Party to Power in 1884.* New York: Columbia University Press, 1919.

Thornton, A. P. *The Imperial Idea and Its Enemies.* New York: Macmillan Company, 1959.

Tischendorf, Alfred P. *Great Britain and Mexico in the Era of Porfirio Diaz.* Durham: Duke University Press, 1961.

Tyler, Alice Felt. *The Foreign Policy of James G. Blaine.* Minneapolis: University of Minnesota Press, 1927.

Unger, Irwin. *The Greenback Era. A Social and Political History of American Finance, 1865 − 1879.* Princeton: Princeton University Press, 1964.

Vail, Walter S. ed. The *Words of James G. Blaine on the Issues of the Day.* Boston: D. L. Guernsey, 1884.

Van Alstyne, Richard W. *The Rising American Empire.* New York: Oxford University Press, 1960.

Van Der Zee, Jacob. *The British in Iowa.* Iowa City: State Historical Society of Iowa, 1922.

Volwiler, Albert T. ed. *The Correspondence Between Benjamin Harrison and James G. Blaine, 1882 − 1893.* Philadelphia: American Philosophical Society, 1940.

Williams, Charles R. *Diary and Letters of Rutherford B. Hayes.* Columbus: Ohio State Archaeological and Historical Society.

Williams, William A. *The Roots of the Modern American Empire.* New York: Random House, 1969.

Woodward, C. Vann. *Tom Watson: Agrarian Rebel.* New York: MacMillan Company, 1938.

INDEX

Adams, Brooks: bimetallist, 196
Adams, Charles E., 208
Adee, Alvey: British West Indies treaty, 130; on German ambitions, 157
Adet, Pierre A., 5
Alabama, 13, 38
—claims: Evarts U.S. negotiator, 46
Alien Land Law: provisions, 104-105; mentioned, 99
Allen, John: tariff views, 37
Allen, William V., 200, 202, 203
Alliance, 103, 112
American Iron and Steel Association, 161
American party: 1887 demands, 15, 101
American Revolution, 4
Andrews, E. Benjamin: bimetallist, 196
Anglophobia: ambivalent aspects, 14, 120, 221-222; passim
Argentina, 52
Arkansas Valley Land and Cattle Company, 98, 99
Arthur, Chester A.: pushes trade expansion, 120-122, 124, 133-135; 1884 message, 125; mentioned, 98, 147, 152, 170, 175, 186
Associated Industries of the United States, 53, 54
Atkinson, Edward, 26
Australia, 38, 52, 123, 153, 154, 177
Austria, 179

Baird, Henry Carey, 20
Balfour, Arthur J.: bimetallist, 210-211; Venezuelan crisis, 212
Balmaceda, Jose Manuel, 181-182
Baltimore incident: discussed, 180-182
Bayard-Chamberlain Treaty, 158-161
Bayard, Thomas F.: calls for American canal, 62; on Samoa, 142-143, 156-157; Anglophile, 144; 1884 campaign, 145; foreign policy, 146-147, 151; monetary policy, 148-150; Hawaiian reciprocity, 152-155; mentioned, 109
Belford, James B., 96
Bell, Clark, 46
Belmont, Perry: on foreign markets, 144
Beveridge, Albert J.: on England, 4
Bismarck, Count Herbert: distrusts U.S., 155-156
Blaine, James G.: views of England, 7,

67, 87; supports Roach subsidy, 50, 71-75; on Latin America, 67, 70-71, 75-76, 166-167; tariff, 69-70, 177; Hawaii, 77, 82-84; isthmian canal, 78-79; 1884 campaign, 86, 99; on Monroe Doctrine and Africa, 135; "Paris letter," 161-162; reciprocity, 169-170, 172-175, 178; 1888 campaign, 171; Pan-American Conference (1889), 172; Chile, 181; commercial policy, 184-186; monetary views, 195; mentioned, 62, 107, 120, 132, 153, 154, 206, 214, 219
Bland-Allison Act, 148, 149, 199, 200
Bland, Richard: silverite, 151
Blodget, Lorin: trade group official, 53
Bookwalter, John W., 136
Boston Bimetallic Club, 196
Boutwell, George: favors Hawaiian renewal, 154
Bowen, Thomas M., 142, 151
Brazil: trade efforts, 47; Roach steamship line to, 50, 71-74; trade pattern, 71-72; mentioned, 146
British West Indies: reciprocity treaty, 126, 147, 178
Brooks, James: supports Wells, 32
Brougham, Henry: on American manufactures, 8
Bryan, William Jennings: 1896 campaign, 213-214; mentioned, 198
Bryce, James, 209
Buchanan, James: fears Britain in Cuba, 11
Burnham, George: trade group official, 53
Butler, Benjamin F.: supports Roach subsidy, 50
Butler, Matthew Calbraith, 183
Butterfield, Carlos: advocate of Latin American trade, 54-55

Cake, Henry L.: ties Wells to British, 31
Calhoun, John C.: against British meddling, 11
Canada, 7, 8, 13, 147, 177, 178, 183, 184
Canadian Pacific Railroad: Asian trade, 136; steamship line, 154
Carey, Henry C.: continues father's program, 9; tariff, 15, 21; economic views, 20, 22-23; soft money thesis, 24-25; attacks Wells, 28, 30; heads